The Libertarian Illusion
Ideology, Public Policy, and the Assault on the Common Good

William E. Hudson
Providence College

CQ PRESS

A Division of Congressional Quarterly Inc.
Washington, D.C.

CQ Press
2300 N Street, NW, Suite 800
Washington, DC 20037

Phone: 202-729-1900; toll-free, 1-866-4CQ-PRESS (1-866-427-7737)

Web: www.cqpress.com

Image credits:
AP Images: 2, 24 (top, bottom), 39, 64, 87, 110, 120, 171, 175, 201, 215
Corbis: 124
Landov/Reuters (Shannon Stapleton): 104
Politicalcartoons.com: (R. J. Matson) 48, 139; (Jimmy Margulies) 199
Washington Post Writers Group (Nick Anderson): 180

Cover design: McGaughy Design
Cover photo: Corbis (Denis Scott)

∞ The paper used in this publication exceeds the requirements of the American National
Standard for Information Sciences—Permanence of Paper for Printed Library Materials,
ANSI Z39.48-1992.

Printed and bound in the United States of America

11   10   09   08   07   1   2   3   4   5

Library of Congress Cataloging-in-Publication Data

Hudson, William E.
  The libertarian illusion : ideology, public policy, and the assault on the common good /
William E. Hudson.
     p. cm.
  Includes index.
  ISBN 978-1-933116-50-1 (alk. paper)
  1. Libertarianism—United States. 2. Communitarianism—United States. 3. Industrial
policy—United States. 4. Welfare state—United States. 5. United States—Social policy.
I. Title.

  JC599.U5H72 2008
  320.51'2—dc22

                                                            2007045638

For Loreto

Contents

Preface

Not many Americans have ever heard of libertarianism. Those who have understand only vaguely what the term means. Even fewer understand something of libertarianism and embrace its goals. And only a handful of American politicians—2008 Republican presidential candidate Ron Paul is one of the exceptional few—adopt the libertarian label. Despite their ongoing obscurity in American mainstream political discourse, libertarians have had enormous and increasing influence in public policy debates over the past thirty years. Thanks to well-funded think tanks, articulate policy proponents, and organized networks linking policymakers, libertarian policy alternatives have been major contenders for enactment in a wide variety of policy arenas and have been adopted in some. After his 2004 presidential victory, President George W. Bush embraced an essentially libertarian vision for the country's future labeled the "Ownership Society." The package of policy initiatives comprising this vision, such as private accounts for Social Security, failed to be enacted—partly due to the collapse of Bush's credibility because of the Iraq war debacle. Nevertheless, libertarian policy alternatives continue to attract attention and support from many politicians. In the 2008 presidential campaign, each of the Republican candidates put forth proposals in areas such as health care, tax policy, Social Security reform, and deregulation drawn from the libertarian well. The libertarian vision, or as I label it in this book, *illusion,* is bound to influence policy debates for many years to come.

In this book, I argue that libertarian policy solutions are illusory in three different ways. First, and most important, policy proposals derived from libertarian ideological principles do not deliver what they promise. Just like the iceberg on this book's cover, libertarian policy claims shine white in the sun when first they appear, but this attractive surface hides a disastrous reality beneath. The reality of libertarian policies, lurking below the water's surface, will be demonstrated through an examination of policy areas in which libertarian proposals have been enacted, such as economic deregulation and tax policy, and through analysis of the likely effect of libertarian proposals to privatize Social Security or establish a "consumer-driven" health care system. The libertarian illusion promises wonderful policy benefits that fail to appear and fails to anticipate the unpleasant consequences that actually result. California politicians and citizens who expected libertarian-inspired electricity deregulation to provide plentiful low-cost electricity found themselves victims of the libertarian illusion when it only produced price spikes and rolling blackouts. Likewise, airline passengers stuck for hours in delayed planes on airport tarmacs in the summer of 2007 were victims of the libertarian illusion that market forces alone could organize an efficient airline industry. For the future, libertarians paint an illusory picture of all Americans purchasing individual health insurance coverage and providing for their retirements through private investment accounts—a recipe, I argue, for a health care disaster and impoverished senior citizens.

Second, libertarian policy proposals are illusory because the manner in which they fulfill libertarian ideological goals is rarely spelled out explicitly in policy debates. Again, like the iceberg on the cover, much of what is being proposed in libertarian policies lies unseen under the water as we sail toward the innocent block of ice on the surface. For example, agreeing to allow individuals to deposit a small part of their Social Security taxes in personal investment accounts is sold as Social Security "reform," but the long-term consequence, as we see in chapter 4, is likely to achieve the libertarian goal of Social Security abolition. Or, as detailed in chapter 2, flat tax proposals are presented merely as a method of "simplifying" the income tax, but they actually place the entire national tax burden on the shoulders of ordinary wage earners and eliminate taxes on wealthy investors whose incomes derive from their investments. There is always more than meets the eye to libertarian policy proposals. This book will look under the water to see what is there.

Finally, libertarians claim their policies will lead to a nation of expanded individual freedom and autonomy, of ownership and personal responsibility. Libertarian America is a place where individuals are not dependent on government for their retirement security, but instead own their own retirement accounts. It is a place where each of us chooses our individual health insurance plans (or chooses not to have one at all) according to our own needs and expectations about our health. It also is a place where a much smaller government taxes less and does much less, allowing individuals to determine through the free market how their resources will be used. The illusion here is that such an America would be a better place in which to live. According to the libertarian vision, when it comes to navigating the hazardous sea of life *you are on your own*. Alone on the stark and lonely sea depicted on the cover, you must avoid the icebergs in your path by yourself. If your retirement investments fail to yield an adequate income in your old age, you must bear the consequences. If the health insurance plan you chose proves inadequate to cover the costs of an unforeseen illness, you must either forego treatment or exhaust your savings. In this book, I will advocate an alternative, communitarian vision of an America in which we help each other navigate life's waters. In solidarity with our fellow citizens, we craft policy solutions that share the risks and hazards of life so that no one must face an iceberg alone.

As should be obvious by now, this is a point-of-view text. It subjects libertarian policy proposals to a thorough critique. In doing so, however, I have been careful to present the libertarian position fairly, pointing to its virtues as well as its faults. In addition, in each chapter, I place libertarian policy proposals in context through a description of the history and background of each policy area and what problems exist. A core argument of the book is the need to move beyond the labels "liberal" and "conservative" normally used to describe ideological conflict over public policy in the United States. While these conventional labels offered some meaningful description of political conflicts for many years, they are increasingly cumbersome for providing an enlightened understanding of the values at stake in contemporary policy conflicts.

As is explained in detail in the first chapter, this book recasts our understanding of ideological conflict over public policy as a confrontation of *libertarian* and *communitarian* values. The libertarian-communitarian dichotomy highlights, I believe, the most fundamental conflict animating contemporary public policy debates. The libertarian outlook is rooted in a conception of political life that sees government as an instrument by which autonomous, "unencumbered"—to use Michael Sandel's term—individuals protect and pursue their individual preferences. Communitarians view politics as an opportunity to achieve the broader common good beyond what individuals might prefer for themselves. The common good derives from a variety of sources, including moral or civic values and public goals emerging from democratic deliberation among citizens. One finds within both contemporary conservatism and liberalism a combination of libertarian and communitarian outlooks. American conservatives tend to be libertarian on economic policy and communitarian on social policy, and American liberals the reverse.

This approach intends to show the importance of ideology in contemporary policy debates and also indicate how the language of liberal and conservative alternatives as a way of describing these debates fails to capture the value choices involved. In my view, much public policy discussion can be understood better in terms of conflicting libertarian and communitarian values rather than as conflicts between liberals and conservatives. In each of the policy areas described, students should better understand the values at stake in choosing between competing policy alternatives. The point of view in favor of a communitarian policy underscores the value-laden character of public policy choices. Making public policy is never a neutral technical procedure, as is sometimes implied in texts that present contending views in a neutral way, but rather requires value judgments. The critique of libertarian values in this book draws the readers' attention to that fact.

The point of view of this text also has a pedagogical purpose. In my thirty years of teaching American public policy to undergraduates, I have found the best way to engage students in the subject is to provoke within the class the same policy debates that take place in the real political world. The arguments in this book ought to provoke a reaction from those students who are likely to find libertarian proposals appealing. Pairing this book with one of the many well-written and persuasive books arguing the libertarian case, such as Milton Friedman's *Capitalism and Freedom* or Charles Murray's *Why I Am a Libertarian,* might facilitate student engagement. While most of the book critiques the libertarian position on policy issues that contemporary conservatives are most likely to embrace, the last chapter, on abortion and euthanasia, critiques the views of many contemporary liberals. Students in many classes, if their views reflect those in U.S. society, may find themselves shifting sides on the libertarian-communitarian divide when they take up this chapter. My hope is that such engagement will lead students to examine carefully the values underlying their own policy positions.

Acknowledgments

I have been fortunate in the advice, insight, and encouragement of many friends and colleagues during this book's long period of gestation. Early on, Grant Reeher of Syracuse University provided helpful advice on an early paper on Social Security employing the libertarian-communitarian frame; those comments set the overall project on a productive path. Since that time, he has thoughtfully followed the book's progress and encouraged its author. The collegial environment of the Providence College political science department offers just the ambiance a textbook author needs to refine ideas and test them among teaching professionals. Special thanks to Bob Trudeau and Fr. Ed Cleary, O.P., for reading and commenting on several chapters. I owe Ed thanks, in particular, for modeling diligent scholarship and urging upon me the Cleary "Two-Page-a-Day" Rule. Thanks to several Providence College undergraduates who provided research assistance for the book, including Misa Boker, Nick Cote, Katie Feeney, and Amber Rankin. The many students in my American public policy classes with whom I have discussed and dissected public policy issues over the years have not only helped to hone my understanding of these issues but also continually renew my enthusiasm for the subject. The professional insights of several reviewers—Brian Fife, Indiana University–Purdue University Fort Wayne; Mark Henkels, Western Oregon University; David Schecter, California State University, Fresno; and Bruce Stinebrickner, DePauw University—have strengthened the book's argument at many points.

The good folks at CQ Press continue to provide all the advice, assistance, and encouragement an author needs. I am grateful to Brenda Carter and Charisse Kiino for their sustained enthusiasm for the project and their willingness to publish a provocative, "point-of-view" textbook. The skilled editorial and production work of Dwain Smith, Talia Greenberg, Anna Socrates, and Chris O'Brien has kept me on task, polished my prose, and given the book its professional shine. Thanks to them and the other CQ staff who have helped with this project. Finally, as always, a special note of gratitude to my wife, Loreto Gandara, to whom this book is dedicated. Her insights from a professional career both making and implementing public policy and her work as the first reader on each chapter informed the book throughout. I am fortunate in having a spouse who maintains confidence in my work even when mine flags, makes room in our life together for the demands of authorship, and possesses a gentle knack for reminding her husband of the Cleary Rule. Without those reminders and her inspiration, this book would never have been written.

Chapter 1   **The Libertarian Illusion
in Contemporary Public
Policy and the Case for a
Communitarian Alternative**

Bitter cold engulfed the newly renovated East Front of the Capitol Build-ing that Friday morning on January 20, 1961, in Washington, D.C. The sun reflected strongly from the heavy blanket of snow that had fallen the night before. On the inaugural platform, the newly sworn-in American pres-ident, John Fitzgerald Kennedy, hatless despite the cold, stepped forward to deliver a stirring inaugural address. The speech is full of memorable phrases often quoted nearly fifty years after they were first spoken: "Let the word go forth . . . that the torch has been passed to a new generation of Americans—born in this century . . ."; "we shall pay any price, bear any burden, meet any hardship . . . to assure . . . the success of liberty"; "Let us never negotiate out of fear. But let us never fear to negotiate." The best known came at the end of the speech as Kennedy called on Americans to mobilize and sacrifice for the ambitious goals he had laid out for them. Kennedy challenged his "fellow Americans" to *"ask not what your country can do for you—ask what you can do for your country."* To most of his listeners that morning, his charge was heard as a patriotic call for them to join together on behalf of the common good.

Not everyone understood the phrase that way. The next year, distinguished economist Milton Friedman, who would eventually win a Nobel Prize for his contributions to monetary theory, opened his new book *Capitalism and Freedom* with an attack on the phrase as unworthy of "the ideals of free men in a free society."[1] Friedman went on:

> The paternalistic "what your country can do for you" implies that gov-ernment is the patron, the citizen the ward, a view that is at odds with the free man's belief in his own responsibility for his own destiny. The organismic, "what you can do for your country" implies that govern-ment is the master or the deity, the citizen the servant or the votary. To the free man, the country is the collection of individuals who compose it, not something over and above them.

What many considered an appropriate call to patriotism, Friedman regarded as a potential threat to freedom.

Friedman's concern seems to stem from his understanding of the meaning of the word *country*. In the passage above, he first equates country with government. To Friedman, Kennedy's reference to country doing for citizens or citizens doing for country means citizens either serving or being served by their government. But an alternative understanding, one closer I suspect to what Kennedy actually meant, would be to think of country as a collectivity of citizens joined together in common effort. Even more, for many the idea of country carries with it a sense of the mutual contributions we make for each other in the present and the contributions citizens have made in the past. Most who heard Kennedy would not have thought of him asking that they, as individuals, submit to a government, defined either as a set of institutions or officials, but that they commit themselves to a common purpose—to the common good.

Friedman's misunderstanding results from his failure to recognize the possibility of a common good except as an aggregation of individual goods. Later in the same paragraph, Friedman writes that a "free man" recognizes only "the consensus of the goals that the citizens severally serve" and "the consensus of the purposes for which the citizens severally strive." To the extent that there

THE LATE MILTON FRIEDMAN, A NOBEL PRIZE–WINNING ECONOMIST, WAS A PERSUASIVE ADVO-CATE OF LIBERTARIAN POLICY IDEAS.

might be a common good, it seems, it results only when individually chosen purposes happen to coincide. Goals and purposes, in this view, can belong only to individuals and never to the collectivity as a whole. Concepts such as the common good, public interest, collective endeavor, and perhaps even country itself are abstractions that possess no intrinsic meaning. To call on someone to serve the common good, then, must mean to subject that person to another individual's or group of individuals' good, not to participate in a good that all hold in common. This attitude toward the common good lies at the heart of a libertarian political ideology, one that, since Kennedy gave his speech and Friedman wrote his book, has become increasingly influential in public policy debates in the United States.

When Kennedy became president, the ideas of Friedman and those who agreed with him existed on the margins of American political life, a fact that Friedman himself acknowledges in his book. In the decade following that cold January morning, Americans would be called to numerous common endeavors for the common good, from sending a man to the moon to fighting a war on poverty. Americans mobilized to fight racial injustice and guarantee civil rights for all. They also were called to a disastrous war in Southeast Asia. In part in reaction to these common endeavors, but also for other reasons that will be addressed in this book, the libertarian outlook gained adherents. Sentiments like Friedman's have gained currency, and by the 1980s many of his specific policy recommendations were being adopted. Today, libertarian solutions are invariably major contenders when any policy problem reaches the public agenda, and many have been implemented, transforming profoundly the character of American life. No matter what the issue, proponents of providing individuals with freedom of choice on the matter—an ability to determine for themselves what they want free from governmental interference—will make themselves heard.

Libertarianism versus Communitarianism

Libertarianism has not gone unopposed, however. A Kennedy-like concern for the common good remains strong among many Americans who also believe in a constructive role for government. On most policy issues there are strong advocates for the need to provide for a broader community interest on the issue—that individuals must be held responsible to the common good. This outlook I will label *communitarian* in this book.

Contending libertarian and communitarian views emerge in nearly all policy debates. For example, in recent debates on Social Security, one side argues for giving people individual private accounts in which they can invest as they please in providing for their retirement, while the other cautions that all Americans have a common stake in the future well-being of all retirees and that a public pension program must not leave individuals' basic security to their individual investment skills. In debates over education policy, one side advocates providing individual students with vouchers to use in any school of their choice while the other argues for the need for a common educational experience that all children in a community should share. Underlying most policy debates are fundamental value choices about government's role in society, individual rights and responsibilities, and the extent to which public policy should promote common values and the common good of all.

This book examines the contending ideological and value choices at stake in several important areas of public policy. While most discussions of policy debates usually apply the labels *liberal* and *conservative* to contending ideological perspectives, these labels, for reasons I will explain, do not describe well the contending values and ideological perspectives that divide Americans on most policy issues. In most cases, the values at stake in policy debates derive from competing assumptions about the role of individuals in society and the obligations individuals have to their communities—and that their communities, including the broad national community, have to them. These competing assumptions are rooted in libertarian and communitarian ideologies that cut across the conventional conservative and liberal groupings. If we are to understand ideological conflict in public policy, we need to understand the contrasting libertarian and communitarian ideologies and how they define the value choices presented in public policy debate.

An *ideology,* as one textbook puts it succinctly, is "a set of ideas that link thought to action."[2] In policy terms, an ideology provides the underlying rationale, in terms of political values and principles, for choosing one policy option over another. If this is what an ideology is supposed to do, neither conventional liberalism nor conservatism provides a clear road map for understanding contemporary public policy conflict. The underlying principles and values that justify policy positions typically taken by conservatives and liberals vary from issue to issue.

For example, conservatives in the United States are associated with the notion of reducing the size and involvement of government in American life and liberals with a more interventionist government. Yet if we examine the well-known positions of conservatives and liberals on specific policy issues, we find that their views of the role of government are often reversed. On economic and budgetary issues, conservatives typically advocate smaller government, arguing for tax cuts, reduced government spending on social programs, and less business regulation. Liberals typically desire more social spending, higher taxes if needed to finance them, and closer regulation of business. But if the issues involved relate to matters of personal privacy, religious practice, or free expression, it is the conservatives that typically argue for more government action to regulate sexual behavior, proscribe abortion, promote prayer—even in public facilities—and restrict freedoms of expression, like pornography or flag burning. Liberals usually defend individual rights to be free of government intervention on these issues. Who is more in favor of smaller government, liberals or conservatives? It depends on the issue.

Or, to look at this in another way, it helps to distinguish between stances on issues of material well-being (economics, taxes, business regulation, the environment) and issues of personal privacy and self-expression (abortion, sexual preference, free speech). In this book, I will label the former *economic issues* and the latter *social issues*. In making this distinction, however, we should remember that it oversimplifies both types of issues, as such classifications always do. We need to keep in mind that economic issues all have significant social impacts and most social issues have an economic dimension.

Whether economic or social issues, policy discussion often focuses on the extent to which government should regulate the actions of individuals. Should individuals in their capacities as employers and workers in a free market determine wages and working conditions in society? Or is government regulation needed to enact a minimum wage and make sure that working conditions are safe and fair? These are typical questions about economic issues often debated in the United States. At the same time, on social issues, Americans argue about government regulation of matters of personal privacy and the degree of individual freedom people should have regarding personal choices. Should people who are terminally ill be free to seek physician-assisted suicide? Or can government, in the name of moral or community values, restrict people from taking such an action? Public policy debate on both kinds of issues raises these fundamental questions about individual liberty and the claims of the broader community.

Figure 1-1 shows how we can make sense of the complexity of ideological debate over public policy by comparing stances toward government and community constraints on individual autonomy on these two dimensions, one in regard to social issues and the other economic issues.[3] On the horizontal axis, policy positions toward community/government control versus individual autonomy on economic issues is portrayed; on the vertical axis, community/government control versus individual autonomy on personal privacy and self-expression is shown. The result is a four-fold table that displays how conservatism combines a communitarian outlook on social issues with a libertarian outlook on economic issues while liberalism combines a communitarian position on the economy with a libertarian view on social issues. Both libertarians and communitarians, by contrast, are consistent on both dimensions.

Contemplating this figure is useful because it clarifies the actual ideological division that animates public policy conflict. On most policy issues in recent years, arguments have tended to focus on choosing between libertarian and communitarian policy alternatives. This is not because many American citizens or even policymakers consider themselves communitarians or libertarians. In fact, there are only a very few people who consciously label themselves as either. "Conservative" and "liberal" remain fairly rough but accurate labels for classifying most people's political attitudes, even if they suggest that Americans are not consistent in how they view the appropriate role of government or in their commitment to individual freedom. Yet if we focus on any single policy issue, we find the actual policy choices that people argue about derive from the value assumptions of libertarian and communitarian ideologies. On

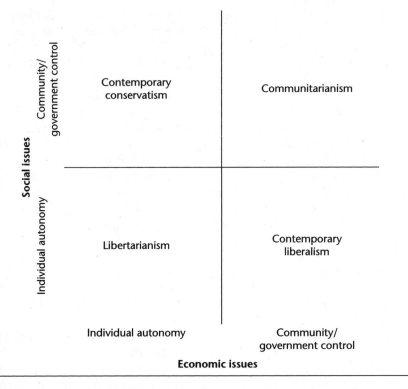

Figure 1-1 FOUR-FOLD CLASSIFICATION OF PUBLIC POLICY IDEOLOGIES

economic issues, contemporary conservatives rely on libertarian arguments and liberals on communitarian ones; on social issues liberals become libertarians and conservatives become communitarians.

In this book I will show how choices between libertarian and communitarian values are at the heart of the important contemporary domestic policy conflict. I will describe different ways these ideologies describe the policy problems facing America today and the contrasting solutions they propose. As the title of the book indicates, I have a particular bias in this ideological squabble. For all the issues that follow, I will argue that the libertarian path to resolving our policy dilemmas, though attractive to many Americans and resonant with our political traditions, is an illusory one. These chapters will document how libertarian solutions have undermined the common good in the United States; they will also dissect the flaws in libertarian proposals in current areas of policy contention. If we are to find policies that address the needs of our country, we will be better off in adopting policies that reflect more communitarian values.

Before proceeding with this goal, I need to explain in more detail what both libertarianism and communitarianism mean, provide a brief history of the role each has played in American political life, and furnish a guide to what is to come in this book. The remainder of this chapter will take up these tasks.

Libertarianism in a Nutshell

Before proceeding with a capsule summary of basic libertarian ideas, a couple of caveats are needed. First, libertarianism comes in many shades and varieties. Those who promote a libertarian position on public policy are not required to sign onto any dogma or absolute loyalty to a single version of libertarian belief. In fact, as we will see, libertarians would be the first to oppose any such dogmatic approach to politics and the restrictions on individual conscience that it implies. While one can summarize the essence of a libertarian outlook, as I do below, that does not mean that all libertarians would agree with every detail in the summary. In boiling libertarianism down to its fundamentals, I have chosen not to get into details about the points of difference and controversy within the movement. Some of those differences will come to the fore when we discuss specific policies in subsequent chapters.

Second, like all people sharing a basic overall political outlook, those who are sympathetic to libertarian policy ideas do not necessarily consciously regard themselves as libertarians, nor do they consistently espouse a libertarian outlook across the board. While many self-conscious libertarians, such as those who support the Libertarian Party, may more consistently adhere to libertarian values in their policy positions, most people are not so totally consistent in their political beliefs. Special circumstances or particular policy commitments may cause them to deviate from their general political position. Politicians especially often find themselves in this position. California governor Arnold Schwarzenegger, for example, who shares many libertarian positions, such as limited government regulation of business and a woman's right to an abortion, and disagrees with the libertarian position that government should not regulate gun ownership. Many conservative politicians are libertarians on tax policy but strongly support government prohibitions on the use of "recreational" drugs. Many members of the American Civil Liberties Union take libertarian positions on civil liberty issues, like freedom of speech or abortion rights, but remove their libertarian hats when it comes to environmental issues. The following summary is meant to identify the basic ideas that inform and are used to justify specific policy proposals when used in debates on particular ideas. So what were the key ideas of libertarianism?

Individual Liberty. The core political value for libertarians is the liberty of the individual. Individuals should be free to live their lives any way they choose so long as they do not violate the equal right of other individuals to do the same. This freedom to choose includes mundane matters such as what career to pursue, where to live, what products to consume, and with whom to associate. It also includes individual freedom to define proper moral and ethical conduct, choose what to value, and determine how best to live one's life. No other individual or societal institution has the right—nor should they have the power—to dictate to individuals what choices to make on these matters.

This individual liberty is based on a conception of human beings as autonomous from one another and equal.[4] At the most fundamental level, individuals *own themselves;* that is, no one else has legitimate control over what they do. Libertarians quote approvingly John Locke, who in his *Second Treatise on Government* said that "every man has a property in his own person; this nobody has any right to but himself."[5] Because individuals are equal in respect to this self-ownership, no one can impose one's conception of the good life or what is best for human flourishing on anyone else. From this right of self-ownership derives the freedoms that individuals require, such as freedom of conscience, speech, and religion, in order to control their own flourishing.[6]

Libertarians, then, are adverse to any public policy that directs what an individual can or cannot do as long as the action does not harm anyone else. This principle provides the basis for opposition to a wide range of public policies, including enforcement of mandatory seat-belt laws and motorcycle helmet laws, restrictions on reproductive autonomy and sexual conduct, prosecution of "victimless" crimes like prostitution or drug or alcohol consumption, enforcement of public access laws on private property, and restrictions on businesses such as sale of alcohol or tobacco. Concern for individual liberty leads libertarians to oppose any policy justified on moral grounds, such as restrictions on abortion, private sexual behavior, access to pornography, alcohol consumption, or drug use. Most libertarians agree that government cannot and should not "legislate morality," because only individuals can determine what is moral for themselves. Yet along with condemnation of morals legislation, libertarians are equally—perhaps even more—opposed to restrictions on economic liberty. They believe that an essential element of individual liberty is the freedom to dispose of one's economic resources according to one's own values, whether in buying products, entering an occupation, starting a business, or selling to particular customers.[7] This concern for economic liberty makes freedom to control individual private property and enter into voluntary exchanges in a free market the next two core principles of libertarianism.

Private Property. For libertarians, ownership of property gives self-owned individuals the means to achieve their individually chosen life goals and put into practice their individual value commitments. As one libertarian puts it, "the ownership of property is a necessary implication of self-ownership because all human action involves property. How else could happiness be pursued? If nothing else, we need a place to stand. We need the right to use land and other property to produce new goods and services."[8] In the modern world, individual property rights include not only rights to land or a business but rights to more abstract and intangible kinds of property, such as ownership of corporate stock. Individual freedom to dispose of such property is justified not only as a fundamental aspect of human liberty, but also on practical grounds. Libertarians believe that a society of individual property owners will more intelligently and efficiently use that property for productive purposes than if it were under collective control or regulation. Individual ownership connects responsibility for the most productive use of property to the individual self-interest of the owner. If the property is used wisely, the individual owner gains; if used unwisely, the individual suffers. Therefore, individual property ownership promotes effective and productive use of societal resources.[9] Most important, private property provides a basis for protecting other individual liberties.[10] It gives individuals resources that can be used to defend themselves if government seeks to deprive them of free speech, freedom of religion, or freedom to participate in politics.

Given this priority that libertarians place on individual control of one's private property, it is no surprise that they oppose most government regulation that places any limits on how individuals control their property. Government regulation might be justified, they would agree, if individual decisions on property use harm others; but they would insist on clear evidence that such harm occurs before agreeing to government regulation. So government may be justified in limiting environmental harms, such as polluting the water or air, that result from production in a factory, but libertarians would insist that the potential harm from the pollution be proven and that any regulation of that pollution be done in a manner that limited overall business decisions in the factory as little as possible. If no clear harm to other individuals can be proven to occur as a result of individual decisions regarding how property is used, then government regulation must be opposed. Certainly, for libertarians, any government regulation of business aimed at achieving a moral or religious objective, such as prohibiting the sale of liquor on Sunday, would be a clear violation of the right of private property.

Perhaps the most important aspect of property rights for libertarians is the understanding that no one, including government, should be allowed to take private property by force. If individuals have acquired their property and wealth justly, through activities that have not violated the rights of other individuals, then they have an absolute right to keep that property for themselves and have no obligation to give it over to anyone else, for any purpose.[11] This means that government should not be able to take private property for what it deems to be a public purpose, such as building a highway, unless it provides the property owner full compensation. And government certainly has no right to take property, wealth, or income from an individual, say through taxation, and turn it over to someone else. Any program that redistributes wealth from one person or group to another—such as the system of progressive taxation, which taxes wealthier people to support government activities at a higher rate than poorer people, programs to help the needy, or even, for some libertarians, public education or public libraries—violates property rights. If the wealthy are to help the less fortunate, for strict libertarians, such charitable acts must be through individual, voluntary choices. The right to own private property makes any governmental program of mandated redistribution illegitimate and unjust.

Voluntary Exchange. For libertarians, the only just and legitimate manner to transfer property from one individual to another is through voluntary exchange. This understanding provides the basis of the libertarian celebration of free markets. According to libertarians, markets—whether a farmers' market where fruits and vegetables are sold, stock markets where stock in corporations are bought and sold, or labor markets where employees find jobs with employers—are all networks of multiple voluntary exchanges. Libertarians esteem such markets for several reasons.

First, libertarians admire markets because their very existence enhances the realm of individual freedom. In the marketplace, individuals are "free to choose" what to buy, whom to employ, where to work, what to produce, and what to sell.[12] All these choices are made without anyone coercing anyone else, and they place individuals in control of what happens to them. By extension, the actions that take place in society as a whole, to the extent that they are the result of market exchanges, reflect the free choices of individuals. To make this point, Milton and his wife and coauthor Rose Friedman contrast the freedom individuals have at the supermarket with the freedom they have in democratic elections.[13] At the supermarket, individuals get to choose precisely the items they want. In elections, individuals must choose between a package of policy proposals (items) that different candidates offer. Even when one's preferred candidate wins, this may result in choosing "items" one did not want in order to obtain those one did. And when the candidate an individual has chosen does not win, that individual gets "items" she or he did not even want. So, if individuals want to maximize their freedom to choose societal outcomes that give them what they want, they should prefer market solutions to obtaining social needs rather than finding solutions through democratic processes.

Second, libertarians praise the efficiency of markets. If market exchanges are voluntary, then self-interested individuals will only agree to exchanges that they believe benefit them.[14] Every exchange, then, involves at least two individuals that get more satisfaction from the allocation of resources after the exchange than before. For example, if I sell my apple to you, after the sale, I get the money that I valued more than the apple and you get the apple that you valued more than your money. Now your hunger is satisfied and I have the money I need to market the Internet search engine that I just invented. Because markets, through networks of such mutually advantageous exchanges, allocate resources to where they are most needed, societal resources are put to their best uses. The overall result will be more economic productivity and greater prosperity.

Finally, libertarians admire how markets coordinate vast and complex human endeavors without any coercion or conscious central direction. No central plan is required for a free market to produce just the number of automobiles, lattes, baseball caps, hip-hop albums, and poetry volumes that people need and want to consume. A favorite anecdote libertarians use to illustrate this point concerns the multitude of activities that the market coordinates to produce a simple lead pencil.[15] Logging camps in Oregon are built and loggers housed and fed to cut cedar logs that are shipped on railroad cars to mills in California, which cut the lumber into small pieces and ship them to a pencil factory in Pennsylvania. Meanwhile, graphite is mined in Sri Lanka for the "lead," rubber trees in the East Indies are grown to produce the factice for the eraser, and copper and zinc are mined in Chile for the bit of brass to attach the eraser to the pencil wood. All these materials are produced and assembled in just the right quantities at the pencil factory without any of their thousands of producers knowing that their work is going into creating a pencil or any single person ordering that each necessary action take place so the pencil can be created. And it all only happens because a child exchanges a part of her allowance at the local drugstore to buy a pencil. The point of this story for libertarians is twofold. One, without free markets such marvelous instances of spontaneous coordination needed to create useful material goods would not occur, and second, interfering with or impeding free markets would prevent the creation of material prosperity, as represented in even mundane items like a good pencil.

Role of Government. A possible agent of harmful interference with the market, of course, is government. When libertarians talk about government they are most concerned with what it should not do. It should not violate individual liberty, it should not legislate morality, it should not redistribute income, and it should not impede the efficient operation of free market exchanges. But, unlike anarchists, libertarians recognize a needed role for government in a libertarian order. Government's job is to prevent force and fraud.[16] If individual liberty is to be secure for all, this requires a collective institution to make sure all are safe from those individuals who might wish to employ force or engage in fraud to violate another's freedom.

This need to secure individual liberty provides justification for a rather wide range of government activities. First, a complex fabric of laws and the institutions required to make them are needed to define clearly the liberties individuals possess and the precise nature of how they are to freely relate to one another. For example, laws defining clearly how individuals enter into contracts with one another are essential if individuals are to trust those with whom they exchange property. Second, institutions to ensure law and order, including the enforcement of contracts, are essential if individuals are to be secure in their freedom. Courts, police, prosecutors, and prisons exist to prevent individuals from interfering with one another's rights through force or fraud and to enforce the contracts that individuals make with one another.

For libertarians, government has an essential role in society, but the great danger is that government action will expand beyond what is needed to simply secure individual rights. Because the government has ultimate coercive power, government officials, usually in league with favored groups within society, may be tempted to use that power to their own advantage or on behalf of their own vision of the common good. In fact, libertarians decry the extent to which modern governments have expanded their powers beyond what is strictly necessary. Most libertarians condemn many of the economic powers government now wields in the name of the "public good." One listing of "tyrannical controls" over economic activity includes: licensing of doctors, plumbers, morticians, and other professions; laws "interfering" with labor contracts such as minimum wage requirements, overtime rules, and workplace safety requirements; and regulation of firms that raise capital in public stock exchanges.[17] Even more objectionable are government subsidies to promote particular industries or worthy social goals whether price supports for farmers, public television programs, or even the promotion of culture and scientific research. Such subsidies not only interfere with the efficiency of the free market and require taxing individuals to support endeavors they might not endorse, they have the further danger of making individuals dependent on government largesse. This dependence poses a grave threat to a free society as government becomes more and more powerful and individuals become afraid to resist government power for fear of losing their government benefits. A government that strays beyond its narrow function of preventing force and fraud ends up undermining individual freedom.[18]

To prevent government from expanding in ways that undermine liberty, libertarians advocate a strict understanding of the "rule of law" that includes clear constitutional restraints on government officials. For libertarian theorist F. A. Hayek, the rule of law means first, government is bound by formal, general rules that treat all individuals equally.[19] This means government cannot provide to any particular group of individuals a subsidy or benefit not available to all. Second, the rule of law means government cannot identify particular *ends* people should pursue individually or collectively; rather, it must be restricted to supporting the means by which individuals pursue their own individual goals. As he put it, "[government should be] a piece of utilitarian machinery intended to help individuals in the fullest development of their individual personality [ends] . . . [and not] . . . a moral institution . . . which imposes on its members its views on all moral questions."[20] To guarantee laws that meet this standard, a constitutional regime, including a written constitution and independent judiciary to enforce it, must be in place to limit government power. The natural tendency of government to expand means continual vigilance is required to keep it within its constitutional boundaries.

Spontaneous Order. Even if the rule of law and constitutional design check government, its very existence poses a threat to liberty. An even better safeguard against government interference with individual liberty would be to find ways to accomplish even legitimate collective action without recourse to government. Many libertarians believe that constructive orderly relationships among individuals can occur spontaneously without any central authority. The operation of the free market, as illustrated above in the pencil anecdote, provides an example. A libertarian society would depend on individuals to organize themselves for joint purposes as the need arises without central control or coercion. Many human institutions such as "language, law, money, and markets," according to libertarians, came into existence spontaneously.[21] If individuals perceive a need for useful collective institutions, libertarians believe they have the capacity to create them. Often, private associations in what is called "civil society" come together through the voluntary actions of individuals to accomplish social goals. Philanthropic associations, fraternal organizations, social clubs, and religious denominations can be relied upon to serve community needs, respond to emergencies, and help needy individuals without government action. If government's role is restricted, then individuals will step up voluntarily and spontaneously to provide for collective and social needs.

Libertarianism and "Liberalism." As any student who has an introductory course in political theory may have noticed, many of the views described here as libertarian bear a striking resemblance to what theory textbooks call classical liberalism. These are the political ideas initially articulated in the works of Thomas Hobbes and John Locke and later elaborated by thinkers such as Adam Smith, Thomas Paine, and John Stuart Mill. In fact, many of the theorists I have labeled libertarian preferred either the classical liberal or just the liberal label. Hayek always referred to himself as a classical liberal, while Friedman insisted on calling himself a liberal; both acknowledged that their work was lodged in the classical liberal tradition. In *Capitalism and Freedom,* Friedman even sought to reclaim the word *liberal* from contemporary liberals who he said had "corrupted" the term.[22] This terminological confusion exists because of modifications to liberal theory that emerged in the latter half of the nineteenth century.

At that time a number of political thinkers who embraced much of the classical liberal tradition, such as J. S. Mill and, most importantly, T. H. Green, began to see that more than just authoritarian governments threatened individual liberty.[23] They worried about how, in the liberal, capitalist societies then developing, poverty and inequality seemed also barriers to individual liberty. Green introduced a distinction between what he called negative and positive freedom. Classical liberals (or today's libertarians) saw freedom only in a negative sense as the absence of government control over individual liberty. But Green thought individual liberty also depended on positive freedom—the ability to obtain what was needed to develop one's capacities and pursue one's goals. Poverty, illness, and ignorance constituted obstacles to obtaining this positive freedom, so Green argued that government needed to step in and provide what today we would call equal opportunity. Public schools and hospitals, promotion of safe working conditions, and the like promoted individual freedom. This outlook came to be called welfare liberalism.

In the United States, beginning in the Progressive Era, just as Friedman laments, welfare liberals had taken over the term *liberal* for themselves. Those favoring a more classical liberal outlook came to be called conservatives. (In Europe, the term liberal or neo-liberal still refers primarily to classical liberal or libertarian views. Those holding "welfare liberal" views tend to be labeled "social democrats.") Eventually welfare liberals tended to adopt a communitarian understanding of the relationship between the individual and community. Today, most welfare liberals would embrace the communitarian views described below, particularly on economic issues. But, as argued earlier, some welfare liberals lean more in the classical liberal or libertarian direction on social issues. But in sorting through this terminological thicket, keep in mind the caveats with which this section began.

Public Policy Implications. How, then, does a libertarian outlook influence public policymaking? First, it reduces the need for public policy. The vision of limited government means libertarians simply will oppose enacting many policies some policymakers might see as desirable. Second, a libertarian approach will be biased toward policies that encourage social outcomes that are produced spontaneously in the market rather than social outcomes created by government. Specifically, this means lower taxes, so that individual decisions guide how money is spent and invested rather than collective decisions; moral and cultural values are determined by individual choices rather than public policy; and government does little planning regarding the direction of economic development. Finally, when public policy is made, a libertarian approach will seek market-based alternatives that place individuals in control, as much as possible, of public policy outcomes. As we will see in subsequent chapters, libertarians have been ingenious in devising market-based public policy approaches in environmental policy, health care, education, and many other policy areas.

Communitarianism in a Nutshell

The same caveats applied to the preceding summary of libertarianism apply to this capsule summary of communitarianism. There are many varieties of communitarianism, and not all communitarians subscribe to a single consistent set of ideas. The following summary describes the fundamental concepts that define communitarianism as a political ideology, but does not capture the many nuances present in communitarian thought. And, like many libertarians, those who propound communitarian policy positions may not be consistent in their advocacy; nor are they necessarily self-conscious of their communitarianism. In fact, unlike libertarianism, which has attracted a core of conscious adherents in recent years, the number of Americans who identify themselves as "communitarians" is extremely small. For example, there is no Communitarian Party in the United States; the closest equivalent is a Communitarian Network, made up of a small number of academics. The influence of the following ideas on public policy comes not from an organized cadre of communitarians, but from people whose positions on particular policy issues are based on the following understandings.

Community. The core communitarian value, equivalent to individual liberty for libertarianism, is the idea of community. For communitarian thinker Philip Selznick, a community is a framework in which people "share a common life."[24] This common life includes a shared history, or what sociologist Robert Bellah calls a "community of meaning," shared beliefs, and common rules for right conduct.[25] This view of community emphasizes the interdependence among individual human beings who require the nurturing and respect of others if they are to live meaningful and satisfying lives. Human beings are not "self-owned," as libertarians would have it, but products of the communities of which they are a part. Among these communities is the national political community in which individuals share a common life with other citizens.

A very different conception of individual human nature divides communitarians and libertarians. Unlike the autonomous, detached individuals libertarians describe, communitarians consider individuals to be "socially embedded persons," the products of the history and culture of their community.[26] Even the individual liberty that libertarians celebrate can only exist within a community that creates and nurtures it. Human liberty, like all human goods, did not arise fully made out of nothing but was a creation of past generations of individuals who suffered and died on its behalf.[27] To preserve liberty, individuals are obliged to support the community institutions and practice that give it life. What is true of liberty applies equally to all other benefits that individuals enjoy. Wealth, education, career success, and satisfying personal lives depend on contributions from social institutions and supports; they are not solely the result of individual effort.

Since all of us benefit from community ties, we have a reciprocal obligation to support the community and other individual members. Communitarians emphasize the responsibilities and obligations that go with community membership, along with its rights and benefits. This is not merely a limited contractual relationship or the sort of voluntary exchanges that sum up societal ties for most libertarians. Individual ties to the community are deeper, more diffuse, and more open-ended than implied in a contract. They may require individuals to sacrifice for the good of the community, including other individual members, without any obvious individual, direct, return compensation. Soldiers who sacrifice their lives for the good of the national political community are a dramatic example. Because human beings are socially embedded creatures, human history is replete with examples of individuals willing to sacrifice for the good of their communities and fellow citizens.

The Common Good. If individuals are socially embedded beings, "enmeshed in [community/societal] institutions that both constrain and empower them," then one can reasonably inquire about whether those societal institutions produce a common good.[28] For libertarians, such talk of a "common good" makes no sense. They believe that only individuals can have goals, purposes, interests, and values; all goods are individual. This is what former British prime minister Margaret Thatcher meant when she famously remarked that "there is no such thing as society." To even claim that there are substantive goods a society or community as a whole should seek to achieve can only be a mask certain individuals use to impose their individual vision of the good on others. Yet if one replaces the libertarian understanding of human beings as totally autonomous and unencumbered with social ties with the more nuanced understanding of individuals as products of their communities, then the common good of those communities must be an important concern.

Even libertarians concede the existence of a common good or interest that all individuals have in fair rules and processes, "the rule of law" described in the previous section, allowing them to freely pursue their individual goods. People can achieve their own vision of the good life only if society provides the freedom and conditions that allow them to do so. Communitarians take this very "thin" conception of the common good further in advocating a "thick" conception encompassing the many other social conditions that give individuals the capacity to live full and satisfying lives, beyond simply fair procedures and rules.[29] As Pope John XXIII writes, the common good is "the sum total of those conditions of social living whereby men and women are enabled more fully and readily to achieve their well-being."[30] Communitarians identify a large number of substantive social and community conditions that are necessary to achieve this goal. A clean and healthy environment; access to good jobs at fair wages; quality education for all; preservation and promotion of cultural goods—such as art, literature, science, and religion; and a wholesome moral climate are some of the substantive goods that may constitute the public good.

A key concern for communitarians has to be deciding what the common good is and what it requires. Most modern communitarians would agree that individual preferences regarding most aspects of life should be respected—a broad range of individual liberty itself is part of and contributes to the common good. But the common good often will require limits of individual preferences or seek to channel preferences in particular directions. For many people, especially libertarians, limiting individual freedom in the name of the common good smacks of autocracy. Communitarians respond that there is nothing autocratic or authoritarian about enforcing community norms established in the name of the common good if they are determined democratically. Democratic institutions and procedures exist to deliberate about what the good life for all requires.[31] Democratic communitarians understand the common good to be defined through a process of dialogue and deliberation, not imposed on individuals based on some particular group's deductions from particular philosophic or religious principles. In pluralistic, liberal democracies, a variety of philosophies and religious outlooks will inform deliberations about the common good, but those deliberations can produce agreements on a vision of what the good of the whole community requires.

Regulated Markets. Because communitarians believe in the common good, they advocate monitoring market outcomes to make sure that the common good is not being undermined. Just because two individuals may agree to a voluntary exchange that they regard as mutually beneficial does not mean it benefits the community as a whole. A drug dealer may find a willing buyer for his product or a real estate developer may find a willing seller of a protected wetland, but that does not mean that society must sanction the drug deal or allow real estate development that harms the common environment. Communitarians value the material prosperity and the efficient production and distribution of goods and services that free markets produce. Nowadays, most of us consider capitalist market economies as a valued element of the common good. But the aggregate of free exchanges in a free marketplace may produce negative outcomes for the community that must be regulated. When markets produce environmental degradation, pornography, excessive inequalities of wealth and income, or a coarse, mindless popular culture, communitarians believe that public action is justified to correct the situation in the name of the common good. This may mean outright prohibitions of some kinds of market activity, such as drug dealing; or tight regulation of the sale and distribution of certain kinds of products, such as cigarettes or pornography; or enforcement of rules mandating fair treatment in the marketplace, such as antidiscrimination laws, protections of worker health and safety, and minimum wages; or subsidies promoting activities insufficiently produced in the market alone, such as public libraries, art museums, radio and TV, theater, art, and music. For communitarians, markets are good, but markets regulated in the public interest and for the common good are better.

As libertarians will be the first to point out, regulations of markets inevitably means limits on property rights, which communitarians are quite willing to allow. Communitarians are likely to share the view of the American legal realist school that emphasized how the distribution of property in any society at any given time depends on the legal rules governing property ownership. They agree with the utilitarian philosopher Jeremy Bentham that "there is no natural property [because] property is entirely the creature of the law."[32] Laws defining property ownership give certain entitlements to holders of property and confer limits on the freedom of those without property.[33] For example, because of property law, hungry people cannot simply squat on unused land and grow the food they need without compensating the landowner. The owner can demand such compensation and the hungry people must pay, even if the land would be unutilized otherwise, because the law demands it. The landowner's right and the obligations of the hungry seem "natural" to us because the conventions of our society happen to assign property rights to land in this fashion. We lose sight of the artificial, conventional aspects of these rights. Could we imagine a society in which landowners lost rights to untilled land after a certain period of time and hungry people were free to take it? A different legal definition of property rights could make it so.

The extent to which such rights reflect legal convention become clearer when we consider those things in which people do not conventionally have property rights. Only the most extreme champions of private property would give mothers property rights in their babies so they could sell them on the market, or individuals such rights over their body organs.[34] People cannot have property rights to such things because communities and the law deny them. Following this understanding of property rights, communitarians regard them as delegations of public power, useful to society but potentially revocable if misused or defined differently if the common good requires. When we see property rights as legal conventions, not absolute entitlements, then a host of limitations on property rights are easily justified: time limits on patents, copyrights, and zoning laws, and public regulation of fair labor practices or the stock market have all become familiar to and accepted by most Americans.

Finally, communitarians understand that market regulation means limits on the choices individuals may make in the marketplace. Together with libertarians, communitarians believe that most of the time individuals should be free to enter into any market exchanges they find mutually beneficial. Being free to choose among the goods, services, and business opportunities in the marketplace usually provides both individual satisfaction and social benefits. But communitarians understand that individual consumers may make choices that lead to social harms. Community efforts to discourage the choice to smoke, overeat, pollute the air, or ride a motorcycle without a helmet may justifiably restrict individual freedom for the sake of public health.[35] Recent measures instituted in many communities that make smoking expensive and inconvenient, such as taxes on cigarettes or prohibitions on smoking in public places, are in the communitarian spirit of molding consumer choices to reduce the health effects of smoking. Similar logic implies regulation of business corporations to ensure that they act in a socially responsible manner. At minimum this means that they do not commit fraud or despoil the environment. Social responsibility also means treating employees well; paying fair wages; adhering to job health and safety standards; and not discriminating against minorities, women, or the disabled. A broader understanding of social responsibility, which most communitarians would favor, demands that corporations consider more than just maximizing the bottom line in making business decisions. Communities must respect the long-term need of corporations to be profitable, but they also can mandate that corporations limit negative impacts on communities, even if some financial loss occurs.

Moral Government. As the discussion of communitarian willingness to regulate the market implies, communitarians view government as a positive force for promoting the common good. It must do more than simply provide a framework of the "rule of law" in which people pursue their individual goods. Government can and should "legislate morality," whether standards of individual moral behavior or collective moral outcomes. Such a government is not automatically authoritarian or a threat to individual liberty. In a liberal democracy, the moral values government promotes are determined through dialogue, debate, and deliberation. They reflect the will of the majority, but with attention to minority rights. Contemporary communitarians accept the need for zones of individual rights and privacy.[36] At the same time, democratic governments need to assert the community moral standards that most people deem necessary for the good of the community.

To see government as a moral agent does not mean that it is an instrument of a particular religious or philosophical point of view. In a pluralistic, liberal democracy like the United States, citizens will draw on different and varied religious and philosophical traditions in developing the common moral values that government should promote. Despite the different sources of moral values upon which Americans draw, most would agree on the immorality of racial discrimination, the morality of strong families, the need to protect individual human dignity, and the moral imperative of respecting human diversity. In fact, most Americans regard tolerance of different religious points of view as an important moral imperative. For communitarians, the First Amendment prohibition of a religious establishment and protections of religious expression are not only guarantees of individual religious freedom but also guarantees of the common good. In a religiously diverse society, the First Amendment religion clauses prevent religious conflict and strife, protect varied religious practices, and permit religion to flourish. Many scholars consider America's tradition of religious freedom, including the right not to believe, to be a major factor in the greater amount of religious observance in the United States than in other Western democracies. Communitarians see no contradiction between divergent moral and religious viewpoints in society and the capacity of government to promote moral views on which there is general agreement.

A moral government is one that promotes social justice. Communitarians reject the libertarian view that government confine itself to providing just processes, a formal "rule of law" equitably applied to all, and not concern itself with the outcomes of those processes. The French writer Anatole France pithily satirized this libertarian view when he wrote: "The law, in its majestic equality, forbids the rich as well as the poor to sleep under bridges, to beg in the streets, and to steal bread."[37] For communitarians, government must concern itself with establishing a just social order that prevents the need for some to live under bridges or steal bread to feed their families. Social justice demands, as a moral imperative, that individuals be able to obtain work at a living wage, health care, quality education, and pensions. When the free market and social institutions fail to produce these outcomes, then government has a moral duty to step in.

Hayek dismissed notions of social justice as a "mirage."[38] He thought that only individuals could be held morally accountable for the conscious choices they made; social outcomes, such as inequalities resulting from market processes, were "spontaneous" and morally neutral. Correcting such outcomes in the name of social justice would lead to despotic governments imposing utopian designs on society. For a communitarian, such a view ignores how social structures, such as market systems, are themselves humanly designed institutions that produce outcomes biased in favor of some and against others. Understanding such structures in this fashion makes asking whether their outcomes meet the requirements of social justice legitimate. Social adjustments to compensate for unjust outcomes, whether those outcomes were intended or unintended—conscious or unconscious—does not mean creating utopian schemes, but rather providing incremental "relief of oppression."[39] Good governments have a moral obligation to make laws and establish social structures that respect the fundamental human dignity of all citizens.

Civil Society. Like libertarians, communitarians believe in the importance of a vibrant civil society. Unlike libertarians, they do not believe civil society to be solely a realm of voluntary and "spontaneous" relationships. Communitarians expect the institutions of civil society to be a primary means for nurturing and enforcing socials norms and establishing social justice. Churches, fraternal societies, social clubs, even choral societies are critical to creating the "social capital" that both bind communities together and help individuals live successful, fulfilling lives. Government alone cannot be responsible for either achieving social justice or enforcing individual obligations to community. In civil society, individuals organize to meet community needs, to pass on the community's cultural heritage, and to help individuals in need. Moreover, through the associational life in civic organizations, individuals learn critical citizenship skills. They learn how to work with one another in a democratic manner to identify and address community needs. This insight undercuts the libertarian fear that communitarianism leads to oppressive government. The creation of a good community or "good society" is not solely a governmental responsibility; nor is it the product of a single, unified vision of the good. The diverse groups within civil society all work to build a strong community from within the various religious, cultural, and ethnic traditions that motivate them.

Also, communitarians recognize that, like all aspects of society, a vibrant civil society does not arise spontaneously but requires good laws and public policies to nurture it. Political scientist Theda Skocpol argues that the many civic organizations that formed in the United States in the early twentieth century, whether fraternal organizations like the Odd Fellows or social service organizations like the Red Cross, depended on governmental encouragement and sound public policies.[40] The decline in the willingness of Americans to join such organizations in recent decades likewise can be attributed to governmental decisions. Public policies that have encouraged suburbanization, failed to support strong families, and ignored wage stagnation all undermine civil society. People who must commute long hours between work and home or work two jobs to earn an adequate income do not have much time left for work with a fraternal or volunteer organization.[41] A key part of the communitarian agenda is the enactment of public policies that encourage rather than discourage participation in civic organizations.

Public Policy Implications. Aside from the sharp differences with libertarians on the role of government, the need for adequate taxes, and the limitations of market-based public policies that should be clear from this discussion, communitarians recognize the need for civic virtue in the making of public policy. Libertarians assume, in fact encourage, self-interested behavior on the part of citizens; they see little need to expect citizens to consider the public good rather than their own self-interest when thinking about public policy. In fact, much of libertarianism derives from a belief that civic virtue is an illusion. From a communitarian perspective, however, citizens should consider not only how they might be affected by a public policy proposal, but also how the proposal affects the broader community. When a public school bond issue is on the ballot, the virtuous citizen asks: "Do the schools need more money to educate the community's children?" not "Do I want to pay more taxes?" Because a communitarian society requires citizens who ask the former, not the latter question, promoting civic virtue itself is a key communitarian public policy issue.

These nutshell summaries show the very contrasting ways libertarians and communitarians view public policy issues. How did these contrasting perspectives come to dominate contemporary public policy debates? The following section traces the emergence of a systematic libertarian worldview—first on the political right, within the 1950s conservative movement, and then on the political left, out of the 1960s counter-culture. The communitarian response begins in the 1980s and gains strength as the Clinton administration draws on its insights in formulating a New Democratic policy agenda. As the new century begins, libertarian and communitarian outlooks face off across the public policy spectrum, as the Bush administration pursues a decidedly libertarian approach toward economic policy and a communitarian one in the social arena.

The Rise of Libertarianism and the Communitarian Response

The modern libertarian movement emerged in the United States after World War II. Over the previous fifty years, in every industrial capitalist society, the role of government in regulating business, providing social benefits to its citizens, and planning industrial and social developments had expanded enormously. In the United States, the growth of government had taken place primarily through the Progressive reforms during the first two decades of the twentieth century and President Franklin D. Roosevelt's New Deal programs of the 1930s. The new "welfare state," as this expanded governmental role was labeled, was seen as an improvement on the brutal, unregulated, "laissez-faire" capitalism of the nineteenth century. As noted earlier, "welfare liberals" were the primary advocates of this expanded role for government. For its proponents, the welfare state softened the sharp edges of capitalism by protecting individuals from the risks of the unregulated marketplace and assuring that businesses served the public interest as well as their owners' interests. The dominant view at mid-century was that the welfare state was a permanent improvement on the capitalist economic model in that it preserved key elements of capitalism, such as private property and a market economy, that brought overall material prosperity while ameliorating capitalism's negative consequences, such as severe poverty and environmental degradation. A well-regulated capitalist welfare state was the "vital center" between unbridled laissez-faire capitalism and the totalitarian dangers of communism or fascism.[42] For some observers of the welfare state, however, it was neither vital nor centrist but rather a step toward the destruction of both capitalist material prosperity and human freedom. For these libertarian thinkers, as they would eventually be labeled, the expansion of government was a grave mistake that could only be corrected through a return to the true principles of liberal capitalism.

Two Austrian economists, both refugees from the Nazi regime, launched the first attacks on the mid-century welfare state in works that gained considerable attention immediately following World War II. For Ludwig von Mises and his student F. A. Hayek, the welfare state, far from being the "vital center," was only a milder version of the socialist totalitarianism that they saw characterizing both Nazi Germany and Soviet Communism. In *The Road to Serfdom*, first published in 1944, Hayek argued that the economic planning going on in liberal democracies undermined individual liberty and the rule of law in much the same way it did under a socialist planned economy. A middle way between a liberal, free market society and socialist system was an illusion; even a partial planning system led eventually to "serfdom."[43] Von Mises not only condemned any attempt to modify market outcomes through economic planning, but argued that any government intervention in market outcomes, however well intentioned, served only to reduce the standard of living in the long run.[44] Even though many mainstream intellectuals would attack von Mises and Hayek as eccentric throwbacks spouting antiquated ideas, their work would provide intellectual underpinnings to the nascent conservative movement slowly gathering strength in the 1950s.

Von Mises's and Hayek's celebration of individual liberty as the supreme political value and their attack on the welfare state as a threat to it appealed to the small but increasingly fervent conservative movement building in postwar America. Until the rise of social and religious conservatism in the 1980s, their libertarian ideas formed the domestic policy doctrine for most conservatives. Conservative publications like William F. Buckley's *National Review*, first published in 1955, found libertarian economic ideas a compatible match with their commitment to anticommunism.[45] In the 1960s, Friedman brilliantly promoted these ideas, first in his best-selling book *Capitalism and Freedom* and then in his column in *Newsweek* magazine.[46] Friedman translated libertarian philosophy into practical policy reforms, such as school vouchers, privatizing Social Security, tax reform, and welfare reform that remain today the core libertarian policy ideas. Assisting in this popularization of libertarianism was the novelist Ayn Rand, who in novels like *The Fountainhead* and *Atlas Shrugged* wrote of heroic individuals struggling to express themselves in the face of the stultifying conformity and mediocrity of society.[47]

Eventually politicians would integrate libertarian-based policy proposals into their campaign platform. Conservative Republican presidential candidate Barry Goldwater translated his personal libertarian outlook into major themes in his 1964 campaign. Although Goldwater endured a massive repudiation at the polls, the conservative activists he inspired and other politicians, such as Ronald Reagan, carried forward the conservative dream and the libertarian ideas that formed a part of it. By the 1970s, libertarian proposals were taken seriously in political debate and well represented in policy discussions in Washington. At this time, policy think tanks like the Cato Institute and the Heritage Foundation were founded to promote these policy ideas. The world of academic scholarship took more respectful regard for libertarian ideas when Harvard political philosopher Robert Nozick formulated a systematic justification of libertarianism in *Anarchy, State, and Utopia,* published in 1974.[48] So when Ronald Reagan took the presidential oath in 1980, libertarianism was no longer an obscure doctrine of eccentric émigré thinkers but a coherent and influential set of ideas that would guide one side of the public policy debate into the next century.

While libertarian ideas were establishing a strong presence on the right in the conservative movement, they were also taking root on the political left. Left-wing libertarianism was one of the products of the political turmoil of the 1960s. Among the many political movements of the era, such as the struggles for civil rights and against the Vietnam War, were demands, especially among young people, for more individual freedom in personal self-expression—a movement that came to be known as the "counterculture." The "beat" writers of the previous decade, including novelists Jack Kerouac and Ken Kesey, and poet Allen Ginsberg, had lampooned the conformity and conventional morality of the 1950s. Inspired by the libertarian strain in these works, as well as that of Rand, many of the sixties generation sought to defy the constraints of social convention in how they conducted their personal behavior. The hippies of the era, with their long hair, gaudy dress, profane language, rock and roll, sexual experimentation, and, especially, drug use, represented a wide rejection, by the young, of conventional social mores. While the counterculture had a strong communitarian strain—hippie communes and other communitarian experiments were a characteristic feature of the era—the broadest political impact was more libertarian. The individualist, more libertarian,

DURING THE 1960S, LIBERTARIAN IDEALS APPEALED TO RIGHT-WING POLITICIANS, LIKE 1964 PRESIDENTIAL CANDIDATE BARRY GOLDWATER (TOP), AND THE COUNTERCULTURAL LEFT, LIKE THESE SAN FRANCISCO HIPPIES DURING THE 1967 "SUMMER OF LOVE" (BOTTOM).

motto to "do your own thing" had the strongest resonance among the young. The libertarian tendencies of the counterculture coincided with other political developments of the time that tended to privilege individual rights and autonomy. Decisions of the Warren Court during the 1950s and 1960s had emphasized expanding the realm of individual rights and autonomy in areas such as religion, free speech, rights of criminal defendants, and sexual relations. Demands for black, women, gay, Hispanic, or native American liberation, while not necessarily libertarian in nature, often were given a libertarian twist into a blanket demand for a free choice of an individual "lifestyle." At the same time, legal theorists began to advocate the assertion of absolute individual rights as an avenue toward progressive reform. For example, Yale University's Charles Reich sought to expand the reach of social welfare programs by reconceptualizing jobs and welfare as a type of property right.[49] Many liberal activists adopted the strategy of asserting rights in court as a primary avenue toward progressive social change rather than seeking legislative remedies.[50] The 1973 *Roe v. Wade* decision that defined a constitutional right to an abortion seemed to vindicate this strategy for many on the left. By the end of the 1970s, liberals were using essentially the same libertarian arguments to expand individual autonomy in social matters, such as sexual identity and behavior, free speech, and lifestyle choices, that conservatives used to seek individual autonomy in economic matters.

The increasing popularity of libertarianism in this era, on both the right and the left, should not be surprising given the American "liberal" tradition.[51] Libertarianism, after all, is an extreme, and some philosophers would argue, distorted version of the classical liberal ideas upon which the American political system was founded. The Enlightenment ideals that informed the American founding were meant to liberate individuals from the stifling, autocratic communitarianism of the time. The traditional celebration of American individualism, whether in the work of American writers like Ralph Waldo Emerson and Henry David Thoreau or in popular culture, also provided fertile ground for the popularity of libertarian ideas. Yet, in the past, American individualism and its embrace of individual liberty had been leavened by the more communitarian strains of small town life or the close community ties in urban ethnic neighborhoods.[52] Social changes in the second half of the twentieth century, including social mobility and suburbanization, had separated many Americans from those communal ties. By the end of the 1970s, many social commentators remarked on the increasing self-centeredness and selfishness that seemed to reflect the rising dominance of libertarian outlooks in what they now called the Me Decade. Pop culture advanced this mentality in books and magazines, such as the best-selling *Looking Out for #1*, a self-help manual encouraging selfishness.[53]

As the social pendulum swung in a libertarian direction it induced a counterreaction in the 1980s that eventually produced the contemporary communitarian movement. A first sign of this pendulum swing came from the political right, among cultural and religious conservatives who associated themselves with the Reagan presidency. Reagan's key political achievement was to unite these communitarian conservatives, appalled at society's libertarian turn on moral, cultural, and social issues, with the economic libertarians who had previously been the core of the conservative movement.[54] Reagan's own political rhetoric often sounded communitarian themes, with references to "building a city on the hill" and the erosion of community ties, even as his administration pursued a thorough libertarian agenda on economic matters and in the area of business deregulation. In the realm of political philosophy, key works were published by Alasdair MacIntyre (*After Virtue*) and Michael Sandel (*Liberalism and the Limits of Justice*), which questioned the libertarian view of government neutrality toward moral ends and the libertarian conception of autonomous and "unencumbered" human nature.[55]

An influential work of social philosophy published in 1984, *Habits of the Heart* by sociologist Robert Bellah and colleagues, created a portrait of the constraint American individualism placed on maintaining a good society.[56] Drawing on Alexis de Tocqueville's insight that success of American democracy required social mores or "habits of the heart" to counter cultural individualism if community ties were to be maintained, Bellah described in detail the erosion of those mores and the absence of community within America's increasingly libertarian culture. Works such as this and others stimulated new efforts to overcome the Me Decade ethos and stimulate more community mindedness on the part of Americans.[57] A number of scholars and prominent Americans began to call for a program of national service to build an ethos of citizenship and community mindedness among young people. In mid-decade, a number of college and university presidents formed Campus Compact to encourage their students to engage in community service and to integrate service-learning into college curricula. Such efforts helped to spark a student community service movement that remains a key component of campus life today. In his first term, President Bill Clinton would draw upon this community experience in creating his AmeriCorps national service program.

In the early 1990s, a number of scholars, led by Amitai Etzioni, a prominent sociologist, came together to form an explicitly communitarian movement. Their manifesto, "The Responsive Communitarian Platform: Rights and Responsibilities," defined this new communitarian perspective. Its aim was to recognize "both individual human dignity and the social dimension of human existence," and it detailed the communitarian view found in the nutshell summary in this chapter. A new journal, *The Responsive Community,* would provide a forum for elaborating on this ideological perspective and offering specific communitarian responses to contemporary public policy issues. Nearly every current policy issue over the next decade, including taxes, family policy, welfare, education, drug abuse, crime, and many others would be addressed in this publication.[58] Communitarian views received a strong hearing in the Clinton administration through one of the founding editors of

The Responsive Community, political philosopher William Galston, who was named a key Clinton policy advisor. Through Galston and others, communitarian views have become more and more influential in American policy debates.

Communitarian and antilibertarian views have received a boost, as well, from evaluations of failures of libertarian-inspired policies. One area in which libertarians succeeded in fostering policy change was in business deregulation. First in the airline industry, then in trucking and railroads, banking, electricity, telecommunications, and prescription drugs, Congress responded to libertarian arguments over the past twenty-five years in removing many of the regulatory restraints on these industries that had been in place since the 1930s. In other areas, such as health care and the environment, libertarian proposals for introducing market incentives had been in effect for some time. By the late 1990s, many of the negative effects of these deregulation and market schemes became apparent in developments such as skyrocketing electric rates, an airline industry in perpetual financial crisis, and a dysfunctional health care system.[59] By the new millennium, a network of journals, such as *The American Prospect,* and think tanks like the Century Foundation, the Economic Policy Institute, and the Campaign for America's Future would contest libertarian and pro-market views on policy issues. While libertarians continue to have the edge in promoting their policy positions among the public and political elites, communitarian alternatives are beginning to gain more attention.

The Plan of the Book

The chapters that follow will document the confrontation between libertarian and communitarian views on the major policy issues confronting Americans today. The reader should be forewarned, however, that each chapter will take a point of view emphasizing the flaws in the libertarian approach. While I recognize many virtues in the libertarian outlook and cherish many of the ends, such as individual liberty, that it promotes, I believe that it is fundamentally flawed as a guide for political life and good public policy. In the chapters that follow, I will show in detail the shortcomings in the libertarian position on each public policy issue. In presenting this point of view, however, I will attempt to present as fairly and completely as possible both the libertarian and communitarian views on each policy issue. The reader will have seen a model of such a presentation in the nutshell summaries of each philosophy in this chapter.

In each of the following chapters, I will begin with a general description of the history, context, and nature of each policy issue. Then, the contrasting libertarian and communitarian proposals for each policy will be presented. I will conclude with my own analysis of the proposals pointing out why a communitarian approach is likely to result in a better outcome than the libertarian one. Here are the issues we will look at: taxing and spending, deregulation,

Social Security, health care, and issues regarding the beginning and ending of life—abortion and euthanasia. On each of these policies, many readers will find the libertarian position logical and appealing. Because of our history and culture, most Americans like to think of themselves as autonomous individuals capable of solving problems without relying on others. Our predilection is to regard government as, like Ronald Reagan used to say, "the problem, not the solution." The argument of this book is that this libertarian view is an illusion. The community ties, including those government provides, that make our country function successfully are not always obvious to us, but they are essential. Policies that recognize them and reinforce them are most likely to succeed. The libertarian illusion is that we can do without government and depend on voluntary exchanges in the market to spontaneously meet community needs. The goal of this book is to lift the veil on these claims to show how illusory they are.

SUGGESTIONS FOR FURTHER READING

Boaz, David. *Libertarianism: A Primer.* New York: The Free Press, 1997. The basics of libertarianism from the Cato Institute, the premiere libertarian think tank.

Doherty, Brian. *Radicals for Capitalism: A Freewheeling History of the Modern American Libertarian Movement.* New York: Public Affairs, 2007. As the title suggests, this book chronicles all the details of the personalities involved in contemporary American libertarianism.

Hayek, F. A. *The Road to Serfdom.* Chicago: University of Chicago Press, 1944. A classic warning of the dangers of the welfare state by a prominent libertarian thinker.

Nozick, Robert. *Anarchy, State, and Utopia.* New York: Basic Books, 1974. A now-classic case for libertarianism from a leading American philosopher.

Selznick, Philip. *The Communitarian Persuasion.* Baltimore: The Johns Hopkins University Press, 2002. A summary of key communitarian principles by one of the leading theorists of communitarianism.

SELECTED WEB SITES

http://world.std.com/~mhuben/libindex.html. A compendium of articles and Web links critical of libertarian ideas.

www.cato.org. Web site of the Cato Institute, the leading libertarian think tank.

www.mises.org. Web site dedicated to the memory of Ludwig von Mises, with articles on libertarian policy ideas.

NOTES

1. Milton Friedman, *Capitalism and Freedom* (Chicago: University of Chicago Press, 1962), 1.
2. Terence Ball and Richard Dagger, *Political Ideologies and the Democratic Ideal,* 4th ed. (New York: Longman, 2002), 5.
3. A number of authors have devised four-fold tables expressing these relationships. See, for example: David Boaz, *Libertarianism: A Primer* (New York: The Free

Press, 1997), 22; Kenneth Janda, Jeffrey M. Berry, and Jerry Goldman, *The Challenge of Democracy: Government in America*, 3rd ed. (Boston: Houghton Mifflin, 1992), 28.

4. Richard Epstein, *Skepticism and Freedom* (Chicago: University of Chicago Press, 2003), 35–38.
5. John Locke, *The Second Treatise of Government* (Indianapolis: Bobbs-Merrill, 1952), 17.
6. Boaz, *Libertarianism*, 64.
7. Milton and Rose Friedman, *Free to Choose* (New York: Avon Books, 1979), 57.
8. Boaz, *Libertarianism*, 65.
9. Epstein, *Skepticism and Freedom*, 39.
10. Boaz, *Libertarianism*, 68.
11. Robert Nozick's *Anarchy, State, and Utopia* (New York: Basic Books, 1974), perhaps the leading philosophical justification of libertarianism, offers this critique of redistribution.
12. The connection between free markets and human freedom is the central theme of Milton and Rose Friedman's *Free to Choose*.
13. Ibid., 57.
14. Epstein, *Skepticism and Freedom*, 42.
15. The origin of this story seems to be an article by Leonard Read published in the December 1958 issue of *The Freeman*, an early libertarian periodical. The story has wide circulation in libertarian circles and writings. See Milton and Rose Friedman, *Free to Choose*, 3–5.
16. Epstein, *Skepticism and Freedom*, 46.
17. Milton and Rose Friedman, *Free to Choose*, 57–58.
18. Ibid., 58–61.
19. F. A. Hayek, *The Road to Serfdom* (Chicago: University of Chicago Press, 1944), 73–79.
20. Ibid., 77.
21. Boaz, *Libertarianism*, 16–17.
22. Friedman, *Capitalism and Freedom*, 6.
23. Ball and Dagger, *Political Ideologies and the Democratic Ideal*, 72–73.
24. Philip Selznick, *The Communitarian Persuasion* (Baltimore: The Johns Hopkins University Press, 2002), 16.
25. Ibid., 19.
26. Ibid., 42.
27. Thomas A. Spragens Jr., "The Limitations of Libertarianism," in *The Essential Communitarian Reader*, ed. Amitai Etzioni (Lanham, Md.: Rowman and Littlefield, 1998), 24.
28. John A. Coleman, "The Common Good and Catholic Social Thought," in *A Distinctive Voice: American Catholics and Civic Engagement*, ed. Margaret O'Brien Steinfels (Lanham, Md.: Rowman and Littlefield, 2004), 5.
29. Selznick, *The Communitarian Persuasion*, 125.
30. Coleman, "The Common Good and Catholic Social Thought," 11.
31. Selznick, *The Communitarian Persuasion*, 125.
32. Quoted in Cass Sunstein, *The Second Bill of Rights: FDR's Unfinished Revolution and Why We Need It More Than Ever* (New York: Basic Books, 2004), 20.
33. Barbara Fried, "Left Libertarianism: A Review Essay," *Philosophy and Public Affairs* 32, no. 1 (Winter 2004): 72.

34. Arguments for a market in human organs by two of the leading advocates of this idea: Virginia Postrel, "Need Transplant Donors? Pay Them," *Los Angeles Times,* June 10, 2006, B17; Sally Satel, "Supply, Demand, and Kidney Transplants," *Policy Review* 144 (August/September, 2007): 59–69.
35. Selznick, *The Communitarian Persuasion,* 97.
36. Ibid., 42, 69–81.
37. Anatole France, *The Red Lily,* trans. Winfred Stephens (London: John Lane, 1914), 95.
38. Hayek's views are discussed in Selznick, *The Communitarian Persuasion,* 107–109.
39. Ibid., 109.
40. Theda Skocpol, *Diminished Democracy: From Membership to Management in American Civic Life* (Norman: University of Oklahoma Press, 2003), 20–73.
41. Robert Putnam, *Bowling Alone* (New York: Simon and Shuster, 2000).
42. Arthur Schlesinger Jr., *The Vital Center* (Boston: Houghton Mifflin, 1949).
43. Hayek, *The Road to Serfdom* (Chicago: University of Chicago Press, 1944), 41.
44. Boaz, *Libertarianism,* 53.
45. George H. Nash, *The Conservative Intellectual Movement in America* (Wilmington, Del.: Intercollegiate Studies Institute, 1996), 134.
46. Boaz, *Libertarianism,* 56.
47. Ibid., 54–56.
48. Nozick, *Anarchy, State, and Utopia.*
49. Charles Reich, "The New Property," *Yale Law Journal* 73 (1964): 785–786.
50. For a critique of this strategy, see William Hudson, *American Democracy in Peril,* 5th ed. (Washington, D.C.: CQ Press, 2006), 95–100.
51. The classic account of this tradition is Louis Hartz, *The Liberal Tradition in America* (New York: Harcourt Brace, 1955).
52. Alan Ehrenhalt describes such community ties in 1950s Chicago in *The Lost City* (New York: Basic Books, 1995).
53. Robert J. Ringer, *Looking Out for #1* (New York: Ballantine Books, 1977).
54. Michael Sandel, Democracy's Discontent (Cambridge: Harvard University Press, 1996), 308–315.
55. Alasdair MacIntyre, *After Virtue* (South Bend: University of Notre Dame Press, 1981); Michael Sandel, *Liberalism and the Limits of Justice* (Cambridge: Cambridge University Press, 1982).
56. Robert Bellah et al., *Habits of the Heart: Individualism and Commitment in American Life* (New York: Harper Row, 1985).
57. See for example, Alan Wolfe, *Whose Keeper? Social Science and Moral Obligation* (Berkeley: University of California Press, 1989).
58. Many of the articles from the *Responsive Community* are collected in two volumes: Amitai Etzioni, ed., *The Essential Communitarian Reader* (Lanham, Md.: Rowman and Littlefield, 1998) and *The Communitarian Reader: Beyond the Essentials* (Lanham, Md.: Rowman and Littlefield, 2004).
59. Robert Kuttner describes these woes in *Everything for Sale* (New York: Alfred A. Knopf, 1997).

Chapter 2   Taxing and Spending: Community Needs versus Private Wants

Budgetary policy concerns how government decides to raise revenue and spend that revenue—in other words, taxing and spending. Since the 1930s, influenced by the theories of British economist John Maynard Keynes, making government budgets also has involved judgments about the impact of government budget decisions on macroeconomic performance including policy decisions for adjusting taxes and spending to promote prosperity—what is called fiscal policy. We will examine the fiscal policy side of budgeting later in this chapter. In the main, however, the fundamental goal of budgetary policy has to be, as one eminent economist has put it, "to plan what the community wants to do through government . . . [and] to plan tax rates so as to provide sufficient revenues to cover planned expenditures."[1]

First, on the spending side, budgetary policy requires answers to significant questions. What total amount of government spending is needed? What are the various public needs that should be met and what services provided? How should spending be allocated among various needs and services? Second, to fund these government activities, budget policy involves deciding what kinds of taxes to impose on citizens and the form that taxation will take. Will government tax people's incomes? The value of their property? Or some combination? Should government tax the sale of products? Whether the tax is on sales, income, or property, what tax rate—the percentage of whatever to be taxed is taken by government—is appropriate? Should all pay the same rate or should it vary depending on individual circumstances? Will government impose special taxes on particular forms of economic activity, such as on the purchase of certain products, like cigarettes or luxury goods, or on goods imported from abroad? Both taxing and spending decisions have enormous impacts on the kind of society we will have, from how income and wealth are distributed to what sorts of lives citizens lead. In sum, budgetary policy decisions ought to reflect the goals and purposes a democratic citizenry determines for its common good.

Under the spell of the libertarian illusion, budgetary policy, in particular tax policy, has undermined the common good. Libertarian misconceptions about government's role in a complex society have fostered an antigovernment mentality that underestimates the need for effective government in a complex society. And it has led to tax policies that deprive the government of what it needs to provide public goods. Massive reductions in revenue have produced large increases in government debt that threaten both economic prosperity and the government's ability to meet public needs far into the future. Moreover, the wealthy and powerful have found libertarian arguments helpful in altering the tax structure to serve their interests, in the process, exacerbating growing inequality in this country. Tax reduction policies favoring the wealthiest Americans since the 1980s, particularly the massive cuts enacted under President George W. Bush, have shifted onto the backs of middle- and low-income citizens the bulk of the tax burden. If libertarian proposals for further tax reform were to be adopted, the wealthy, whose income derives primarily from investment, would escape taxation altogether, leaving the burden for financing our common endeavors solely on men and women who depend on salary and wages. This marrying of libertarian ideology and the interests of the wealthy has the potential of drastically altering the American dream of a society of middle-class citizens where equality of opportunity prevails.

This chapter explores the rising influence of libertarian values over budgetary policy and how they have placed a priority on satisfying private wants through the market over meeting community needs through government programs. The first section traces briefly the evolution of budget and fiscal policy since the 1930s, ending with the impact of the George W. Bush tax cuts of 2001–2004. Then we will examine libertarian ideas regarding the role of government and of taxation and their implications for public policy. This will allow a review of how these values have been detrimental to American society, chiefly in the form of high levels of debt and growing inequality. Libertarian proposals for further "tax reform" would exacerbate these problems and further undermine the government's ability to meet future needs. Finally, we will conclude with an alternative, more communitarian vision that would distribute more equitably the burden of providing for the common good.

Libertarians in Power: Discarding Keynes, the Supply-Side, and Starve the Beast

Recent budgetary and fiscal policy reflects a libertarian mindset that had been gaining ground since the 1970s. Prior to that time, budgetary and fiscal policy reflected the post–World War II "Keynesian consensus" that looked to John Maynard Keynes's analysis of the Great Depression as the touchstone for managing the macro-economy. The problem with that consensus, from a libertarian point of view, was that it ratified a growing public sector and a permanent role for government in managing the capitalist market economy. Overturning that consensus and public support for public policies associated with it has been a prerequisite for advancing a libertarian policy agenda. In recent decades, libertarian ideas have become more and more influential in justifying tax cuts and shaping fiscal policy. This section offers a brief account of the evolution of budgetary and fiscal policy since the 1930s, describing the rise of the Keynesian consensus and how misgivings about it in the 1970s opened the door for a more libertarian turn, culminating in the Bush tax cuts.

When the Great Depression struck in 1929, economic analysis of the business cycle—periods of economic growth followed by economic recessions followed in turn by renewed growth—was based on Say's Law. The eighteenth-century French physiocrat Jean Baptiste Say explained fluctuations in the supply and demand of all commodities with the doctrine that "supply creates its own demand." If demand—the willingness of buyers to purchase a commodity—were ever to diminish, that would result by definition of an increase in the supply of the commodity in the marketplace waiting to be purchased. As the supply of the commodity grew, its price would gradually fall until potential consumers would come along willing to pay the price offered. Soon sufficient demand for the commodity would diminish the available supply, prices would rise now that scarcity of the commodity produced competition among buyers, and rising prices induced producers to supply more. This idea, applied to the business cycle, indicated that the increasing supply of unemployed workers in a recession or depression would automatically correct itself as wages fell to a point where employers would spend their capital to hire workers. At this point employment would rise, along with wages, until an equilibrium was reached with enough jobs to employ all workers willing to work. The policy implication of Say's Law was "laissez-faire"—the best government policy during economic downturns was to leave things alone as the increasing supply of workers eventually would create the demand for them. Keeping a balanced budget—that is, reducing spending to match recession-induced tax revenues—was the appropriate laissez-faire policy.

The prolonged worldwide depression after 1929, with its ever-growing supply of unemployed workers and no sign of any demand for their services despite plummeting average wages, called both Say's Law and laissez-faire into question. Keynes's *The General Theory of Employment, Interest, and Money* sought to explain why capitalist economies seemed to have reached a possibly permanent equilibrium despite the presence of an ever-growing supply of the unemployed.[2] For Keynes, the answer to the mystery lay on the "demand side" of the economy and the psychology of business investment. To summarize Keynes's complex analysis quite simply: the reason the high level of unemployment persisted was that with so many consumers unemployed and unable to demand new products, business owners had little incentive to invest in new production. Why employ workers to make products that were unlikely to be sold? The result was a circular, self-fulfilling prophecy where unemployment prevented the consumer demand that employers needed to expect in order to hire new workers. With declining expectations of demand, employers tended to lay off even more workers, further undermining future demand in a never-ending spiral.

This view of the economy had enormous implications for government. Rather than leaving the economy alone, Keynes's analysis required government action to stimulate the economic demand needed to lift a country out of a depression. Instead of balancing the budget, economic downturns required governments to run a deficit through either higher spending, tax reduction, or a combination of the two. Although U.S. policymakers were slow to adopt Keynes's policy prescriptions in the 1930s, probably thereby prolonging the depression, World War II induced spending increases, and large deficits confirmed Keynes's analysis as the U.S. economy sprang back to life and unemployment disappeared. In the years following the war, the Keynesian consensus emerged as the dominant outlook, positing a need for government fiscal policy to manage the economy. Laissez-faire and the bias toward balanced budgets were rejected in favor of active government management of consumer demand. Both unemployment and inflation, Keynesianism suggested, could be managed through a fiscal policy that ran deficits when recession appeared on the horizon and did the opposite—produced surpluses—when the economy boomed and inflation threatened. Along with fiscal policy, monetary policy, the expansion or contraction of the supply of money in the economy (the responsibility of the Federal Reserve Board in the United States) could be called upon to manage economic demand. In fact, in normal times some Keynesians looked to monetary policy as a primary instrument for managing demand.[3] At all times, however, Keynesian orthodoxy required that fiscal and monetary policy work in tandem—stimulate demand when recession threatened and dampen demand when a booming economy produced inflation.

Although prominent critics of Keynesianism, such as the libertarian economist Milton Friedman, continued to make themselves heard during this period, the steady economic expansion of the late 1940s into the early 1970s seemed to confirm Keynesianism.[4] During this period economic productivity had doubled, making Americans twice as prosperous in 1970 as they had been in the 1940s.[5] Keynesianism's triumph seemed complete when in 1968 a conservative Republican candidate running for the presidency, Richard M. Nixon, proclaimed, "We're all Keynesians now!" As is often the case in history, just as Keynesianism seemed triumphant the economic crises of the 1970s called into question its fundamental premises and opened the door to a libertarian turn in fiscal policy.

Before describing the economic crises of the 1970s, another component of the Keynesian consensus needs to be presented. The Keynesian consensus after World War II went beyond simply an analysis of how to manage the business cycle—it included a whole new outlook on the role of government in society. Americans' experience of the New Deal and the war had transformed their attitudes toward the size and scope of government activity. During the New Deal major new government programs had been enacted, ranging from Social Security to extensive business regulation. During the war the federal government organized the entire war effort, mobilizing nearly all of industry and employing millions of Americans directly as soldiers. Both ventures seemed, from the perspective of the late 1940s and 1950s, to be great successes—thanks to an activist government. This expansion of government endeavors continued through the 1950s and 1960s through popular programs such as the GI Bill, the creation of an interstate highway system, and the establishment of Medicare and Medicaid in 1965. Between 1932 and 1970, government's share of the gross domestic product (GDP) grew from less than 5 percent to about 20 percent.[6] Astute observers of this expansion, like Friedman, saw a clear connection between economists' acceptance of Keynesian macro-economic management, the notion that government had a positive role to play in maintaining economic prosperity, and the willingness of most Americans to embrace an expanded government role in many aspects of their lives.[7] The conventional wisdom in public policy circles around 1970, among policy experts and politicians alike, assumed an expanding role for government to solve society's problems. By 1980, the conventional wisdom in the United States, with the assistance of libertarian journalists and allied politicians, would change dramatically in a direction more amenable to libertarian ideals.

For reasons still not well understood, economic productivity in the United States slowed dramatically around 1973. By mid-decade, the country experienced its most severe economic recession since the Great Depression, followed by a feeble recovery and another recession at decade's end. What called into question the Keynesian consensus during this period was that the high unemployment of this period was accompanied by high inflation. According to Keynesian doctrine, high inflation combined with high unemployment—what came to be known as *stagflation*—should not happen. During the 1960s, most Keynesians had embraced the Phillips curve, named for British economist A. W. Phillips, which posited a direct trade-off between inflation and unemployment. The Phillips curve tracked this relationship so accurately during the 1960s that some economists advocated fine-tuning the economy by targeting a given rate of inflation, say 3 or 4 percent, in order to keep unemployment at a low level.[8] As inflation approached the double digits along with unemployment in the 7 to 8 percent range in the mid-1970s, the stable trade-off of the Phillips curve had vanished.

Stagflation had tremendous implications for fiscal policy. The simple Keynesian formula of boosting demand in a recession through economic stimulation could not work if that same stimulation would send inflation through the roof. Just as the economic reality of the Great Depression had called into question balanced budget policies four decades earlier, the economic reality of the 1970s called into question Keynesian policy prescriptions. Some economists attempted to craft alternative visions of the business cycle in response to the seeming failure of the Keynesian vision, but the greatest challenge to the Keynesian consensus came not from mainstream economists, but from libertarian journalists associated with the editorial page of the *Wall Street*

Journal and an obscure maverick economist named Arthur Laffer.[9] They labeled their alternative to Keynesianism "supply-side economics," cleverly highlighting it as a contrast to Keynes's focus on economic demand. Their alternative gained a place on the policy agenda when it caught the attention of a Republican presidential candidate named Ronald Reagan.

The supply-siders took an economic truism, made a logical leap, and then elevated the truism into a supposedly new approach to fiscal policy. The truism says that tax rates conceivably could be raised so high that they generate less rather than more revenue for government. If marginal tax rates (the rate at which each new dollar invested or earned is taxed) reach such a high level that most of what people earn from additional work or investment is confiscated from them, then the supply of work and investment in the economy would decline, depressing economic activity and reducing government revenues. In such a situation, reducing tax rates, counterintuitively, actually would increase government revenues through the fruits of the increased supply of savings, work, and investment that lower marginal tax rates would stimulate. The logical leap was to move from this truism to the claim that high tax rates (and too much business regulation—an issue to be examined in the next chapter) in the U.S. economy explained the economic doldrums of the 1970s, although the supply-siders offered no convincing empirical evidence that this was the case.[10] The supply-side policy prescription was to radically reduce taxes to stimulate more economic activity coupled with the claim that this could be done without increasing government deficits. The increased savings, work, and investment resulting from lower marginal tax rates, the supply-siders claimed, would generate additional revenue for government, not less. They were offering, in effect, a free lunch—Americans could receive a large tax cut without having to pay for it with cuts in government programs or an increase in national debt.

Offering a free lunch provides an attractive option for someone seeking election to the presidency, and Reagan embraced the supply-side nostrum with gusto. Beyond the benefits of offering a pain-free formula for curing stagflation, cutting taxes fit nicely with Reagan's libertarian-influenced ideas of minimalist government.[11] Declaring, as he came into office, that "government was not the solution, it was the problem" and addressing the "government problem" of high taxes fit perfectly Reagan's ideological orientation. His first domestic policy achievement, *The Economic Recovery Tax Act of 1981,* adopted the supply-side prescription with an average tax rate reduction in all brackets of about 23 percent plus a dramatic reduction in the highest bracket affecting only the richest tax payers.[12]

Meanwhile, the Federal Reserve Board, under its chair, Paul Volcker, was taking a conventional Keynesian approach to reducing inflation. Appointed by President Jimmy Carter in 1978, Volcker considered the double-digit inflation of the late 1970s a greater evil than the unemployment component of stagflation. He resolved to tighten the money supply and raise interest rates to fight inflation no matter what the impact on employment. The result was a Fed-induced prolonged economic recession in 1981–1982 with record-high unemployment levels for the post–World War II period, but that did succeed in reducing inflation. Reagan's supply-side tax cuts, then, were implemented in the midst of a deep recession, making them, ironically, the precise Keynesian medicine for stimulating economic demand. Higher military spending also stimulated demand. The result was renewed economic growth beginning in 1983 and continuing through the decade, combined with much lower inflation—the Reagan boom.

In the end, traditional Keynesian-style demand stimulus, not any supply-side effect, revived the economy in the 1980s just as the earlier Keynesian-style tightening of the money supply had cooled inflation. It seems that the 1981 tax cuts did little to stimulate savings and investment as the supply-siders predicted. The proportion of personal income saved declined during the 1980s; Americans seem to have spent their tax cuts rather than used them for investment.[13] Nor did the predicted supply-side effect bring in additional government revenue. Economic expansion did not make up for the loss of revenue created in the 1981 cuts. By the end of the 1980s, *Reaganomics*—tax cuts combined with expanded military spending—had doubled the government budget deficit as a percentage of GDP, creating the central problem budget policymakers had to face for the next ten years.[14] Reagan's policies had produced a huge *structural deficit*—one that persisted even when a full employment economy generated the maximum revenue that tax rates allowed. This meant that rather than produce the supply-side effect predicted, they were denying the government sufficient revenue to support its activities. Not only had the tax cuts failed to produce the predicted supply-side effects, they produced a substantial shift in the burden of taxation from the wealthiest Americans to the middle class.[15] The dramatic reduction in marginal income tax rates primarily benefited those with high incomes just as regressive Social Security taxes, which take a larger proportion of the salaries of lower-income workers, were increasing in the 1980s. In 2001, President George W. Bush's tax cuts would exacerbate this shift in tax burden.

The budget policies of both of Reagan's successors, George H. W. Bush and Bill Clinton, centered on raising taxes and cutting spending in order to get the structural deficit under control. Despite his campaign pledge not to raise taxes, the first President Bush thought it prudent to sign a deficit reduction package including some tax increases sent to him by a Democratic Congress in 1990. In this first year in office, concern over the deficit caused Clinton to jettison campaign promises for new programs in favor of the Omnibus Budget Reconciliation Act of 1993 that provided for both spending cuts and substantial tax increases. This legislation barely passed a sharply divided Congress without a single Republican vote. Supply-siders predicted that the Clinton tax increase would so undermine the incentive to save and invest as to destroy the economy. Despite this prediction of doom, the U.S.

economy in the 1990s underwent its longest sustained economic expansion since World War II.[16] The Clinton economic boom, combined with sustained policy attention to deficit reduction during the 1990s, solved the structural deficit problem created by Reaganomics. In 1998, for the first time in thirty years, the federal government ran a budget surplus, a feat Clinton would repeat in his final two budgets.

This was the context within which presidential candidate George W. Bush formulated his plans to emulate Ronald Reagan and promote a new massive reduction in tax rates. Whereas Reagan had advocated his tax cuts as a formula for dealing with economic stagnation, Bush pointed to the budget surplus produced in the Clinton boom as the rationale for a tax cut—proving that for the libertarian minded, both good times and bad called for cutting taxes. Although many experts at the time, concerned with future budget obligations for entitlement programs such as Social Security, cautioned against expecting surpluses to last, Bush proposed a $1.6 trillion tax cut over ten years. Arguing in regard to the surplus that "it's not the government's money, it's the people's money," and that his proposal was merely returning to people what was already theirs, Bush made the tax cut his priority domestic policy proposal.[17] As we will see below, these arguments, favoring redistribution of the surplus to individuals rather than using it for common public purposes—as a majority of the public preferred—reflect what is an essentially libertarian conception of the nature of taxes and the role of government. Few Americans at the time supported tax cuts as their preferred option for the surplus. Instead, polls showed large majorities favoring investing the surplus in paying down the national debt or on new programs such as expanding education spending.[18] In early 2001, when Bush took office, the U.S. economy had dipped into a recession, reducing projected government revenues and diminishing prospects for future surpluses; nevertheless, the new administration stuck to its tax cut proposals, now arguing that they were needed to stimulate the economy.

The passage of *The Economic Growth and Tax Relief Reconciliation Act of 2001*, enacted in the spring of that year, provided a massive reduction in federal taxes that has defined the parameters of fiscal policymaking for the first two decades of this century. In the legislation, Congress embraced the essentials of the administration's proposal, providing $1.35 trillion in tax reductions over ten years, a phasing out of the estate tax, and some pro-family measures such as increased child tax credits. Two additional major tax cuts followed in 2002 and 2003. Altogether, the Bush tax cuts were bigger than Reagan's.[19] The administration claimed the tax cuts would benefit average Americans, but impartial analyses of their effects show that most benefits went to the richest Americans. A 2004 study showed that individuals in the bottom 20 percent of the income distribution received only $230 on average from the tax cut, while those in the top 20 percent received an average $4,890 cut.[20] The greatest beneficiaries were the super-rich, those in the top 1 percent of the

TAX RELIEF FOR AMERICA

PRESIDENT GEORGE W. BUSH SIGNING THE 2001 TAX CUT BILL THAT BROUGHT BACK STRUCTURAL DEFICITS AND SHIFTED THE TAX BURDEN TO THE MIDDLE CLASS.

income distribution earning over $1 million in annual income; they garnered an average tax cut of $40,990. Moreover, the richest 1 percent saw a 5.3 percent increase in after-tax income thanks to the tax cut, double the average increase of 80 percent of American households.

The Bush administration justified the measure's bias toward the wealthy, claiming it stimulated investment and promoted economic growth—the supply-side argument again. Yet this did not prove to be the case. The tax cuts failed to stimulate the economy; in fact, most Americans experienced a real decline in their household income between 2001 and 2004.[21] Rather than · stimulate additional growth, the tax cut brought back the structural deficit. A $236 billion budget surplus in 2000, President Clinton's last year in office, had become a $412 billion budget deficit in 2004.[22] In effect, the American people collectively, through their government, were going into debt in order to deliver a windfall to the richest Americans. Viewed from the point of view of the common good, the Bush tax cut agenda amounts to a disastrous budget policy.

The shift from surpluses to deficits was not, however, detrimental to a libertarian policy agenda. The prospect of government budget surpluses had posed a new dilemma for advocates of minimalist government like libertarians. The political dynamics since the onset of the huge Reagan deficits in the 1980s had been quite favorable to those advocating smaller government. With the looming deficit hanging over the economy, liberal advocates of new or expanding government programs were at a disadvantage. Any proposal to expand government could be stopped with the admonition that it would "increase the deficit." When Clinton contemplated proposing universal health care in 1993, for example, a government-funded single payer plan was off the table because it would require either a large tax increase or deficit increase.[23] During the 1980s tax cut advocates had propounded this political advantage to deficits when the supply-side budget benefits failed to materialize. David Stockman, Reagan's budget director, dubbed this view "starve the beast," that is, deny government revenue through massive tax cuts as a way of reducing the size of government. Libertarian activist Grover Norquist would later justify President Bush's massive tax cut in exactly these terms, claiming its goal to be "reducing the size and scope of government by draining its lifeblood."[24] A continuing large structural deficit also interferes with any reduction in the national debt to accommodate future financial pressures on Social Security and Medicare. Libertarians hope these pressures will allow for privatizing these programs (see chapters 4 and 5). So the return of the deficit problem with Bush's repeated tax cuts served perfectly the libertarian ideological agenda.

For libertarians, large tax rate cuts are only part of their agenda. Not only do they want to dramatically cut the revenue going to the federal government, they want to revamp how and from whom it is collected. Since 1913, when the federal income tax was created, it has been both progressive—that is, placing the highest tax burden on those most able to pay, the rich—and has taxed both capital and labor. Consistent with their ideological perspective on the role of government, libertarians seek to eliminate both progressivity and taxation of capital from the tax code. Libertarian-leaning organizations like Norquist's Americans for Tax Reform and the Club for Growth, a Washington lobby group representing wealthy investors, have pushed hard for making the Bush tax cuts permanent, including the elimination of the estate tax. Yet the ultimate aim for these tax cuts is to eliminate taxation of all income from savings, investments, and dividends; that is, tax only labor, not capital.[25] These goals are encompassed in the campaign for a flat tax. Before going into the details of flat tax proposals and the impact of the "starve the beast" deficit strategy, we need to review libertarian principles regarding the role of government and taxation.

The Libertarian Critique of Big Government and Taxes

The Bush administration's agenda of radical tax reduction fits perfectly with a libertarian outlook on the role of government in society. As we saw in the introduction, the libertarians' overarching commitment to liberty as the primary political value couples with an assumption that government action poses the greatest threat to individual freedom and autonomy. What better way to diminish this threat than by starving it of revenue? Tax cuts represent, for libertarians, not simply a fiscal policy strategy but a blow for individual liberty. The "starve the beast" rhetoric of Norquist and other libertarians made this point clear.[26] The libertarian vision of government as a voracious beast, on the prowl to restrict individual liberty, justifies tax-cutting, at any time and whatever the circumstances, as worthwhile. The beast metaphor, however, interferes with a fiscal policy that calculates realistically the revenue needs required to accomplish what government needs to do in the modern world. For government, even though it might sometimes restrict liberty, is also a necessary means for achieving tasks essential to the common good. The libertarian illusion ignores that fact.

Libertarians believe that they can dispense with government because of the seduction of their vision of the unfettered market. They expect the free market to spontaneously supply essential human needs if only government will get out of the way. In the previous chapter we saw that libertarians make several interrelated arguments about the virtues of markets. One of the most compelling of these is that markets efficiently and spontaneously produce and allocate the goods that people want and need. Even nonlibertarians can acknowledge the virtue of markets as efficient engines of material prosperity. Yet libertarians go beyond viewing markets as mere economic instruments; they conceive of them as democratic—more responsive to individual preferences, seemingly the libertarian definition of democracy—than possibly can occur through democratic institutions based on majority rule. Elections and government legislation enact only the majority's preferences, creating by definition a minority whose preferences are not enacted. In markets, each individual "buys" what she wants irrespective of what other individuals buy. Finally, and this argument influences most directly libertarian attitudes toward government taxing and spending, market outcomes are based on voluntary exchanges between individuals while government actions, because they require taxation, are based on coercion. For libertarians, individuals have an absolute entitlement to the property they acquire through market exchanges that government inevitably violates when it taxes away a portion of that property for public purposes.

A sophisticated defense of this latter notion can be found in libertarian philosopher Robert Nozick's book *Anarchy, State, and Utopia.*[27] Nozick argues that if individuals have acquired their property justly—not through force, coercion, fraud, or dishonest manipulation of others—they have an absolute right to that property. For example, if individuals engage in free and voluntary exchanges in the marketplace and some, because of their ingenuity, effort, or luck, emerge richer than others, there are no grounds for claiming that disparities among the winners and losers, no matter how great, are unjust. Government, certainly, has no right to tax justly acquired individual income and wealth to redistribute it to other individuals or for purposes the taxed individuals have not voluntarily endorsed. Even if an overwhelming majority of citizens favor a particular public program, taxing the minority who oppose the program, according to Nozick, "is on the par with forced labor."[28] No one, not even the state, can take property without violating individual rights.

Nozick recognizes, of course, that rights, including those to justly acquired property, need protection. Some individuals in any society, even one governed according to libertarian principles, may try to gain property unjustly, through force or fraud. A minimal state that provides only protection against force and fraud can be justified. Rational individuals will agree voluntarily to pay fees in order to protect their rights. In fact, Nozick claims that in a truly libertarian "state of nature" individuals would voluntarily hire such protection from entrepreneurs selling it in the free market. Eventually the protection firm most capable of providing such protection would acquire all the business in a given territory and become the "government." Such a government would violate no one's rights, since all it governed would be voluntarily paying it for protection. But if the government would go beyond mere protection, say to provide public education or health care or unemployment compensation, then it must violate the rights of those it taxes to provide those benefits. The point of libertarian arguments like Nozick's is to make the case that our current government does violate individual property rights because it engages in a vast range of activities that go beyond simply protecting those rights. People are forced to support through their taxes the well-being of others, say those who are unemployed or receive subsidized loans for college tuition, and activities they might not favor, whether a foreign war or public television programming.

Few Americans, even many libertarians, would endorse the radical libertarian views of Nozick, but the underlying sensibility conveyed in these arguments has been increasingly influential in molding budgetary policy. First, the idea that taxes take from us property to which we are entitled seems superficially unassailable. When tax cuts advocates say they are just letting us keep what is ours, they assume this libertarian understanding of the justice of market allocation of income and wealth. The pretax income I hold is assumed to be the sole result of my individual effort. This outlook introduces a bias against raising revenue adequate to meeting public needs. Second, the impact of large tax cuts on government services is ignored because of a libertarian assumption that only minimal government is necessary. People begin to believe that the social outcomes of the market are always superior to what democratic citizens might determine to pursue collectively. We overlook the ways in which market exchanges alone fail to meet many important public needs.

The notion that the money I have earned legally and through my efforts is mine has enormous resonance. Who has not looked at the sums deducted from a paycheck for taxes as a loss of what was their own? Each month I receive a paycheck from the college where I teach that certainly constitutes justly acquired property in Nozick's terms. I work diligently, competently, and honestly to teach my students in return for compensation contractually agreed upon with my employer. The college derives the assets from which I am paid justly through tuition payments that students and their parents voluntarily contract to provide in exchange for the educational services provided. It seems only just that I should get to keep the income I produce through my honest efforts. Considered in this way, my annoyance at those large deductions from my paycheck to pay taxes seems justified.

All of us are susceptible to this way of thinking about income and taxes, but it is based on a mistaken understanding of the nature of income, wealth, and property in a complex capitalist society. The ability that any of us have to earn income and acquire wealth depends only partly on our own individual efforts. It relies as well on the operation of political, economic, and social institutions that make it possible for any of us to "earn a living." The market system itself is a social construct that could not exist without the structure of laws and government policies. Anyone's ability to earn income and own property depends on a host of laws—criminal, contract, corporate, and property—and a host of institutions required for their enforcement, police forces and judicial institutions. Beyond these, an infrastructure of transportation, regulatory, and educational institutions, many a part of government, are needed. My private college could not exist without an extensive public education system that prepares many of our students or the government grants and subsidized loans that support their tuition payments. Viewed in this light, those deductions from my paycheck can be seen as reimbursement to society for that portion of my earnings derived from social goods.

This more communitarian understanding of the nature of income and wealth extends to the nature of private property itself. Libertarians tend to assume that property is a naturally occurring entity, like an acre of land I come upon and make productive. But private property is a legal convention that only exists in the context of a legal system that defines it.[29] Even that acre of land I plow will be my private property only if some government gives me a title of ownership. The artificial character of private property becomes clear when we think of the many abstract forms of property that many of us own in modern capitalist societies. If I buy stock in a corporation, for example, my property consists of partial ownership of the corporate assets, to the extent of my investment, from which I am legally entitled to dividends the corporation might pay out of corporate profits. My ownership stake in the corporation, however, comes with an understanding of limited liability; that is, I am personally liable for the financial obligations of the corporation only to the extent of my investment. For example, should the corporation become bankrupt, I will lose the money I have invested but no more. Anyone who has a claim against the bankrupt corporation's assets, say a supplier who never got paid for materials provided or a bank that loaned money, cannot sue me personally for what they lost.

Limited liability defines the meaning of property in corporate stock; U.S. courts assigned this meaning in the nineteenth century. As a matter of government policy, providing limited liability in corporate ownership probably was a good idea. It is hard to imagine the flourishing of U.S. corporations and the material prosperity they engendered without it. But it is important to remember that it is a convention defining corporate property ownership, not a natural entity. The same applies to existence of corporations as economic actors. Although any existing pattern of private property, if well established, can appear as products of the laws of nature, they are based on conventions rooted in political choices. That once, in the United States, one could hold private property in human beings proves how conventions defining private property can change.

What are the implications for the conventional character of private property for how we think about taxation? It underlines how any distribution of property and income depends on the structure of political and policy choices. The libertarians cannot claim that the distribution of income, wealth, and property ownership derives solely from the outcomes of individuals' voluntary exchanges. That is partly the case, but they also reflect the legal system in which the market operates, including the tax system, and access to a variety of social goods.[30] My pretax income, then, should not be considered something to which I am individually entitled, but as a combined product of my efforts and the operation of the overall social system. Instead of viewing taxation as taking what belongs to individuals, taxes should be evaluated in terms of the collective goals they aim to achieve. This includes both policy judgments about the division of what the economy produces between individual private control and governmental control and about the appropriate distribution of societal wealth and income.

Tax policy, then, ought to be made on the basis of what revenue government needs to perform the tasks citizens want it to rather than on the basis of an abstract theory of property entitlements. The spending side of budgetary policy will reflect what role we want government to play in society. A basic assumption in the United States' liberal democracy is that many social goods, including much of our individual material prosperity, will be produced through the operations of a capitalist market economy. Other goods will be produced through what is often called "civil society," activities carried out through volunteer efforts or funded through charitable contributions. These range from social services provided by local churches to the activities of large social service agencies such as the Red Cross or Habitat for Humanity. While most productivity activity in the United States happens through these two sectors—the private/market and nonprofit/voluntary—the size of the government sector as a proportion of GDP has remained stable at about

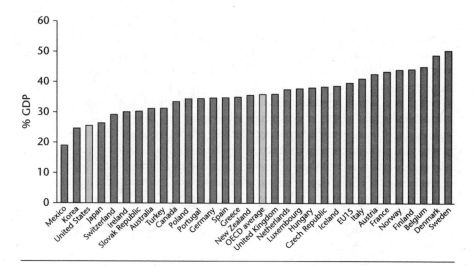

Figure 2-1 TAX REVENUES AS PERCENTAGE OF GDP FOR OECD COUNTRIES

SOURCE: OECD Factbook, http://caliban.sourceoecd.org/vl=14742923/cl=26/nw=1/rpsv/factbook/10-03=01.htm.

NOTE: OECD = Organization for Economic Cooperation and Development. EU15 = European Union prior to May 1, 2004.

one-third for the past several decades. That one-third includes all levels of government; federal government portion constitutes about 20 percent of GDP. The Organization for Economic Cooperation and Development (OECD) provides comparative statistics on the relative size of government in developed countries based on tax revenues collected. As Figure 2-1 shows, government as a proportion of GDP for all levels of government in the United States is much smaller than most other industrial democracies. At least compared to most of the rest of the world, the U.S. government hardly seems the huge beast gobbling up the rest of society that libertarians conjure up.

Government's Role in Promoting the Common Good

For libertarians, the levels of taxation in other countries are just evidence that their governments are too large. Campaigns to reduce taxes are premised on the assumption that much of what government does can be dispensed with. The goal for libertarians like Norquist is to "cut the government in half in 25 years, to get it down to the size where we can drown it in the bathtub."[31] This view assumes a minimal need for government activity in modern America, but most Americans would find such a pruning an unacceptable alteration in what they expect from their government. This becomes clear if we examine what the federal government actually does in modern America, as well as public opinion on the role of government. But before we look at that empirical evidence, we need to look at some theoretical arguments about the appropriate role of government in a predominantly capitalist liberal democracy.

Most libertarians, as we saw earlier, acknowledge the need for a minimal governmental role in maintaining a functioning market economy. Markets cannot exist without defining and protecting property rights, providing public order, enforcing contracts, and creating and managing a money supply.[32] Some libertarians also acknowledge some need to regulate the market to maintain competition through preventing private monopolies. They tend, however, to downplay the extent of regulation needed to maintain orderly, fair, and competitive markets.[33] In recent years, libertarians have been strong supporters of deregulation efforts to dismantle government oversight of market activity, an issue examined in detail in the next chapter. Economists would label many activities related to maintaining the market system, such as enforcing contracts, as *public goods*, activities government must undertake because markets alone will not provide them.

Why do markets fail to provide "public goods"? In nontechnical terms, in a market no one would have an incentive to produce a public good because it is a kind of good that when provided to one individual is available to anyone else to consume, as well, without payment. A classic movie western scenario provides an example. Suppose a Clint Eastwood character, say the Man with No Name, rides into town offering to sell his services to round up the desperados bedeviling the citizenry. Would he find a market for his services? Would anyone voluntarily hire him to free the town of crime? No individual citizen rationally attentive to his individual self-interest, characteristics assumed of market exchanges, would do so. If any one citizen or group of citizens paid No Name's price, everyone else in town also would get the satisfaction of seeing, at no cost to themselves, their town freed of crime. Since all have an incentive to be "free riders"—beneficiaries of public order without paying for it, the market would fail to provide it. The desperados would breathe easy as No Name rode out of town having failed to sell his services. The only way citizens could clean up crime would be to impose a tax on everyone and hire No Name as town sheriff.[34] This scenario illustrates why the usual institutions that guarantee public order—police, courts, public prosecutors—are a part of government. Even in a capitalist market society where the expectation is that the market will produce just the right amount of most of what we want and need, government needs provide those things the market itself will fail to produce. Along with public order, national defense, clean air, and clean water are classic examples of public goods mentioned in economics texts.

Another kind of failure requiring government action involves the market producing too much or too little of a particular good. This can happen when voluntary market transactions among individuals result in positive or negative externalities—benefits and costs imposed on others not involved (external to) the transaction. The classic example of a negative externality is pollution. In an unregulated free market, a textile factory will dump the dyes used in coloring its textiles rather than dispose of them in an environmentally safe way. Why? Because if the factory owner invested in pollution control, his higher prices would send his customers across the river to buy from the factory that continued to pollute. In a free market neither producers nor consumers have an incentive to pay for pollution cleanup. In fact, both benefit in their individual transactions with each other from the pollution, even if all collectively suffer from it in the long run. Market competition, in the case of negative externalities, prevents individuals from voluntarily tackling a problem like pollution, even if they see the need. The only way to keep the river clean is for a government-enforced law preventing any factory from dumping dyes in the river. If government regulation imposes the same cost of pollution control on all producers, then there is no longer any market incentive to pollute. Government intervention also is necessary when market incentives alone do not induce individuals to produce a sufficient amount of a particular good.

Education offers a good example of this kind of situation—a positive externality. Individuals usually earn higher incomes as a result of more education, a prime reason many students end up reading assigned college texts like this one. Markets provide strong incentives for individuals to invest in education. However, would you invest in finishing this chapter if you knew that doing so would bring you no additional individual benefit, not add a penny to your future earning potential, but would result in a social benefit—perhaps inspire you to abandon your planned career on Wall Street in order to be a lower-paid public servant? Market theory suggests you would not—the individual incentive is to buy only the amount of education that provides an individual benefit. If society at large is to receive the benefits from a more educated citizenry, in terms of higher economic productivity and the social benefits educated people provide, then the government must subsidize education to induce individuals to obtain more education than they might be able or willing to purchase for themselves.

Most libertarians recognize the need for government sometimes to provide for public goods and deal with externalities, but they prefer some market failure to government action.[35] They consider the "government failures," waste, inefficiency, and loss of individual liberty that often come with regulating market failure as more costly to us all in the long run. Concepts like public good and externalities, they point out, also are quite elastic and can be used in a long list of government programs well beyond national defense and pollution control. And this is true. One can identify a long list of "public goods" that some might argue free markets fail to provide and, therefore, government must do. This list might include public health, education, transportation infrastructure, scientific research, historic preservation, national parks and forests maintenance, space exploration, promotion of moral behavior, or support of arts and culture, for a start. In fact, in the United States government is currently

Source: © 2007, R. J. Matson. All Rights Reserved.

involved to some degree in all of these activities. This long list provides the libertarian grounds for complaint about big government and the desirability of reducing or eliminating government programs in many of these areas. Communitarians see promotion of this list of public goods and more as necessary for a good society. The basic conflict with more communitarian-minded citizens involves a different attitude toward what the common good requires government to do. We can see this conflict over differing attitudes toward the need for a national park system.

For most of us, America's network of national parks is just the sort of public good that government should provide. Not to libertarians. In *Capitalism and Freedom,* Milton Friedman argued that since it is possible to control entry and charge an admission fee, parks like Yellowstone or Yosemite could be run as private enterprises.[36] These parks now charge fees to defray a portion of the cost of maintaining the parks, but taxpayer funds cover most of the costs. Friedman believed entrepreneurs would readily invest in purchasing the parkland, maintaining the parks, and earning profits by charging admission. After all, private parks such as Disneyland do quite well offering an experience for which consumers are willing to pay. If the free market could provide the pleasurable experience of seeing nature in what is now a government-funded national park, then there is no reason why government should be involved in running parks.

Friedman's argument misunderstands the purpose of a national park system and reflects his myopia about why we need government. If you visit the National Park Service Web site you will find that the government maintains parks not primarily to provide a fun vacation site, but to "set aside by the American people to preserve, protect, and share, the legacies of this land."[37] Private entrepreneurs might do a great job running parks as vacation destinations, but could they be counted on to preserve, protect, and maintain a park as a legacy for future generations? Imagine a privatized Yellowstone. What would prevent its owners from installing a sound-and-light show to accompany Old Faithful? They might even add artificial pumps to boost the height of the geyser to make it seem more impressive to visitors, probably disrupting the natural geyser in the process. In a privatized park system, there would be nothing to prevent owners from modifying or destroying natural attractions if they thought it would attract more paying customers. Protecting a legacy, however, does not produce private profits, and that is why a national park system is a public good government must provide if we are to have it. The libertarian bias discounts the importance of such public goods, thereby underestimating our need for government.

More than programs like national parks that offer a public good, programs that redistribute income and wealth are the ones libertarians hate the most. Their faith in the absolute justice of market distributions leads them to regard redistribution as a kind of theft. Libertarian accounts tend to paint government redistribution as taking money out of the pockets of the rich and handing it to the poor in Robin Hood fashion. Yet government programs that involve redistribution in the United States do not fit this image. Most exist for one of two reasons: to provide equal opportunity or to ensure a "safety net." Equal opportunity recognizes that, in a capitalist market economy, personal resources advantageous to economic and social success are unequally distributed. Some are born into families that can provide the education, cultural advantages, and social connections. Add to these individual effort and good jobs and productive lives easily follow. But people without the same advantages of birth are less likely to succeed. Government efforts to provide education or overcome discrimination that disadvantage some people are intended to compensate for the inequality of opportunity that occurs naturally in a market economy.

A good example of a historic government effort to provide economic opportunity was the GI Bill. Enacted after World War II, the GI Bill provided servicemen (and some women) returning from the war a package of benefits aimed at easing their reintegration into society.[38] These included a period of unemployment benefits, guaranteed low-interest loans to purchase homes, and—most important—generous financial assistance to attend college or a vocational school. This was a program of economic redistribution—money was taken from taxpayers and given to the GIs in benefits—but it resulted in one of the best economic investments the United States ever made. A total of

7.8 million veterans took advantage of the education benefit flooding the country's colleges, universities, and vocational schools. About half of all students enrolled in college in the late 1940s were there thanks to the GI Bill. The program altered the very idea of a college education from a luxury reserved for a rich elite to an opportunity available to the vast middle class. The GI Bill transformed its recipients, and it transformed the country. In one fell swoop, the program raised the educational level and productivity of a major portion of the workforce and provided it with better housing in new suburbs. This had an enormous, positive impact on the economy as a whole—undoubtedly a factor in the prosperity of the 1950s and 1960s. Political scientist Suzanne Metzler shows that the GI Bill also produced a boom in political and citizen activism that raised voting levels, created a generation of public officials, and stimulated voluntary organizations.[39] None of this would have happened had returning World War II GIs been left to the mercy of the free market alone.

Besides fostering economic opportunity, redistribution is needed to ensure that all Americans obtain a minimal standard of living. Market forces alone will not necessarily provide a minimally adequate income to everyone. Whether due to personal circumstance or ill fortune, some people inevitably will be unable to earn sufficient income to care for themselves or their families. Even for libertarians, leaving some citizens destitute and starving is not acceptable. In fact, one of the most effective "safety net" programs, the Earned Income Tax Credit (EITC), derives from Friedman's proposal, in the 1960s, for a negative income tax. The idea is to use the tax system to supplement the incomes of those earning very low wages. Under the EITC, low-wage earners submit a tax return like everyone else, but instead of being assessed a tax, they receive from the IRS a check to raise their income. This program compensates somewhat for the fact that not all wages offered in the marketplace, even if one works long hours, are sufficient to support a decent standard of living. In this case, government does not replace the market but supplements it activity.

Libertarian attitudes toward both taxing and the role of government in society interfere with clear thought about government budgets. If individuals are regarded as absolutely entitled to their property, if the existing market distribution is sacrosanct and taxation is, in effect, theft, then government can never raise revenue adequate to satisfy public needs. If government is considered largely unnecessary, then starving it of revenue seems unlikely to cause any substantial problems. Radical tax reduction will produce only the elimination of government programs no one really needs. But if government action is needed to provide essential public goods, deal with externalities, and redistribute the market's unequal distribution of income and wealth, then smaller government will harm the public good. A communitarian perspective sees the need for a government large enough to meet public needs and a level of taxation to pay for it. Since the 1980s, the rise in libertarian values in public policymaking has muddled U.S. budgetary policy in ways that seriously threaten the United States' future. The libertarian legacy of irresponsible budget policy, astronomical deficits and debt, and growing economic inequality has reduced the prospects for better lives for most Americans.

Mortgaging Our Future and Stifling the American Dream

Since 1980, the United States has conducted two massive social experiments with the libertarian approach to budgetary policy: the large, "supply-side" tax cuts of the Reagan era and the even larger Bush tax cuts of 2001–2003. In neither case did any of the predicted benefits of these tax cuts materialize. The claims of the supply-side stimulus of savings and investments proved illusory. The Reagan boom resulted mainly from a Keynesian-style stimulus of demand first from the demand-side stimulus of the tax cuts themselves, then from a large expansion in military spending. As mentioned earlier, Americans' rate of saving actually declined in the Reagan era. By the end of the 1980s, the Reagan boom had fizzled out into another recession. Bush's even-larger tax cuts had no visible supply-side impact.[40] Neither did the tax cuts in either era reduce government spending as the "starve the beast" advocates had hoped. They did succeed in restraining government expansion—fear of the structural deficit clearly compromised some of Clinton's hopes for new government initiatives like universal health insurance—but actual cuts in spending occurred in neither case. In fact, periods of government spending growth followed both the Reagan and Bush cuts. What both eras of tax-cutting produced were huge structural deficits, undermining the country's capacity to meet future public needs (perhaps the main purpose of starving the beast, anyway), and, because their tax cuts benefited the wealthy, exacerbating growing economic inequality. In this section, I will document the future fiscal crisis Bush's tax cuts have stimulated and show how they have contributed to one of the United States' most serious problems—growing economic inequality.

Not only political activists like Grover Norquist embraced the "starve the beast" idea; certain distinguished economists of libertarian bent did as well. Both Milton Friedman and Gary Becker in separate articles in the *Wall Street Journal* in 2003 defended the Bush tax cuts on the ground that they would induce lower government spending.[41] Friedman characterized tax cuts as cutting the allowance of "spendthrift children." As this comparison implies, the libertarian confidence in tax reduction as a means of reducing government spending depended on their philosophical assumption that most government activity is superfluous. But what if government spends on real public needs? And what if the public supports those needs? If most government spending supports priorities most people find important, then the libertarian premise that government will quickly shrink in response to tax cuts collapses. Some facts on how the federal budget is allocated can offer some perspective on how feasible shrinking government might be and what the costs will be if it is forced to shrink.

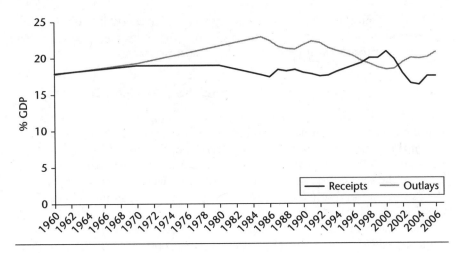

Figure 2-2 FEDERAL BUDGET: REVENUES AND OUTLAYS, 1960–2006

SOURCES: U.S. Office of Management and Budget, *Budget of the United States Government. Historical Tables,* annual; http://whitehouse.gov/omb/budget/fy2007; www.census.gov/compendia/statab/2007 edition.html.

First, however, we need to get some perspective on long-term trends in government taxing and spending. If we go back to 1960, the year John F. Kennedy was elected president, revenues roughly balanced spending at a level of just under 18 percent of GDP (see Figure 2-2). During the subsequent decade, the federal government expanded, with spending rising 1 percent and revenues keeping pace. The economic stagnation of the 1970s checked growth in federal revenues, but spending growth continued. By 1980, at the end of a recession, the deficit reached almost 3 percent of GDP. As the figure shows, Reagan's supply-side experiment exacerbated the deficit as revenues fell and spending rose. In 1986, at the height of the Reagan boom—a time when revenues ought to have kept pace with spending, the 1981 tax rate cuts produced a drop in the inflow of tax revenue relative to GDP compared to 1980 levels (when the economy had been weak), yet spending now reached a new high. The result was a structural deficit equivalent to about 5 percent of GDP. Several tax hikes in the following years, particularly a rather sharp rise in 1993—Clinton's first year in office—eventually succeeded in wiping out the structural deficit, producing a near-balanced budget in 1997 with budget surpluses the following three years. When George W. Bush was elected president in 2000, the surplus amounted to 2.5 percent of GDP. In the following years, Bush's tax cuts brought about a return of the structural deficit; in 2003 and 2004 government revenues declined relative to GDP to levels not seen since the 1950s. As we will see below, once Bush's tax cuts begin to be fully implemented, and if they are made permanent, the eventual structural mismatch between revenues and spending will far exceed that of the Reagan years.

The preceding paragraph reads Figure 2-2 with a focus on the fluctuation of revenues and expenditures over the past four decades. But the pattern shown tells another story, as well, one of stability rather than change. Notice that since 1970 government spending as percent of GDP has fluctuated around 19 to 20 percent. Over nearly four decades, presidents and Congresses of different political parties and differing ideologies seem to put together budgets producing a government with a fairly constant relative size. This stability may offer a clue to the limits of any libertarian strategy for drastically shrinking government. First, it undermines libertarian portrayals of exploding government growth. They may not support a federal establishment equivalent to about one-fifth of GDP, but they cannot claim that government expansion is uncontrolled. Second, the people's representatives may be providing a government offering a consensus package of programs and services that meet settled public needs. This becomes clearer if we examine some of the specific components of the federal budget.

In 2006, the federal government spent $2.7 trillion dollars. As Figure 2-3 indicates, three programs—national defense, health, and Social Security—account for 61 percent of spending.[42] Add interest on the national debt and the proportion comes to 70 percent—over two-thirds of the entire budget. What is significant about this two-thirds is that it is basically immune from reduction in any given budget year. Interest on the debt must be paid to those who have loaned the government money through purchase of Treasury and savings bonds. Social Security, Medicare, Medicaid, and the State Children's

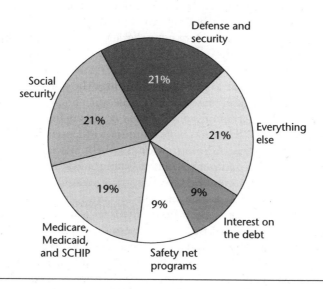

Figure 2-3 COMPOSITION OF THE FEDERAL BUDGET IN 2006

SOURCE: Office of Management and Budget data, Center on Budget and Policy Priorities, www.cbpp.org/pubs/fedbud.htm.

NOTE: SCHIP = State Children's Health Insurance Program.

Health Insurance Program (SCHIP), often called "entitlement" programs because those receiving benefits under the programs are legally entitled to them, cannot be cut unless Congress agrees to revise the underlying law. For example, annual Social Security costs represent the amount of money needed to provide the legally designated benefits to those entitled to them in a given year. Social Security provides retirement benefits to thirty-four million elderly and surviving spouses and children of Social Security beneficiaries and disability benefits to fifteen million additional people. Medicare provides health insurance to people over age 65 ($330 billion in 2006); Medicaid provides health care to the very poor, including nursing home care to the elderly; and SCHIP supports state-level programs that insure children. National defense expenditures reflect international commitments the nation has made and generally not viewed as easily trimmed. "Funding our troops" usually places this part of the budget off limits—at least in the short term. So over two-thirds of the federal budget is essentially immune from consideration if Congress wants to trim spending in response to any tax cuts it may have enacted.

The 9 percent of the budget ($250 billion) comprised of safety net programs offers one area where the budget might be trimmed, but spending cuts are difficult here, as well. First, some of these too are entitlements—such as food stamps—that can be cut only by changing eligibility rules in existing law. Second, except for the hardest of hearts, low-income housing assistance, child care, energy assistance, school meals, and the EITC are programs generally agreed to ease some of the distress of poverty for our poorest citizens. Taken together, these programs lift nearly thirteen million Americans out of poverty. Since the 1980s, many of the budget cuts aimed at bringing deficits under control have come from these safety net programs. Today, they represent the bare bones of assistance a decent society ought to offer its least well-off citizens. These expenditures comprise a much smaller amount of the budget than many Americans, who tend to greatly overestimate the portion of the federal budget devoted to "welfare," usually imagine.

That leaves the 21 percent of spending for everything else that government does, ranging from the FBI to air traffic control, the Centers for Disease Control to the Food and Drug Administration, or the National Parks Service to the space program. This part of the budget supports federal retiree and veterans' benefits, education, scientific research, roads, transportation infrastructure including the national system of highways, and foreign aid. This latter item, a popular target for those who decry "big government," comprises only 1 percent of the federal budget and less than 0.2 percent of GDP—significantly lower than that of most other industrial democracies.[43]

Once we look at what the federal government spends its money on, the difficulty of shrinking government becomes clear. Government spends its money on items that, except perhaps for diehard libertarians, represent reasonable contributions to the common good. Politicians find attacking government spending in the abstract easy; such charges are a convenient twin to a tax-cutting agenda. But the experience of both the Reagan and George W. Bush years shows that actually identifying what parts of government can be easily cut is not easy. The politicians' experience here tracks public opinion. While Americans consistently say they prefer smaller government, when specific programs are named, they invariably wish to maintain or increase spending on those programs. In 2003, for example, a Harvard Kennedy School of Government poll found 80 percent of respondents preferring "maintaining spending levels on domestic programs such as education, health care, and Social Security" to "lowering your taxes."[44] Public support is especially strong for programs like Social Security, Medicare, and—in a post–9/11 world—national defense spending that comprise the bulk of the federal budget. At the same time, Americans are mindful of government's responsibilities to the less fortunate, with 69 percent preferring safety net programs and a majority favoring helping the needy even if such expenditures increase the deficit.[45] Both political experience and public opinion suggest that the libertarian dream that government can be reduced so that it can be "drowned in a bathtub" is an illusion. Large tax cuts have not "starved the beast" but, instead, have induced a fiscal crisis—an ominous structural deficit that places the United States' economic future in jeopardy.

Even had there been no Bush tax cuts, fiscal problems loom on the United States' horizon in the form of aging baby boomers. The huge demographic cohort born in the years after World War II is on the cusp of reaching eligibility for the two largest federal programs, Social Security and Medicare. For the past two decades, policymakers have understood that baby boom retirements would place a strain on these programs. As we will discuss in more detail in chapter 4, reformers in 1983 established Social Security and Medicare trust funds to begin preparing for this eventuality. But the capacity of these funds to support program finances always has depended on a strong fiscal position for the federal government as a whole. Meeting the obligations to the retiring boomers would require a capacity to generate sufficient revenue—a task simplified if government debt is at reasonable levels and the overall economy is growing briskly. Complicating this picture are the rapidly rising health care costs that recent studies suggest will be a larger factor in rising budget costs in this century than demographic changes.[46]

Many analysts viewed the elimination of the structural deficit achieved in the 1990s as precisely the formula for coping with these fiscal challenges. Its return with the Bush tax cuts has worsened the current outlook. There can be no doubt that the tax cuts account for a major portion of the current reversal of the deficit situation. Sometimes increased government spending for the Iraq war and Homeland Security, as well as weak economic performance since 2000, are cited as major factors in higher deficits. These certainly have contributed to the deficit, but most analysts cite the tax cuts as accounting for the substantial portion of recent deficits.[47] A recent study by three leading economists calculated that the Bush tax cuts were the single largest factor accounting for the deficits between 2001 and 2007.[48] Looking to the future, the tax law changes enacted in 2001–2003, according to Brookings Institution budget experts Alice Rivlin and Isabel Sawhill, will become a growing factor in expanding deficits as they take full effect in the second half of the decade.[49]

In order to understand our current fiscal dilemma, a couple of elements of existing tax policy need to be explained. First, the tax cut law enacted in 2001 contained a bizarre "sunset" provision that says that all of its reductions, including the lower tax rates and the elimination of the estate tax, will expire in 2011. The Republican congressional leadership and the Bush administration included this provision to allow them to claim a lower revenue cost for the bill and make it more politically palatable, although they expected from the first to extend these provisions.[50] Bush and his libertarian supporters have called repeatedly for making the tax cuts permanent since they were enacted. Their opponents are at a political disadvantage because opposition to making the cuts permanent can now be portrayed as "raising taxes." The second feature concerns a quirk in the tax code called the *alternative minimum tax* (AMT), first enacted in 1969. Its purpose, at that time, was to ensure that wealthy taxpayers, who take advantage of the technicalities of the tax code to reduce their liability, would always be forced to pay some tax. The AMT required high-income taxpayers to calculate their tax liability two ways—according to the regular tax schedule, which allows for deductions, and the AMT schedule, which does not. The taxpayer has to pay the higher amount. The AMT, however, was not indexed for inflation, so, over time, rising incomes began to make even middle-income taxpayers susceptible to the AMT. If left unchanged, in 2010, 50 percent of households earning between $50,000 and $100,000 will be subject to the tax, turning it into a tax on the middle class.[51] The AMT relates to our story, again, because of the politics surrounding the Bush tax cuts. In calculating the impact of the cuts on overall federal revenues, the administration also assumed the AMT would remain unchanged, although everyone who understood the politics of letting the AMT become a middle-class tax knew Congress would prevent this from happening either through outright repeal or raising the income levels. And the latter is exactly what Congress has done: as middle-class taxpayers come under the AMT provisions.

In calculating future deficits and debt, one needs to assume that revenue from neither the AMT nor the 2001 tax law sunset provisions will be available. This is precisely what the Center for Budget and Policy Priorities does in its analysis of the country's long-term budget prospects. Its projection, based on data from the Congressional Budget Office, is sobering. By 2050, if current budget policies are unchanged, the tax cuts are made permanent, and AMT relief continues, the federal budget deficit will be 20 percent of GDP (remember that is the level of all federal government expenditures today) and the total debt 231 percent of GDP—about twice as high as debt reached during World War II.[52] To avoid this development and keep debt at current manageable levels, a combination of permanent tax increases and spending cuts equivalent to 3.2 percent of GDP, the fiscal gap, would be needed. This would mean, in 2008, tax increases and spending cuts of about $461 billion. To consider this figure in perspective, in 2006, the entire defense budget was $557 billion, Social Security cost $549 billion, and Medicare $516 billion, meaning this size of a cut would entail nearly eliminating any one of these major federal government commitments. While these long-range estimates of the fiscal gap are alarming, we should keep in mind that they are based on a range of assumptions about future economic performance. Predictions about what will happen with the economy fifty or so years into the future are uncertain—a matter we will take up in more detail when we look at predictions about the fate of Social Security in chapter 4. Nevertheless, the magnitude of current estimates of the fiscal gap would lead prudent policymakers to take careful steps today to avoid the consequences of an out-of-control national debt.

What would be the impact of such huge deficits? Rivlin and Sawhill identify five consequences of consistent high deficits that need to be avoided.[53] First, government deficits and debt require greater government borrowing that reduces potential investment in the private economy. This lower investment means slower economic growth and reduced incomes for all Americans. Second, households will not only earn less income, their expenses will rise to cover higher interest rates. Third, deficits increase U.S. dependence on foreigners to purchase our debt. In recent years, foreigners, including the Chinese and other foreign governments, have purchased a majority of newly issued Treasury debt. This puts the United States at risk of rapid withdrawal of foreign investments should the value of the dollar fall, making dollar investments less valuable. Fourth, interest payments on the debt will become a larger proportion of annual budgets, leaving less revenue to pay for other public needs. And finally, continuing deficits today place a burden on future generations that will be forced to pay higher taxes and enjoy fewer government benefits.

This final point brings us back to "starve the beast." Many libertarians have been disappointed that neither the tax cuts of the 1980s nor the more recent Bush cuts resulted in immediate spending reductions. Their tendency to underestimate the value of government programs led them to believe that government spending can be quickly and easily reduced. It may be that they need to be more patient. As pointed out earlier, concerns over keeping the deficit in check, even if they have not drastically reduced government spending, do seem to have had an impact in preventing government expansion and the introduction of new programs. Also, average government spending as a percentage of GDP since the late 1980s has been slightly below the average since the 1960s.[54] If the Bush tax cuts are made permanent, as libertarians advocate, and other tax changes they favor are enacted, the resulting huge deficits will undoubtedly place enormous pressure on existing budgetary commitments. Already both Social Security and Medicare are in the libertarians' sights. As we will see in chapters 4 and 5, they usually cite projected government spending on these programs as an argument for privatizing them. Inducing a fiscal crisis might be a successful strategy for overcoming public resistance to such privatization that currently seems to be blocking their efforts.

Even if "starve the beast" never fulfills libertarian dreams of a drastically smaller government, higher deficits are sure to harm the public good. Many communitarians would point to unmet public needs in health care, education, and transportation that are threatened by large deficits. Already, concern for deficits has meant substantial reductions in programs for the poor, as politicians feel little political pressure from this weakest of constituencies.[55] As Rivlin and Sawhill point out, "deficits are likely to put downward pressure on spending for education, nutrition, and health care that could make today's children more productive."[56] As the example of the GI Bill shows, public investment matters as much as private investment in stimulating the economy and building a good society. Government cutbacks in financing scientific research have produced a decline in the United States' share in the number of global patents. And, for years now, the country has failed to maintain our national highways, resulting in crumbling roads, collapsing bridges as occurred in Minneapolis–St. Paul in 2007, and increasing gridlock.[57] Nor has the federal government invested sufficiently in the maintenance of the national parks and forests where one is likely to encounter these days potted roads and washed-out trails.[58] These investments are on the decline and will decline further if the country's fiscal house is not put in order.

The example of Colorado offers a lesson in where a libertarian approach of radical tax cuts and fiscal pressure might lead.[59] In 1992 Colorado passed a Taxpayer's Bill of Rights (TABOR) that placed rigid limits on tax and spending growth—even in times of economic prosperity. Norquist labeled the law the "holy grail" of libertarian budget policy. Even though Colorado is the country's tenth-richest state, TABOR quickly pushed it toward the bottom in providing health protection and education to its citizens. By 2004, the number of children lacking health insurance had doubled as state government failed to adequately fund its portion of Medicaid spending; this placed the state last among the fifty states in covering low-income children. In 2005 Colorado had more cases of whooping cough—a potentially deadly disease for children—than any other state except Texas, even though it has a fifth the population. This is not surprising, since TABOR caused the state government to reduce funding of childhood vaccinations. Education was especially hard hit: the state dropped to forty-seventh in the nation for support of K–12 education. Because of education-spending cuts, the student-teacher ratio is now among the highest in the country. Colorado has shown what ignoring the value of public investment and government programs can produce.

Libertarian budget policies also are likely to exacerbate another social trend that has substantially undermined the American Dream—growing economic inequality. Since the 1970s U.S. society has changed from one becoming more economically equal to one becoming more unequal. As Figure 2-4

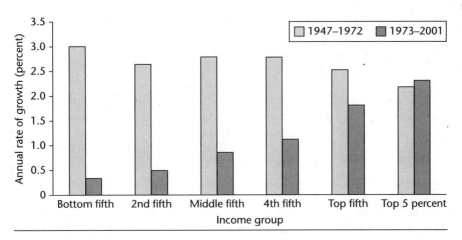

Figure 2-4 ANNUAL GROWTH RATE OF REAL INCOME ACROSS THE U.S. FAMILY INCOME DISTRIBUTION, 1947–2001

SOURCES: William E. Hudson, *American Democracy in Peril*, 5th ed. (Washington, D.C.: CQ Press, 2006), 277; Gary Burtless and Christopher Jencks, "American Inequality and Its Consequences," in *Agenda for the Nation*, ed. Henry J. Aaron et al. (Washington, D.C.: Brookings Institution, 2003), 65.

shows, in the post–World War II period, the era of the GI Bill, the prosperity of the era was distributed with remarkable equality across all income classes. Annual income growth was substantial for everyone, but remarkably the poorer 20 percent of Americans saw their incomes rise faster than the richest 20 percent. That situation has changed dramatically in the past four decades. The white bars in Figure 2-4 show a stair-step progression from poorest to richest, with the rich far exceeding the rest in income growth. In addition, annual growth in income in this latter period was much less for everyone than the post–World War II years *except* for the richest 5 percent. The years since the 1970s have been the fat ones for those at the top of the income distribution. By 2000, the distribution of income in this country had grown to resemble what it had been in the 1920s before the Great Depression.[60] Today, the top 1 percents' share of total gross personal income is about 17.4 percent and increase from 8.2 percent in 1980.[61] The richest 0.01 percent of Americans, about thirteen thousand taxpayers, earn an average of $17 million—three hundred times that of the average wage earner—and a total amount equal to the incomes of the twenty million poorest Americans. The wealthiest 1 percent of Americans not only capture a larger share of annual income, they now control a total of 40 percent of the country's total assets. Wealth is now more highly concentrated in the United States than in most European countries.[62]

What accounts for this shift toward greater inequality? Structural changes in the market economy and shifts in public policy have worked in tandem to create a less-equal America.[63] Beginning in the 1970s, corporate leaders adopted a series of policies to "modernize" the U.S. economy, make it more competitive globally, and increase corporate profitability. This process involved reducing dramatically the size of the country's manufacturing base, especially in key industries such as steel and automobiles, through transferring production abroad, where lower wages could be paid. At the same time, major corporate reorganization occurred through mergers, acquisitions, and financial buyouts. Generally, corporate "downsizing," laying off large numbers of employees, and selling off less-profitable parts of a corporation accompanied these financial maneuvers. When they lost their manufacturing jobs or were downsized, workers were forced to take jobs at lower pay in service industries. Globalization has been a key aspect of these developments, as corporate titans moved investment capital around the world, seeking the cheapest way of producing goods. This means that many American workers find themselves in competition with workers worldwide, from Bangalore to South Africa, who are willing to work for less. Corporate employers have encouraged this competition through aggressive anti-union efforts to undercut the domestic bargaining power of workers. In the 1950s, close to 35 percent of nonfarm employees belonged to a labor union; by 2000 only about 8 percent did. Unlike their grandparents, workers are on their own in negotiating wages and benefits with their employers, who can easily offer much less than they would if faced with workers organized collectively in a union.

Of course, none of this economic reorganization could have occurred without favorable public policies that politicians since the 1980s have been eager to provide them. To begin, starting with the Reagan administration, labor laws have been consistently administered in a manner favoring employers over workers. As they pursued aggressive tactics to decertify unions or prevent workers from organizing, corporate leaders could count on favorable decisions from a National Labor Relations Board usually controlled by Republican appointees. Politicians also have refused to increase the minimum wage in line with inflation, making it much lower—even with some belated increases in the past decade—when adjusted for inflation than it was in the 1960s. Public policy also has shifted in favor of financial deregulation, allowing deindustrialization, downsizing, and corporate reorganization. Corporate America also has found that Republican and Democratic politicians alike have responded to its desire to find the lowest production costs worldwide through the negotiation of trade agreements like the North American Free Trade Agreement (NAFTA) and the World Trade Organization (WTO). These global trade policies have facilitated the movement of capital and profits around the globe, but have not concerned ensuring fair wages and working conditions or environmental standards. Finally, tax policy has contributed substantially to growing inequality. Between 1979 and 2000, change in after-tax household income has delivered higher incomes in the same stair-step fashion across the income distribution as the pretax increases shown in Figure 2-4. Only when the impact of the tax law on incomes is taken into account are the steps at the higher end of the distribution giant sized. Increases in after-tax income for

80 percent of Americans ranged from the meager 9 percent increase for the poorest 20 percent to a more respectable 24 percent for the next to the highest 20 percent. But the richest 20 percent gained 68 percent—well over three times as much as the rest of Americans and the very top 1 percent saw their after-tax incomes grow an amazing 200 percent. The Bush tax cuts have exacerbated this trend, delivering over a short period of time a 7.5 percent increase in the incomes of millionaires compared to only just over 2 percent for middle-income earners. Clearly, tax policy changes since the time of Reagan's supply-side tax cuts have been regressive, making economic inequality worse.

Libertarians are likely to be quite satisfied with the rising inequality in the United States because the changes in economic structure and public policy described here have made economic distribution more responsive to market forces. Greater inequality, they would argue, means individuals are simply reaping their just compensation based upon their economic performance—without the market distorting effects of unions and misguided public policies like minimum-wage laws. In fact, economists report that in this new entrepreneurial economy, corporations are able to measure what employees contribute and compensate them accordingly. Quite a different world than when union collective bargaining determined compensation for much of the workforce, and according to Columbia economist W. Bentley MacLeod, "people with different abilities and capabilities were frequently paid the same amount for doing similar jobs."[64] The fact that inequalities in income correlate ever more strongly with differences in education only underscores that the market is delivering its rewards according to individual merit. And if investors derive large benefits from their global investments, even if this means an increasing share of income goes to capital rather than labor, that is just an inevitable result of a globalized market. Furthermore, market forces have produced strong economic growth through greater efficiency and incentives to work and excel, which inequality encourages; that will bring overall prosperity for everyone. The United States today, including its greater inequality, seems to be moving in a direction more consistent with a libertarian vision.

Communitarians view this growing inequality with alarm. First, they would question the libertarian assumption that the inequalities that the market produces are automatically a reflection of differences in individual "merit." They would point out the extent to which individual economic rewards also derive from social arrangements and sheer luck. Second, even if individual compensation can be related more closely to contributions to a corporation's profits, that does necessarily make the resulting income distribution just. Tying one's compensation solely to the corporation's bottom line in the short term may be a formula for anxiety and adversely impact the rest of one's life. Most of us need some level of stability and security in income to live a happy and productive life. Finally, since Aristotle, political philosophers have warned of the deleterious impact of extreme economic inequality on community life. Economic and social differences divide citizens from one another to such a degree that they become unable to understand each other or live together in peace. This can be especially dangerous for democracy, which depends on citizens' ability to respect one another as mutual participants in a common enterprise. Only when we have some capacity to understand one another's concerns and lives can we hope to devise mutually acceptable solutions to common problems. Political scientists have found a strong connection between economic resources and political influence—one that has been increasing with rising inequality. In today's politics, according to a task force of the American Political Science Association, "ordinary Americans speak with a whisper while the most advantaged roar."[65] If this situation persists, the wealthy are likely to understand less and less the needs of the rest of society as they amass increased power to determine our collective destiny. The common good will not be achieved if only the voices of those who prosper most are heard. Nor does a society sharply divided between the haves and the rest conform to the American Dream of a middle-class society with prosperity for all.

Unfortunately, the libertarian thrust of a federal budget policy with huge tax cuts and a large structural deficit undermines public policies that might reduce inequality. Many economists argue that the structural economic changes of recent years—including globalization—have strengthened the ability of the free market to deliver greater economic growth and, anyway, are unstoppable. We cannot turn back the clock to the American industrial age of the 1950s, when inequality was diminishing.[66] What might be done, however, would be to let the winners in today's market economy compensate the losers. This requires the sort of economic redistribution that is anathema to libertarians, but it works. European countries that have been subject to the same global market forces as the United States have experienced much less inequality because of redistributive social welfare programs. The very safety net programs that have eroded in this country due to structural deficit pressures have been maintained there. To accomplish similar redistribution here would mean increasing public spending for the poor, such as a more generous EITC program; shoring up, not privatizing, social insurance programs that provide economic security to the middle class, like Social Security and Medicare; and creating new programs such as universal health insurance or universal child care. The large structural deficit we now face makes accomplishing this quite difficult. One way to address it will require reversing the tax policies of recent years and returning to a more progressive tax system to generate additional public revenue. As a reader might now expect, this is not the libertarian agenda for the future of our tax system.

Shifting the Tax Burden: Flat Taxes, Death Taxes, and No Taxes on Capital

Since the passage of the Sixteenth Amendment in 1913, which provided for an income tax, American taxation has been based on the principle of progressivity—those with higher incomes should pay a higher proportion in taxes than those with lower incomes. In practical terms, this is expressed in the increase in the percentage of income taxed on higher margins of income. Progressive taxation can be justified philosophically on several grounds.[67] One relies on what is called the benefit principle, the notion that every taxpayer should pay in proportion to the benefits they receive from government. At first glance this seems to imply taxing the same proportion of everyone's income, but since the rich can be seen as benefiting more from government protection, payment in proportion to benefit received demands that the rich pay more. The rich benefit most from the order and safety government provides, and they would have more to lose from a foreign invasion or criminal anarchy than those with less property. In terms of political obligation, the rich have a greater responsibility to return to the community the wealth they derive from living in it. A second philosophical argument relies on the "ability to pay principle." The rich can tolerate providing a larger proportion of their income to support government because they sacrifice less in doing so than someone with a lower income. A rich family, as this reasoning goes, has more discretionary income—income left over after paying for necessities—than a poor person. Paying a higher proportional tax may prevent the rich from enjoying a week in the Bahamas this year, but, unlike the poor, they will not have to skip a meal as a result. Finally, the concept of social justice supports progressive taxation because ensuring a minimal standard of living to all and preventing large inequalities of wealth in society requires redistribution. Taxing a greater proportion of the incomes of the rich in itself limits how much they can accumulate ensuring greater equality. Taking a larger proportion from the rich makes available the revenue for public programs to support the incomes of the poor and open up economic opportunities through education or job training. All three of these arguments reflect a communitarian understanding that sees individuals intimately connected to their communities, deriving their individual well-being as much from others and community ties as from anything they possess by themselves. This is quite different from the libertarian view of and absolute individual entitlement to income and wealth.

Given this fundamentally different philosophical premise, libertarians oppose progressive taxation in principle. That is why libertarian think tanks, activists, and politicians coalesced by the 1980s around a long-term aim of abolishing progressive taxation altogether. A first step was the radical reduction in marginal income tax rates achieved first in the Reagan tax cuts and then in the more substantial George W. Bush cuts. These alone made U.S. taxation less progressive, but they were only the first step. The antitax coalition formed within the Republican Party had next pursued a "five easy pieces" tax reform plan: repeal of the estate tax, ending the taxation on capital gains, allowing businesses to write off investments in a single tax year, abolishing the Alternative Minimum Tax, and making all income from savings tax free.[68] The Bush tax laws in 2002 and 2003 made major strides in allowing business investment write-offs and slashing taxes on dividends and capital gains. The ATM is in the process of being gradually phased out as more middle-class taxpayers come within its purview. The Bush administration has proposed a range of tax savings accounts intended to allow sheltering of taxation—the first for Health

Savings Accounts enacted as a part of the Medicare Prescription Drug Act in 2003. And an estate tax phaseout was included in the 2001 tax legislation that libertarians want made permanent. The culmination of these steps would occur with enactment of the abolition of the progressive income tax altogether and its replacement with a flat tax that alone accomplishes the "five easy pieces" agenda.

Prior to this onslaught against the progressive income tax, the idea of progressive taxation seemed as unassailable a part of U.S. tradition, as a recent book put it, as "no taxation without representation."[69] The well-orchestrated campaign to repeal the estate tax, the country's most progressive tax, demonstrates the vulnerability of the idea in today's more libertarian America. The estate tax has existed since the early twentieth century to provide a limit on the size of the fortunes that the richest 1 to 2 percent of Americans could pass on to their heirs. Republican president Theodore Roosevelt, who feared that the huge Gilded Age fortunes accumulated over time would turn the United States into a plutocracy, was one of its strongest early advocates. Philanthropist and steel magnate Andrew Carnegie was another advocate who thought the children of the very rich undeserving of a fortune they had not earned themselves would become "idle and profligate" from inherited money.[70] In 2001, the estate tax affected only assets in excess of $650,000—an amount scheduled to rise to $1 million in 2002. Of those who died in 1999, 97.7 percent

REPUBLICAN POLITICAL LEADERS, LIKE THEN-HOUSE SPEAKER DENNIS HASTERT OF ILLINOIS, FOUND THE DEATH TAX LABEL EFFECTIVE IN THEIR CAMPAIGN TO REPEAL THE ESTATE TAX.

paid no estate tax, and those 2.3 percent of estates that were taxed averaged about $2.3 million. Despite the small number of Americans taxed, the estate tax generated $24.4 billion—an amount sufficient to fund half the budget of the whole Department of Education.[71]

Although the tax provided an important source of revenue from only the very richest of Americans, by the late 1990s a well-funded and savvy coalition had convinced most Americans that the estate tax threatened them and turned its repeal into a populist cause. Funded by some of the nation's wealthiest families, including the Mars family, the Gallo family, the Walton family (Wal-Mart), and the heirs of Campbell Soup, the Family Business Estate Tax Coalition (FBETC) brought together libertarian-leaning members of Congress like Phil Crane of Illinois and Christopher Cox of California, libertarian think tankers such as Bill Beach of the Heritage Foundation, and a variety of business and farm organizations. Cleverly the FBETC relabeled the estate tax as the Death Tax, implying that it was a tax on death itself rather than on large estates. The Death Tax label became instrumental in convincing a large majority of Americans that they eventually would have to pay a tax at death.[72] In addition, the coalition publicized a handful of anecdotes, usually exaggerated, of individuals that the tax had adversely affected to personalize the issue. False claims about the estate tax forcing families to sell off farms rather than pass them to the next generation gained further public sympathy, although, when challenged, repeal advocates could not produce a single example of this occurring.[73] Central to the repeal advocates' campaign was the libertarian argument that an absolute property right attached to an estate implied that the tax amounted to theft from a dead person's heirs. In the end, estate tax repeal easily made it into the 2001 tax cut package. The tax is scheduled to phase out by 2010, but due to the strange "sunset" provision of the 2001 law, it will return in 2011 as it existed in 2001. (As a result, some wags have suggested that we can anticipate a wave of deaths, somehow encouraged, among the elderly rich in 2010.) However, it is likely, given how public opinion has been shaped on the issue and the skill of the repeal coalition in deploying the death tax label that the repeal will be made permanent. Estate tax repeal definitely has been a major victory for libertarians opposed to progressive taxation.

Progressive taxation will take another major hit if libertarian-inspired proposals for sheltering savings from taxation are enacted. In 2005, the Bush administration proposed three principal vehicles for accomplishing this—Retirement Savings Accounts (RSAs), Lifetime Savings Accounts (LSAs), and Individual Development Accounts (IDAs).[74] RSAs would replace the existing Roth IRA program and, like Roths, would permit individuals to invest up to $5,000 per year in taxed income into a retirement fund that would accumulate tax-free and could be disbursed tax-free after age 58. Unlike Roth IRAs, however, there would be no income limits on participating in the program, making wealthier people eligible to participate in sheltering their retirement income. LSAs would allow contributing up to $5,000 per year in post-tax income that would accumulate tax-free and withdrawals would be tax-free. Withdrawals from these accounts could be made at any time in one's lifetime and used for any purpose. One interesting twist allows anyone to contribute, up to the $5,000 limit, to any other individual's LSA account. Presumably, this would allow people to invest in accounts for their children—or any other individual they wish to support, creating a nest egg for the recipients' futures. The administration admits that through a combination of RSAs and LSAs a majority of taxpayers would be able to shelter all of their savings and investment income from taxation.[75] For low-income earners, the administration has recently proposed IDAs. These accounts would provide federal matching contributions for investments up to $500 per year for individuals with incomes up to $20,000 per year and families up to $40,000.[76] Participating financial institutions would administer the accounts and receive a $50 per year per account subsidy to cover administrative costs. Interestingly, unlike RSAs and LSAs, income earned in these funds would be taxable. Also, disbursements would be limited to higher education purchases, first-time home purchases, or small business startup. So far, partly due to the collapse in Bush's popularity due to the Iraq war, these proposals have not been enacted. The administration did succeed in inserting a provision for Health Care Savings Accounts (HSAs), allowing sheltering income for health expenses, into the 2003 Medicare prescription drug bill. The other, more ambitious plan for tax-sheltered savings remains a key part of the libertarian agenda, however, and will surely return to the fore in the administration of a future Republican president.

The crown jewel in the libertarian campaign to abolish progressive taxation is the flat tax. As we have seen, libertarians believe that if individuals must pay taxes a proportional levy is preferable to a progressive rate. In recent years, many have come to advocate abolishing the current progressive income tax and replacing it with a flat-rate tax on wages and salaries and on business earnings. First developed by two Stanford University economists, Robert Hall and Alvin Rabushka, libertarian think tanks, like the Cato Institute, and libertarian-leaning politicians, like former Republican House majority leader Dick Armey, embraced the flat tax as their preferred reform.[77] In both the 1996 and 2000 presidential campaigns, Steve Forbes, publisher of *Forbes* magazine, made a flat tax the centerpiece of his campaign for the Republican nomination. Supporters contrast their proposal as simpler than the current system because it involves for individuals only a flat tax (usually set at around 20 percent) on wage, salary, and pension income. There would be no need to report any income from interest, savings, or dividends because they are not taxed and there are no deductions. As a concession to some progressivity, the plans typically allow an exemption up to a certain amount depending on the number of dependents. Simplicity is deemed the chief advantage of the system— so simple its advocates say that most taxpayers could file their return on a postcard.

The part of the flat tax that tends to get less attention in political speeches is the business flat tax. Like wage earners, any business, whether a corporation, individual proprietorship (say the local pizza shop), or partnership (such as a law firm), also pays a tax on its earnings, at the exact same flat rate workers pay on their wages. These earnings include all the money the business takes in after deductions for money invested; the cost of plant and equipment; the cost of "inputs," or what a business needs to purchase to do its work (for example, what the pizza shop pays for its pepperoni); and the wages paid to workers. When we take into account the business aspect of the flat tax, it becomes clear that the flat tax is not an income tax, but what economists call a consumption tax. Because the tax excludes from taxation all income from savings, investment, and capital gains on assets, its base is only that part of total income earned in the economy that goes for consumption.

Many economists believe consumption taxes are advantageous for economic growth because they provide an incentive to save and invest. As we have seen, under a flat tax, the more a corporation allocates its total receipts to investment, the lower its tax bill. Theoretically, the savings incentive for the individual wage earner is similarly enhanced. Although all his wages are taxed, when deciding how to spend them, money put into a savings account eventually will earn tax-free interest. That means he will get to keep more of the fruits of good savings habits than he would under an income tax that takes away a portion of that interest. Enthusiasts for the flat tax claim it would also increase incentives for savings and investment because it would eliminate so-called "double taxation." The profits of businesses would be taxed, but they would not be taxed when distributed to shareholders in the form of dividends or capital gains.

The problem with consumption taxes, such as the sales tax, the value added tax (a tax common in European countries), and the flat tax is that they are regressive. Since people earning lower incomes must devote more of their money to consumption than wealthier people, they end up paying a larger proportion of their total income in taxes than the rich. Most flat tax proposals try to ameliorate this problem by making wages exempt up to a certain amount (for Hall-Rabushka that amount is $20,000), but even with the exemption the flat tax shifts the tax burden substantially to wage earners. This becomes clear if we consider the effect of the elimination of the so-called "double taxation." Since investment earnings of individuals are not taxed, earnings of the super-wealthy who garner huge dividends and capital gains cannot be tapped at a progressive rate. True, according to the double taxation argument, their investments have already been taxed through the business tax, but that flat rate taxed what came to them at the same rate as what a retired widow drawing on modest (401)k earnings received. Tapping into the incomes of those most well off, as a progressive income tax does, to meet social needs becomes impossible under a flat tax. Hall and Rabushka themselves admit that their flat tax, compared to the current income tax, would raise taxes on middle-income wage earners while those families "with incomes around $285,000 receive tax breaks of about 7 percent of income, those with incomes of $1.5 million get 10 percent, and the handful with incomes approaching $4 million get 13 percent."[78]

As we can see, even if we assume the validity of the "double taxation" argument, the flat tax's effects are unfair. But is taxing the same asset unfair, and does this only happen with taxation of corporate dividends (or estates—another place where the unfairness of "double taxation" is claimed)? Not according to analysts Michael Graetz and Ian Shapiro. As they point out, "finding double taxation is child's play; double and even triple taxation are everywhere. Our salaries are taxed by the wage tax to finance Social Security, another wage tax to finance Medicare, by both state and federal income taxes, and again by sales taxes when we spend whatever is left."[79] The flat tax would leave multiple taxation of wage and salary income in place even while it prevented "double taxation" of investment income. As a practical matter, then, what the flat tax does is tax more heavily the ordinary workers who earn most of their income from wages and salaries, while freeing most of the income of the very wealthy from taxation. Cries about the unfairness of "double taxation" hardly compare to the unfairness of a flat tax regime where the assistant manager of the local grocery store would see his annual $50,000 salary taxed at the flat tax 20 percent rate, while his rich uncle across town would pay zero on his $500,000 income from his investments.

All these tax changes taken together—estate tax repeal, lifetime savings accounts, reducing taxation of capital gains, and the ultimate flat tax—are part of a libertarian vision where poor and middle-income Americans who earn their livings from wages and salaries bear the burden of taxation. As Graetz and Shapiro put it, they are "key pieces of a three-decade effort to fundamentally re-structure our nation's tax system by eliminating all taxes on wealth and income from wealth."[80] The aim seems to be a dream world for an idle heir or heiress—one where they can be confident of receiving intact their entire share of the fortune from their parents with no "death tax" to "steal it for the government." And they can rest easy that they will never have to pay a dime in income tax on all the dividends that will come their way as their investments grow in value. As a libertarian might put it, their entitlement to their private property will remain untouched. (Well earned is the implication, though their only role in creating it was a lucky choice of parents.) Can we be sure they will put this "entitlement" to good use? I certainly would not count on it.

This libertarian vision of taxation probably would have, in the long run, the effect of "starving the beast." As the wealthy saw their obligations to support the common good decline, more and more of a burden would be placed on people earning low and middle incomes. Given the sharp inequality in the distribution of wealth, something a libertarian tax regime would make worse, an increasing share of the country's assets would be shielded from taxation. This would require raising funds for public purposes from the smaller share controlled by ordinary citizens. Those subject to tax simply will be unable to finance public expenditures, from national defense to national parks. The libertarian illusion is that this shrunken government will permit a better society. A society without a government capable of offering a safety net to the destitute, providing educational opportunities to future generations, ensuring a dignified life to those in their final years, preserving our cultural heritage for posterity, assisting those caught up in natural disasters, and protecting us all from foreign enemies will not be a good society. In eighteenth-century France, the government of Europe's richest country found itself in a fiscal crisis because aristocratic privilege prevented it from taxing those who possessed the greatest part of its wealth. The revolution that resulted provided a bloody resolution to the crisis. To similarly insulate America's wealthy from their obligations to their country may ultimately produce for them a similar disaster.

Conclusion: Paying for the Government We Need and Want

Protecting the common good for us and posterity requires rejecting the libertarian approach to budgetary and fiscal policy. Massive tax cuts combined with false assumptions about government's role in society have produced only structural deficits, growing inequality, and an impending future fiscal crisis. Starving government of revenue has produced inadequately funded agencies incapable of meeting urgent needs, as the dismal response in 2005 to Hurricane Katrina in New Orleans demonstrated. Four basic principles ought to guide budgetary policy to produce a more communitarian pattern of taxing and spending. First, the government must look first and foremost to imposing a level of taxation needed to meet public needs. Second, progressive taxation is required to raise the revenues needed for those needs from those best equipped to pay. Third, obligations to programs such as Social Security, Medicare, and a safety net for the poor must be met. And finally, public investments in education; infrastructure for transportation and communications, research, and development; and protection of our nation's heritage must be made to ensure a good life for future generations.

The United States needs to return to basics when contemplating taxing and spending. Rather than the seduction of supply-side snake oil that promises continued spending despite lowering taxes or "starve the beast" illusions about shrinking government, a democratic citizenry must tax itself to accomplish what it wants its government to do. As a recent Brookings Institution report says, "the fundamental purpose of the tax system is to raise the money government needs to pay for the spending it has chosen to undertake."[81] Not imposing taxes adequate now to meet spending needs requires borrowing that automatically imposes taxes on future generations. Occasional deficits to fight an economic downturn or some debt for investments in infrastructure that benefit future generations can be justified. But the kind of structural deficits the United States incurred in the 1980s and today cannot be. These deficits have not been needed for economic stimulus, nor have they been used for investments in the future. On the contrary, while taxes have been lowered to permit the private consumption of the wealthy—on multiple homes, yachts, and private jets—important public investments for the future have been neglected. In the short term, misguided cuts in the budgets of government agencies for fundamental services, from processing passport applications to responding to natural disasters, have undermined public confidence in the efficiency and capacity of government.[82] Policymakers must make a realistic assessment of what revenues are needed for government to operate, impose the taxes needed to raise them, and fund the government services citizens want and need.

The libertarian brief against progressive taxation is based on mistaken assumptions. The distribution of income and wealth cannot be regarded as sacrosanct and inherently fair. Some rewards from the market are due to individual effort and skill, but they also are a consequence of luck, opportunities made available because of government-provided benefits—at minimum law and order, and the investments other people now and in the past have made to permit earning income and accumulating wealth. Markets also tend to lead to unequal outcomes that accumulate over time. Those who benefit today usually can invest market success in future success. Progressive taxation allows both tapping into the incomes of those best able to pay for public needs and permits some redistribution of market outcomes. Restoring more progressivity to the tax code needs to be a priority for serving the future common good.

A first step in restoring more progressive taxation would be to reverse the tax cuts enacted between 2001 and 2003, including the lowering of marginal rates, repealing of the estate tax, and lowering of capital gains taxes. Perhaps to counter the "death tax" rhetoric, the estate tax, now imposed on estates after death, ought to be replaced with an inheritance tax, imposed on only the largest fortunes—say more than $2 million—of the people who inherit the transferred wealth. This no longer will be a tax imposed on the estate of someone who dies, but a levy on those who receive a windfall, much as is now done with lottery winners. Opponents of such a reversal will claim that it will harm incentives to save and invest, the standard argument made against progressive taxation. Yet the experience with tax increases of the early 1990s that were followed by an economic boom shows that there is room for raising marginal tax rates without undermining economic productivity. Libertarians are correct to warn that if taxes are too high and if the system becomes too progressive, economic growth might be stalled. However, historical experience suggests that there is considerable room for taxing progressively without threatening economic growth.

One strong reason for shoring up the federal government's revenue base through more adequate and progressive taxation is the impending costs of baby boom retirements in the coming decades. As we will see in chapter 4, addressing these costs will require a package of policy changes, but meeting the obligations of Social Security and Medicare cannot occur without a fiscally sound federal government. The historical commitments made to those who have contributed to these programs and have counted on them for retirement demands taking the fiscal measures needed to meet them. Social justice also requires that an affluent society like ours ensure a minimally decent standard of living for the elderly and all people. Social Security and Medicare are the pillars for such a living standard for the old, but we also need to be mindful of those in need who are not old—the safety net for our least well-off citizens. Budget deficits in recent years have created large holes in that safety net that must be repaired. Along with shoring up existing portions of the social compact, a major contribution from government revenues will be required to address the crisis in U.S. health care (see chapter 5). The United States cannot much longer afford a health system that both costs more and produces worse average health outcomes—such as life expectancy and infant mortality—than those in other industrial countries, plus fails to insure over 40 million of its citizens. A major investment in meeting this crisis must be factored into future budget policy.

Finally, as a society, we need to invest in the future. Since the emergence of large structural deficits in the 1980s, governments at all levels have failed to make adequate investments in the infrastructure for future economic growth and prosperity. Greater investments in education must be made if our future citizens are to compete successfully in a global economy. As *New York Times* columnist Thomas Friedman has argued, in the "flat world" we now live in, economic success will increasingly follow skills and knowledge.[83] Higher levels of public investment in education will be needed if our citizens are to have the knowledge and skills to compete in the flat world. Besides investments in human capital, we need to refurbish the physical capital of the country. Transportation will be one area of needed investment in years to come—to repair highways and bridges, modernize air transport infrastructure, and build an adequate passenger rail system. In recent years, congestion on the highways and in the air points to the need for building high-speed intercity rail systems comparable to those in Europe. Such a rail system also would reduce pollution and be more energy efficient. This brings us to environmental needs, especially the threat of global warming, and energy needs. Both also will need to be important priorities in future budgets, along with many other investment needs.

The long list of public needs underscores the libertarian illusion that we can expect smaller government in the future. Although government probably will never comprise as large a proportion of GDP as it does in Europe, government in the United States may need to expand to accomplish even part of what has been mentioned here. It certainly cannot be expected to shrink below current levels. Moreover, this chapter has not discussed the military and foreign policy costs the United States faces as the world's only super power. The United States' federal, state, and local government will have expanding responsibilities, not shrinking ones, in the years to come. Libertarians have sought to place a priority of the private wants of the marketplace over the larger needs of the community for many years now. Indiscriminate tax cuts and unwise constraints on government programs have starved the public sector of the resources it needs to invest in a prosperous future for all Americans. Budget policy must face the reality of the necessity for a vigorous public sector to meet community needs and ensure that taxing and spending decisions allow government to promote the common good.

SUGGESTIONS FOR FURTHER READING

Altman, Daniel. *Neoconomy: George Bush's Revolutionary Gamble with America's Future.* New York: Public Affairs, 2004. A journalist's account of the politics surrounding the enactment of George W. Bush's first-term tax cuts.

Fried, Charles. *Modern Liberty and the Limits of Government.* New York: W. W. Norton, 2007. One of the most thoughtful libertarian-minded legal theorists in the country makes his case for protecting liberty through smaller government.

Friedman, Milton, and Rose Friedman. *Capitalism and Freedom.* Chicago: University of Chicago Press, 1962; *Free To Choose.* New York: Avon Books, 1980. These two well-written and well-argued polemics by the late Nobel Prize–winning economist and his wife make classic libertarian arguments about the need for less government in the United States.

Graetz, Michael J., and Ian Shapiro. *Death by a Thousand Cuts: The Fight over Taxing Inherited Wealth.* Princeton: Princeton University Press, 2005. A detailed and entertaining account of the successful campaign to repeal the estate tax.

Murphy, Liam, and Thomas Nagel. *The Myth of Ownership: Taxes and Justice.* New York: Oxford University Press, 2002. Two philosophers take apart the libertarian assumptions about property rights and taxation.

Slemrod, Joel, and Jon Bakija. *Taxing Ourselves: A Citizen's Guide to the Debate over Taxes.* Cambridge: MIT Press, 2004. A comprehensive survey of U.S. taxation.

SELECTED WEB SITES

http://world.std.com/~mhuben/libindex.html. The libertarian Cato Institute's Web site for tax and budget issues.

www.ctj.org. Citizens for Tax Justice offers well-respected analyses of tax policy that are critical of most libertarian proposals.

www.taxpolicycenter.org/home. A joint venture of the Brookings Institution and the Urban Institute, the Tax Policy Center gathers well-respected policy experts for largely middle-of-the-road discussion.

NOTES

1. Milton Friedman, *Capitalism and Freedom* (Chicago: University of Chicago Press, 1962), 79.
2. James W. Lindeen, *Governing America's Economy* (Englewood Cliffs, N.J.: Prentice Hall, 1994), 19.

3. Paul Krugman, *Peddling Prosperity* (New York: Norton, 1994), 29–34.
4. Friedman argued against using either monetary or fiscal policy to manage business cycles. The best monetary policy, he thought, would be to expand the money supply steadily according to a fixed rule tied to increases in productivity. As regards fiscal policy, he argued simply for balanced budgets. See *Capitalism and Freedom*, 75–84.
5. Krugman, *Peddling Prosperity*, 57.
6. Harold W. Stanley and Richard B. Niemi, *Vital Statistics on American Politics: 2003–2004.* (Washington D.C.: CQ Press, 2005), 398.
7. Milton Friedman, *Capitalism and Freedom*, 77–78. Liberal economist Krugman also makes the connection. See his *Pedding Prosperity*, 53.
8. Krugman, *Peddling Prosperity*, 42–43.
9. Ibid., 82–89.
10. Some mainstream economists in the 1970s such as Martin Feldstein, Michael Boskin, and Larry Summers did provide evidence that some of the high marginal tax rates at the time, particularly on capital gains, did depress some savings and investment. They did not claim, however, that this explained all of slower economic growth in the 1970s and never embraced the supply-side analysis or policy prescriptions. See the discussion in Krugman, *Peddling Prosperity*, 69–75.
11. For a review of Reagan's ideas regarding minimalist government, see Walter Williams, *Reaganism and the Death of Representative Democracy* (Washington, D.C.: Georgetown University Press, 2003), 51–56.
12. Joel Slemrod and Jon Bakija, *Taxing Ourselves: A Citizen's Guide to the Debate over Taxes* (Cambridge: MIT Press, 2004), 24.
13. James J. Gosling, *Politics and the American Economy* (New York: Longman, 2000), 12.
14. Krugman, *Peddling Prosperity*, 154.
15. Ibid., 155.
16. Charles L. Cochran and Eloise B. Malone, *Public Policy: Perspectives and Choices* (Boulder, Colo.: Lynne Reiner, 2005), 203.
17. Liam Murphy and Thomas Nagel, *The Myth of Ownership: Taxes and Justice* (New York: Oxford University Press, 2002), 35.
18. Jacob S. Hacker and Paul Pierson, *Off Center: The Republican Evolution and the Erosion of American Democracy* (New Haven: Yale University Press, 2005), 80.
19. John Cassidy, "Tax Code," *The New Yorker,* September 6, 2004, 71.
20. Cochran and Malone, *Public Policy*, 204.
21. Ibid., 206.
22. Ibid., 204.
23. Theda Skocpol, *Boomerang: Health Care Reform and the Turn against Government* (New York: Norton, 1997), 64.
24. Quoted in Paul Krugman, "The Tax-Cut Con," *New York Times Magazine,* September 14, 2003.
25. Cassidy, "Tax Code," 76.
26. Jared Bernstein, "Ballad of the Beast-Starvers," *American Prospect* Online, March 15, 2005, www.prospect.org/cs/articles?articleId=9335.
27. Robert Nozick, *Anarchy, State, and Utopia* (New York: Basic Books), 1974.
28. Ibid., 169.

29. Liam Murphy and Thomas Nagel, *The Myth of Ownership* (New York: Oxford University Press, 2002), 8.
30. Ibid., 8.
31. Quoted in Michael J. Graetz and Ian Shapiro, *Death by a Thousand Cuts: The Fight over Taxing Inherited Wealth* (Princeton: Princeton University Press, 2005), 27.
32. Benjamin Page and James R. Simmons, *What Government Can Do* (Chicago: University of Chicago Press, 2000), 34.
33. Friedman, *Capitalism and Freedom*, 28; see also David Boaz, *Libertarianism: A Primer* (New York: Free Press, 1997), 172–177.
34. My example roughly meets the economists' theoretical requirement that a pure public good be nonrival and nonexcludable. Assuming a constant number of desperados, No Name's price for disposing of them will be the same whether the town population is one thousand or two thousand. And there is no way to exclude any group of burghers from the greater security the desperados' demise produces.
35. Page and Simmons, *What Government Can Do*, 39.
36. Friedman, *Capitalism and Freedom*, 31.
37. National Park Service, www.nps.gov/aboutus/index.htm.
38. Suzanne Metzler, *Soldiers to Citizens: The G.I. Bill and the Making of the Greatest Generation* (New York: Oxford University Press, 2005), 6–7.
39. Ibid., 121–143.
40. For a good, readable summary of the research on supply-effects, see Norton Garfinkle, *The American Dream vs. the Gospel of Wealth: The Fight for a Productive Middle-Class Economy* (New Haven: Yale University Press, 2006), 179–188.
41. Gary Becker, Edward P. Lazaer, and Kevin M. Murphy, "The Double Benefit of Tax Cuts," *Wall Street Journal*, October 7, 2003, A20; Milton Friedman, "What Every American Wants," *Wall Street Journal*, January 15, 2003, A10.
42. This discussion, like the figure, is drawn from Matt Fiedlier, "Where Do Our Tax Dollars Go?" Center on Budget and Policy Priorities, May 15, 2007, www.cbpp.org.
43. OECD Factbook 2007, http://fiordiliji.sourceoecd.org/vl=1825269/cl=23/nw=1/rpsv/factbook/.
44. Cited in Slemrod and Bakija, *Taxing Ourselves*, 113.
45. Pew Research Center for the People and the Press, "Trend in Political Values and Core Attitudes 1987–2007," March 22, 2007.
46. Richard Kogan, Matt Fiedler, Aviva Aron-Dine, and James Horney, "The Long-Term Fiscal Outlook Is Bleak," Center on Budget and Policy Priorities, January 29, 2007, 1.
47. Alan J. Auerbach, William G. Gale, and Peter Orszag, "New Estimates of the Budget Outlook: Plus Ca Change, Plus C'est la Meme Chose," Tax Policy Center, Urban Institute, April 17, 2006.
48. Jason Furman, Lawrence H. Summers, and Jason Bordoff, "Achieving Progressive Tax Reform in an Increasingly Global Economy," Hamilton Project of the Brookings Institution, June 2007, 4.
49. Alice Rivlin and Isabel Sawhill, *Restoring Fiscal Sanity: How to Balance the Budget* (Washington, D.C.: Brookings Institution Press, 2004), 20.

50. Slemrod and Bakija, *Taxing Ourselves,* 27.
51. Ibid., 46.
52. Kogan et al., "The Long-Term Fiscal Outlook Is Bleak," 2; Stanley and Niemi, *Vital Statistics on American Politics,* 401.
53. Rivlin and Sawhill, *Restoring Fiscal Sanity,* 24–27.
54. Auerbach, Gale, and Orszag, "New Estimates of the Budget Outlook."
55. Robert H. Frank, *Falling Behind: How Rising Inequality Harms the Middle Class* (Berkeley: University of California Press, 2007), 113.
56. Rivlin and Sawhill, *Restoring Fiscal Sanity,* 27.
57. Frank, *Falling Behind,* 113.
58. Timothy Egan, "This Land Was My Land," *New York Times,* June 23, 2007, A27.
59. Greg Anrig Jr., "Discrediting Fiscal Conservatism," TPMCafe, The Century Foundation, March 23, 2006.
60. William Hudson, *American Democracy in Peril,* 5th ed. (Washington, D.C.: CQ Press, 2006), 279.
61. Daniel Gross, "Income Inequality, Writ Larger," *New York Times,* June 10, 2007, BU7.
62. Hudson, *American Democracy in Peril,* 281.
63. For a more detailed account of these developments, see ibid., 283–291.
64. Gross, "Income Inequality, Writ Larger."
65. APSA Task Force on Inequality and American Democracy, "American Democracy in an Age of Rising Inequality," Report Summary (Washington, D.C.: American Political Science Association, August 2004), 11.
66. This argument is summarized in Roger Lowenstein, "The Inequality Conundrum," *New York Times Magazine,* June 10, 2007, 11–14.
67. This discussion relies on Slemrod and Bakija, *Taxing Ourselves,* 59–65.
68. John Cassidy, "Tax Code," 72.
69. Graetz and Shapiro, *Death by a Thousand Cuts,* 267.
70. Ibid., 8.
71. Statistics in this paragraph are from ibid., 6.
72. Graetz and Shapiro provide a detailed and fascinating picture of the complexity of public opinion on the issue and the value of the death tax label to the repeal coalition, 118–130.
73. Ibid.,126.
74. U.S. Department of the Treasury, 2005, *Blue Book: General Explanations of the Administration's Fiscal Year 2006 Revenue Proposals* (Washington D.C.: U.S. Department of the Treasury, 2005), 8–11.
75. U.S. Department of the Treasury, Office of Public Affairs, "The President's Savings Proposals: Tax-Free Savings and Retirement Security Opportunities for All Americans" (Washington, D.C.: U.S. Department of the Treasury, February 2, 2005).
76. Ibid.
77. Graetz and Shapiro, *Death by a Thousand Cuts,* 270; Robert E. Hall and Alvin Rabushka, *The Flat Tax,* 2d ed. (Stanford, Calif.: Hoover Institution Press, 2007).
78. Robert S. McIntyre, "The Flat Taxers' Flat Distortions," *The American Prospect* (Summer 1995).

79. Graetz and Shapiro, *Death by a Thousand Cuts*, 229.
80. Ibid., 277.
81. Furman, Summers, and Bordoff, "Achieving Progressive Tax Reform," 4.
82. Stanley B. Greenberg, "Democrats are Back—But . . ." *The American Prospect* (July/August, 2007): 20.
83. Friedman, *The World Is Flat: A Brief History of the Twenty-first Century* (New York: Farrar, Straus, and Giroux, 2005).

Chapter 3 Deregulation: From Crowded Skies to Rolling Blackouts

Blackout. In the past, most Americans associated electricity blackouts with either bad weather or third world countries. The steady, secure supply of relatively cheap electrical power seemed a given in a prosperous, modern, industrial country like the United States. Sure, a temporary loss of electrical power caused by an occasional snowstorm, severe thunderstorm, overloaded circuits on an especially hot day, or even a pesky squirrel gnawing on an electrical line is a familiar inconvenience to just about everyone, but power stoppages due to an insufficient supply of energy are things one might experience in Guatemala or Bangladesh, but never in the U.S. of A. Imagine the astonishment of California residents in 2001 when over a period of months they experienced repeated periods of rolling blackouts because of a lack of a sufficient supply of generated power.[1] Their surprise was particularly great because only five years earlier, the California legislature had unanimously enacted new electricity deregulation legislation promising a future of cheaper and more abundant electrical power for all courtesy of market competition. Yet in 2001 the state was in an electricity crisis that, besides the blackouts, would produce the bankruptcy of one of its three private utilities, a gubernatorial declaration of a state of emergency, and, eventually, a $71 billion dollar bailout of the private utilities. All this happened because state politicians bought the libertarian illusion that markets producing any goods are most effective and efficient if left free from government regulation.

Prior to 1996, private utilities in California, as was the case in most of the United States, were considered *natural monopolies* that produced electrical power and distributed it to their customers with prices and profits regulated by public utility commissions. (Later in this chapter we will examine the rationale for regulation of natural monopolies and the reasons why the electricity industry was considered one.) A few California cities, for example Los Angeles, operated their own municipal power companies that provided electrical power on a nonprofit basis. (None of the municipal systems in California were deregulated and none experienced any power problems in 2001.) Under electricity deregulation, the private utility companies would continue to sell electricity to homes and businesses, but rather than produce the power in generating plants they owned themselves, they were to purchase the power in the competitive market. Competition among power generators was supposed to drive down the wholesale price of power that, eventually, would lead to lower prices for consumers. As a temporary measure, the private utilities were permitted to charge their customers up to 6.5 cents per kilowatt, a price that was supposed to permit them to earn a fair profit, pay for the power purchased in the wholesale market, and recover the cost of investments they had made in the past expecting a return from the regulated system—so-called "stranded costs." Deregulation advocates had convinced the state government and the utilities in 1996 that with competition the wholesale price per kilowatt would drop well below the 6.5 cent cap. This proved to be the fatal miscalculation.

Deregulators, with their absolute faith in markets, simply assumed competition among producers inevitably would lead to lower prices. As it turned out, electricity generators chose to make money through collusion rather than competition. Free of any regulation or oversight, by 2000, the companies that sold electricity in the wholesale market learned they could drive up prices through creating artificial shortages in electricity. During periods of high demand, they would take power plants off line for repair or maintenance or otherwise withhold supplies driving up the price. They then would release the power at the higher price. Soon California utilities found they had to pay more than 6.5 cents per kilowatt to obtain energy and, when supply was especially tight, they had to institute rolling blackouts to prevent system collapse. At the time, deregulation defenders blamed the wholesale electricity shortage on too little new construction of power plants due to environmental regulations, but the Federal Energy Regulatory Commission (FERC) eventually concluded that producer market manipulation was the major factor in the crisis.[2] Because of the cap on the retail price, California's private utilities soon found themselves in a financial crisis. In April the largest, Pacific Gas and Electric, declared bankruptcy.

The infamous Enron Corporation proved to be a key player in the wholesale electricity market manipulation that brought on the California crisis. Although Enron, originally a gas pipeline company, did not own any electricity generation facilities directly, its specialty by the late 1990s was trading in a wide variety of commodities, including wholesale electricity. All during the decade, Enron CEO Ken Lay had been a major advocate of electricity deregulation and used his political connections, including close ties to Texas governor, then president, George W. Bush to promote the idea. Prior to the California crisis, Enron developed a large business in packaging purchases of electricity from electrical power generators for sale to California utilities. After Enron collapsed in late 2001 in the wake of a scandal involving manipulating its stock price through falsification of its earnings statements, investigators discovered documents and tapes of various strategies Enron traders used to withhold power from California.[3] The tapes included profanity-laden phone conversations among Enron traders, bragging about stealing from "Grandma Millie" in California. Without regulatory oversight, the California case proved that unscrupulous corporations, like Enron, could use their market power to manipulate prices. Later in this chapter, we will take a closer look at why electricity is naturally prone to such market manipulation, and why regulation will always be needed to prevent it.

Although the California case is the most dramatic example of the failures of deregulating electricity, blackouts and rising prices have occurred in other parts of the country that embraced this illusion. The failure of adequate maintenance of transmission capacity in the deregulated system contributed to a major power failure in the Northeast in August 2003.[4] Little competition has materialized in the system, as mergers have concentrated production capacity among a few large producers; neither have the low prices deregulation advocates promised. In fact, in 2007, consumers in deregulated systems saw their rates increased from 20 to 72 percent.[5] Americans should not expect this new libertarian vision of deregulated electricity to deliver on its promises.

The mania for deregulation in the electricity industry and elsewhere reflects a blind adherence to ideology rather than a sensible recognition of the limits of the free market to work in certain industries and contexts. The experience with electricity deregulation in California and elsewhere demonstrates these limits. For decades in the United States, policymakers understood the need to balance market values with other common values and compensate for market failures. Regulation has been the mechanism used to make certain that markets served the public interest. This chapter explores the history of U.S. regulation, the rationales that led policymakers to institute government regulation, and the recent movement to take apart traditional regulation. Basic libertarian attitudes toward the role of government and the magic of markets have fueled the contemporary deregulation movement. We will see how they have undermined the common good in a variety of economic sectors and discuss what needs to be done to bring more communitarian values into the deregulation debate.

Regulation: The 1880s to the 1970s

The creation in 1887 of the Interstate Commerce Commission (ICC), the first independent federal regulatory commission, to regulate the railroads provides the starting point for any history of economic regulation in the United States. Nationally, the railroad industry was extremely competitive, as multiple firms vied with one another to connect the towns and cities across a vast continent. The typical farmer who sought to ship his goods to market through the railroad junction in most farming communities, however, usually faced a local railroad monopoly.[6] Because of the high investment required to build rail lines, business in most towns would not justify service from more than one line. Consequently, in the towns they served, railroads had the ability to demand exorbitant rates. In the 1870s and 1880s, farmers, who had grown increasingly dependent on railroads for shipping their goods, protested the monopoly power of railroads in setting shipping rates, and they demanded government action. The initial action came at the state level with the formation of state railroad commissions, but given the national character of the U.S. economy and the interstate rail network that served it, eventually pressure built for federal regulation. By the late 1880s, even the railroad companies accepted the need for federal regulation as a better alternative to coping with multiple regulatory regimes in different states.

The formation of the ICC established a model of economic regulation that would dominate how it is done up to the present day. The new regulatory agency was empowered "in the public interest" to set railroad rates, protect consumers from price discrimination and anticompetitive practices, and establish routes for passenger and rail traffic. In setting the rates, however, the commission was mandated to ensure a "fair rate of return" to railroad investors—a standard provision in subsequent enactments of business regulation. Thus, the ICC would regulate railroads and the markets in which they operated, but railroad assets would remain private and railroad firms under the control of their managers. Critics, as we shall see, eventually would see this arrangement as one that benefited railroad corporations and executives most of all as their business became insulated from market competition and ensured steady profits. (Eventually the ICC would acquire the power also to regulate trucking, passenger bus service, and inland waterway transportation.) The form of a politically "independent commission" was chosen to avoid direct partisan interference and favoritism in how such an important industry would be regulated. The ICC and subsequent independent commissions would have multiple members, usually five to seven, each appointed to fixed terms by the U.S. president with Senate confirmation. Most commission structures require a bipartisan membership with a single party having no more than a simple majority. The terms on commissions are staggered to prevent a president from appointing an entire commission at a single time. Because of the staggered fixed terms, presidents are able to appoint the majority membership of commissions only if reelected for a second term. This design aimed at insulating commission decisions from day-to-day politics and allowing the commissioners to be impartial in making their regulatory decisions.

Concern about the monopoly power of railroads was only one issue motivating reformers in the 1880s. This was the era of growth and consolidation of giant industrial firms into "trusts" in industries such as oil, steel, and banking. These trusts clearly were intended to attain monopoly power to reduce competition and control prices in a particular industry. Reformers worried not only about the economic impact of such industrial behemoths, they also were concerned about the growing political power the industrial might of the trusts brought to their owners. In 1890, the Sherman Anti-trust Act was passed to prohibit "every contract, combination in the form of trust or otherwise, or conspiracy, in restraint of trade or commerce."[7] Rather than assign the general authority to regulate trusts to an administrative commission, this time the legislation relied on the Justice Department to take monopolists to court (an antitrust division would eventually be formed for this purpose). Trust-busting in this manner proved an elusive task. In the first decade after its enactment, the government failed to break up a single trust in court; its first success came after a twenty-year battle that resulted in the breakup of John D. Rockefeller's Standard Oil Trust in 1911. In response to these difficulties, Progressive Era reformers succeeded in passing the Clayton Act in 1914, creating the Federal Trade Commission (FTC), which has authority to regulate monopolistic and other unfair business practices. This was part of a wave of Progressive reforms that instituted new federal regulation of banking with the creation of the Federal Reserve Board in 1913 and the passage of the Pure Food and Drug Act and Meat Inspection Act in 1906, which lodged responsibility for a safe food supply in the Department of Agriculture.

Much of the work of Progressive reformers occurred at the state and local level. One important area of regulation concerned the licensure of professionals. At the instigation of associations of trained professionals, state legislatures passed laws requiring doctors, lawyers, accountants, teachers, and other professionals to obtain licenses based on proof of competence, either through educational credentials or examination, before being able to practice a profession. Usually the professions themselves, through state medical boards or law boards, administered the procedures for obtaining licenses. The goal was to ensure the competence of all practicing a profession in the state, but critics also would point out that state licensing allowed a profession to restrict entry and regulate the supply of professionals—a factor instrumental in ensuring high levels of compensation for licensed professionals. Soon, such licensure extended to many trades such as plumbing, electrical work, barbering and hair styling, or selling real estate. Today, such professional and occupational licensing is the norm for a wide variety of work.

The other major area of Progressive Era regulation at the state and local level involved public utilities. Progressives recognized that the provision of electrical power, telephone service, and natural gas in local communities constituted what economists call "natural monopolies." The most economically efficient way to provide these utilities was not through competition among multiple providers, but through a single entity. Competing electrical and telephone companies stringing multiple sets of wires in neighborhoods clearly made no sense. Also, economies of scale resulting from a single large producer with many customers allowed service at lower rates. In some cases, municipalities established their own utilities to provide these services. (Municipally owned electrical power companies still are common in many parts of the country today.) Most, however, relied on private monopolies to provide the service that public utility commissions regulated to ensure fair prices (and adequate profits to investors). Eventually, the interstate movement of electrical power, telephone communication, and natural gas came under federal regulation.

The New Deal produced the next wave of regulatory activity.[8] Much of it came about because the Great Depression had destroyed Americans' confidence in a number of industries, as well as in the virtues of an unregulated free market. Two newly created regulatory agencies, the Federal Deposit Insurance Corporation (FDIC) and Federal Home Loan Bank Board (FHLBB), provided government-guaranteed insurance on banking deposits—a measure meant to prevent bank panics like the one that consumed the nation in 1933. Another important banking measure, the Glass-Steagall Act of 1933, prohibited commercial banks from involvement in the stock market through ownership of stock brokerage houses or investment banking. Some at the time attributed the 1929 stock market crash partly to easy credit from banks for the purchase of securities, also making the banks financially vulnerable when their loans defaulted in the crash.[9] Also, in response to the crash, a new Securities and Exchange Commission (SEC) was created to regulate financial markets and ensure truthful disclosure of financial information to investors. The 1935 Wagner Act created a National Labor Relations Board (NLRB) meant to protect the right of workers to form labor unions and regulate labor-management disputes. Two of the New Deal agencies concerned brand-new industries created as a result of new technologies. For these new, technology-driven industries, the goal of market regulation complemented the national interest in promoting technological innovation and a financially stable industry in these areas. The Federal Communications Commission (FCC), replacing an earlier Federal Radio Commission (FRC), was charged with regulating the new broadcast industry—allocating frequencies in the broadcast spectrum to broadcasters and ensuring adequate capital investment to permit future expansion and technological innovation. The Civil Aeronautics Board (CAB) was responsible for the nascent airline industry, regulating entry into the market and pricing to ensure strong and profitable passenger airlines. After World War II, responsibility for air traffic control and the regulation of airports would be spun off in a new Federal Aviation Administration (FAA).

The next wave of regulation came in the 1960s and early 1970s, but it focused on different sorts of concerns than those typical of most government regulation prior to the period. Before the 1960s, most regulation was economic; that is, its primary goal was to ensure that particular industries such as railroads, utilities, and securities firms did not take advantage of their market power to abuse consumers or operate in ways that undermined economic efficiency. In the 1960s, a new social regulation would emerge focused more on achieving certain social goals, such as a clean environment, safe consumer products, and safe workplaces, rather than economic efficiency.[10] First on the list was an expansion of the powers of the Food and Drug Administration (FDA) to regulate the safety of prescription drugs in the wake of a scandal involving the drug Thalidomide, prescribed to pregnant women, which produced deformities in their babies. These events contributed to a more widespread worry over safety of consumer products, resulting in the creation of the Consumer Product Safety Commission (CPSC) and the National Highway Traffic Safety Administration (NHTSA). The existence of both of these agencies owed much to the activism of Ralph Nader, who first gained national prominence with his 1965 book, *Unsafe at Any Speed*, which documented how General Motors produced and marketed the Corvair, a compact car that it knew to be subject to roll-over accidents.[11] Similar concerns about safety at the workplace would produce the Occupational Safety and Health Administration (OSHA) a few years later. A major new regulatory development came with a more prominent federal role in environmental regulation through several pieces of environmental legislation and the creation of the Environmental Protection Agency (EPA) in 1970. And the civil rights movement produced its own demands for regulations to prevent discrimination on the basis of race, religion, gender, or disability.

The rapid expansion of federal regulatory authority in all of these areas would soon produce a backlash. Over the decades, big business had become accustomed and, in general, supportive of much of the economic regulation enacted in the Progressive Era and the New Deal. Because those regulations included calculations of business profitability in assessing the "public interest," most regulated businesses fared quite well. In fact, regulation critics— whose views we will examine in more detail—would claim that regulated industries, whose profitability was protected by regulation, benefited more from regulation than did consumers, who were said to pay higher prices than they would pay in an unregulated marketplace. From a business point of view, the new social regulation was different. Environmental regulations and those requiring worker and consumer safety raised costs of production that had to come from either higher prices or out of profits. Workers, consumers, and the general public received the benefits of these regulations, which many businesses viewed as harmful to their bottom lines. By the mid-1970s, business began to organize systematically to resist this new regulatory expansion and, using many libertarian arguments, began to press for massive deregulation across the economy.[12] Business contributions fueled the growth of antiregulation think tanks in Washington, such as the Heritage Foundation, the American Enterprise Institute, and the libertarian Cato Institute, and supported the careers of sympathetic politicians. Businesses also increased substantially their lobbying activity—working more closely with one another to promote a common business agenda.[13] By the 1980s, the regulatory pendulum had swung decisively away from increased federal regulatory power, inaugurating the era of deregulation that continues to this day. Before examining this new era, we will review the traditional rationales for regulation and the libertarian critique of these rationales that have provided the intellectual justification for deregulatory policies.

The Rationale for Regulation

Economic justifications for regulation derive from the theories of *market failure* that were introduced in the last chapter. To review, even if we assume that most goods and services will be produced as a result of private voluntary transactions among individuals in a free market, there are certain situations when the market by itself will fail to produce certain goods and services adequately and efficiently. We already have examined how the market fails to produce certain *public goods,* in general, and the need for a range of government actions to provide for them. Government regulation is usually justified in the case of three particular market failures: monopolies—natural and anticompetitive, imperfect information, and externalities.

As noted earlier in the case of utilities, a natural monopoly is a product or service that a single producer can create more efficiently and cheaply than if multiple producers competed to provide the service. Economists point out that, unlike goods produced in competitive markets, in natural monopolies the average cost of goods produced declines as output increases.[14] For example, once I invest in the generators and transmission lines for providing electricity to a town each customer added to the grid makes the cost per person served lower. In this situation, I always could offer a lower price for my service than any competing company that might want to make the huge investment in a second grid to serve the customers not yet connected to my grid or to lure any of my customers away. The existence of natural monopolies poses a problem for consumers who are supposedly "sovereign" in market economies because they have no alternative providers of goods they consume. In the case of natural monopolies, that market sovereignty dissolves, as they are at the mercy of a single firm and any price it wants to charge. Regulation, in this case, is expected to replace the absence of market competition. Government regulators make sure that the monopoly good is produced in a way that is fair to both the producer, in the form of fair return on investment, and the consumer, in the form of an affordable price.

Markets where one or a few firms obtain overwhelming control as a result of competitive forces also justify regulation. This sort of monopoly places consumers at the mercy of a single or handful of firms that, without significant competition, can set high prices and are under no pressure to produce quality products or services. Anticompetitive monopoly power also places such firms in a position to engage in predatory pricing—prices set temporarily below the actual cost of production—to prevent any potential competitors from entering the market. The purpose of antitrust laws is to prevent such a situation from developing in a particular industry. These and other regulations, also, aim to regulate practices, like predatory pricing, that interfere with healthy competition.

Just as natural and anticompetitive monopolies undermine consumer sovereignty in unregulated markets, consumers who lack information about the products they buy cannot control adequately the quality of products or services available to them. When the pipes in my house start to leak, I will want to hire a plumber whom I know will be competent to fix them (and not do additional damage to the plumbing in my old house). For someone as unhandy and unknowledgeable about plumbing as I am, state licensure of plumbers offers some assurance that hiring a licensed plumber to do the work will result in a competent job. Of course, if plumbers were not licensed I could rely on recommendations from friends or referrals from previous customers, data available in a market (and that I would use even in hiring a licensed plumber); but in an emergency obtaining such information may not be possible, nor may the advice of my equally plumbing-challenged friends be all that reliable. State licensure of plumbers provides some assurance that those offering their services in this area meet certain minimal standards of competence. Moreover, the plumber I hire will know that failure to do a competent job might put his license in jeopardy—an incentive for conscientious work. What applies when I want some pipes fixed applies as well to the heart surgeon who might be needed to unclog my internal plumbing.

With many technically complex products on the market in a modern economy, none of us has the competence or ability to evaluate the quality and effectiveness of many of the things we buy. Market theory assumes that consumers will be competent to judge by themselves whether product A or product B best satisfies their wants and needs. This competence may come from previous experience with a product or an ability to evaluate its quality directly. For much of what we consume today, this cannot happen because of the complicated character of a product and the complexity of production systems. Much of the food we consume today, for example, includes additives and ingredients we cannot be aware of unless regulations require their disclosure. In the case of medicines, no one can be sure that a pill taken to treat a disease will be safe and effective without some regulatory oversight. Few of us would be willing to acquire information about our medications based on trial and error—such a strategy might prove fatal! Often, requiring disclosure of information regarding ingredients or methods of production may be adequate for addressing this market failure, but review of products prior to sale or mandatory withdrawals of products proven unsafe are needed. Agencies like the FDA and CPSC utilize these methods to compensate for the market's failure to provide sufficient consumer information.

Finally, the concept of externality, as described in chapter 2, provides a further justification for regulation. The individual costs and benefits achieved in market exchanges often do not absorb all of the social costs and benefits of the exchange. The coal-burning power plants of Midwest industries will include in the prices of their products the cost of the power needed to produce them, but unregulated they are not likely to include the cost of preventing their emissions from entering the atmosphere and returning to Earth in the form of acid rain in the Northeast. The only way to prevent the environmental

damage of acid rain is to require those power plants to invest in pollution control devices, rather than impose the social cost of their emissions on people in
the Northeast. A host of environmental and other kinds of regulations can be
justified in these terms.

While most economics texts typically cite market failure as the sole justification for government regulation, many of us can identify nonmarket reasons
why government needs to regulate the behavior of businesses and individuals.
The language included in many regulatory statutes regarding serving the
"public interest" reflects something more than just the goal of economic efficiency. In communitarian terms, the reference to public interest means making sure that regulations ensure that the common good is protected and
enhanced. To serve the common good, regulation may be needed to achieve
at least the following four goals: correct imbalances of power and influence
within the market, ensure and promote individual safety and well-being, nurture the attributes of a good society, and promote social justice and equality.

Historians point out that concerns about the political power of big business and trusts fueled the Populist and Progressive movements to regulate
business more than worries about "market failure."[15] As Woodrow Wilson
argued at the time, government regulation was needed to ensure that democratic government responsive to the people remained "master of masterful corporations."[16] Markets allocate more than just goods, services, and money; they
also allocate power. The common good sometimes means regulation is
required to balance that market power. For example, the need to balance the
power of employers to determine wages and working conditions needed to be
balanced by the power of workers organized collectively into labor unions
motivated the creation of the National Labor Relations Board in 1935.
Although NLRB policies in recent years have failed to fulfill this key regulatory task, the promise of regulation in this area traditionally was to assist labor
in providing, in the words of economist John Kenneth Galbraith, "counter-
vailing" power to that of big business. As we shall see, one dismal consequence
of extensive deregulation in recent years has been to open American society
up to the abuses of unscrupulous corporate executives, such as Enron's Ken
Lay and Jeffery Skilling, who used power derived in the marketplace and
deployed in the political system to serve themselves at the expense of the
common good.

Regulation can be used also as an instrument to protect individuals from
harm and promote their morality. This rationale for regulation is sometimes
referred to pejoratively, in libertarian works, as "paternalism," which implies
government looking out, as a parent does, for its childlike citizens. A better
and more communitarian way of thinking about this regulatory rationale is in
terms of the community as a whole acting to ensure the well-being of all its
members. Regulations requiring people to use seat belts or wear motorcycle
helmets fall, at least partly, in this category. Such regulation can be justified in
terms of market failure—even if a person wishes to take the individual risk of

THE CONVICTION FOR FRAUDULENT FINANCIAL MANIPULATION OF FORMER ENRON CEO JEFF SKILLING, SHOWN HERE AT HIS ARREST IN 2004, SYMBOLIZED THE EXCESSES OF THE ERA OF BUSINESS DEREGULATION.

not wearing a seat belt, there are externalities involved in the costs to society of death and injuries resulting from such reckless behavior. But beyond externalities, most of us would regard providing an incentive to careless individuals to act so as to protect their lives is a value in itself. In a community, we have a moral obligation to watch out for one another. Regulations that assist us in doing what we ought to choose for ourselves promote the common good. A community that encourages its members, sometimes through regulation, to wear seat belts and motorcycle helmets, avoid abusing drugs and alcohol, and not smoke is a better community as a result. This same argument applies to efforts to promote moral behavior and protect the community from indecency. When FCC chair Michael Powell responded to the infamous Justin Timberlake/Janet Jackson "clothing malfunction" in the 2004 Superbowl half-time show broadcast with new regulations regarding permissible content of broadcasts, most American parents applauded. Powell's action only raised some eyebrows because, while willing to expand FCC regulation over program content, he had been a fanatical advocate of telecommunications deregulation. Despite his inconsistency, Powell recognized the value of government regulation for the promotion of community values in the action he took.

Promoting community values also may involve regulations that foster certain institutions and activities we expect in a good society. Regulations with aesthetic or cultural goals fall into this category. In the 1960s, thanks to the highway beautification efforts of Lady Bird Johnson, wife of President Lyndon Johnson, the federal highway legislation was amended to require limits on billboards and imposing landscaping standards for all federally funded highways. For most of its history, the FCC mandated that broadcasters devote a certain number of programming hours to public affairs and educational and children's programs. While such requirements remain, libertarian (at least in this area) regulators like Michael Powell have watered down these regulations, demanding much less from broadcasters in this area. Once content regulations were eased, broadcasters responded to commercial pressures, turning most of their children's programs into cartoons featuring characters associated with sugary cereals and candy. They reduced dramatically public service programming. In recent years, the amount of time devoted to political and public issues on broadcast television has dropped dramatically.[17] While out of favor in the current deregulation atmosphere, regulations demanding that businesses and institutions promote aesthetic and cultural goals remain a reasonable justification for government regulation.

Finally, regulation can be a means to promote greater equality and social justice. Much of the architecture of antidiscrimination, affirmative action, and equal opportunity regulation is justified in these terms. While one can point to the market inefficiencies of discrimination, legislation since the 1960s prohibiting it have rarely been promoted for reasons of economic efficiency, but because of what a fair, equitable, and just society requires. Some regulations instituted for reasons of equity and social justice are imposed even though economists consider them to produce market inefficiencies. Rules for universal access, to telephone, and other telecommunications services through subsidized low rates for basic service are in this category, yet the FCC has imposed these requirements despite strictly economic considerations.[18] Even the 1996 Telecommunications Act that promoted deregulation throughout the industry, universal access was retained in principle and through specific measures included mandated free Internet access in public libraries. In the past, the FCC also promoted a measure of political equality through the "fairness doctrine," which required that radio and television broadcasters offer contrasting views in discussion of political candidates and public policy issues. In line with broadcast deregulation, the fairness doctrine was dropped in the 1980s, encouraging the openly partisan broadcasting on talk radio and cable TV that enlightens all of us today.

Both market failure and non-market arguments can be made to justify regulation. Although these arguments continue to have many adherents and inform much regulation policy, beginning in the late 1970s they fell out of favor. Instead, advocates drawing largely on a libertarian worldview began a wholesale assault on these justifications for regulation. Powerful interests in business and elsewhere found the critique of regulation helpful, as they promoted deregulation in industry after industry. While the success of the movement cannot be explained as a result of the power of ideas alone, the libertarian critique of regulation assisted the agenda of deregulators by providing them with seductive rationales for what they wanted to accomplish.

The Libertarian Critique of Regulation

As readers of this book can predict, libertarians are not fans of government regulation of any sort. For them, regulation threatens liberty, undermines market efficiency, and fails, even on its own terms, to protect the public interest. At the center of the libertarian critique is its assumption of the superiority of market organization over any government action. Because regulation seeks to produce outcomes through government action that the market by itself will not achieve, it is suspect in libertarian eyes. Although most libertarians accept that market failure is conceivable, they view the impact of those failures to be exaggerated and believe that any attempt to correct those failures through government action will produce worse outcomes than the "failures" themselves. Libertarians counter discussion of market failure with discussion of "government failure" through regulation. Dangers from monopoly (either natural or anticompetitive), inadequate information, or externalities do not justify a regulatory response and, of course, any regulation intended to achieve non-market outcomes simply constitute government paternalism anathema to a free society. The need for social regulations to protect consumers or ensure worker safety are dismissed as both unnecessary and overly costly in a market system that supposedly automatically weeds out unsafe products and compensates workers in risky jobs. To libertarians, regulation should not be understood as good faith efforts to achieve public goals, but rather as attempts on the part of special interests to avoid the discipline of the marketplace and gain through the use of government power what they cannot achieve through honest competition.

Regulating and preventing monopoly would seem, at first glance, not nec-essarily at odds with a libertarian worldview. After all, the ostensible purpose of antitrust laws and regulation of natural monopolies is to help the free market work better. Libertarians, however, do not think that government can be trusted to perform the task. Milton Friedman, for example, when reviewing the three alternative ways of coping with a natural monopoly: private monop-oly (such as an unregulated private electrical company), public monopoly (such as a municipal power company), or public regulation opts for the first alternative as the "least of the evils."[19] Why? It seems because any option involving government action, by definition, has to be inferior to the unregu-lated private market. The social conditions that create natural monopolies, Friedman claims, are apt to change as the market introduces new technolo-gies. To prove his point, he argues that the monopoly position of railroads at the end of the nineteenth century would have been temporary once alterna-tive forms of transportation, such as trucks and airplanes, emerged in the twen-tieth century. Friedman never says how Midwestern farmers would have fared for the fifty to seventy-five years before these new alternatives to transporting their goods by rail emerged. Nor does he consider that the railroad industry might have used both its market power and political clout to prevent or delay these alternatives from becoming competitive. Under Friedman's scenario, new trucking firms would have had to establish themselves in competition with established rail lines with their financial capacity to selectively underprice any new trucking competitor and drive them out of business. Moreover, trucks cannot compete without good public roads, adequate to bear the weight of large trucks, which the rail industry might have lobbied governments not to build. In this example, as in many others we will look at, libertarians, like Friedman, seem blind to how power can be wielded in markets as well as through government and how powerful market actors influence government not to impose regulations that limit that market power.

Interestingly, in the 1980s the Friedman approach to natural monopoly was tried when the United States' nascent cable TV industry was deregulated. When cable TV was first introduced in most communities, it tended to be reg-ulated by utility commissions in the manner of most local utility monopolies. After revelations of corruption in the awarding of cable franchises in some communities, the Reagan administration intervened, but rather than impose federal regulations to prevent the local corruption, it adopted the Friedman approach and, in the 1984 Cable Television Act, abolished all regulation of cable TV prices.[20] Supposedly, competition from other and emerging tech-nologies, such as home video rentals, over the air broadcasting, and satellite television, would restrain cable prices. For consumers, however, cable access soon became a necessity (alternatives such as satellite TV never became com-petitive), and the industry took advantage by charging exorbitant rates. Even-tually, in 1992, some re-regulation of basic rates had to be restored, but the 1996 Telecommunications Act deregulated the cable industry completely, again based on the argument that new technologies would restrain prices. Again, absent regulation and real competition, cable companies gouged their customers, increasing rates 36 percent by 2002—triple the inflation rate.[21]

The libertarian position regarding anticompetitive monopolies depends on circular reasoning that whatever results from market forces must be good for markets. In a 1978 book, *The Anti-trust Paradox,* Robert Bork argued that antitrust laws actually interfered with competition because they prevented the competitive market from producing optimal outcomes—even if that included one or a handful of firms dominating a particular industry.[22] If the market produced such a result, Bork reasoned, then it must be because, in that industry, superior economies of scale or capacity to invest in superior technologies made the arrangement desirable. Any government intervention to restrain mergers or other anticompetitive practices, such as pricing products to force a competitor out of business, would produce less than optimal market outcomes.[23] This circular reasoning assumes that if market forces lead to a monopoly then that must be the most efficient arrangement, since market forces always produce the most efficient result. The possibility that markets might fail to do so is assumed away. Such views became influential beginning in the 1980s, as government regulators became increasingly tolerant of corporate mergers and consolidation.[24]

For libertarians, the second market failure justifying regulation—inadequate or "asymmetrical" information—simply cannot exist in a well-functioning market. The market itself will send all the information needed for consumers to make judgments about alternative goods or services. Any government regulation to provide information reflects, in this view, a paternalistic attitude toward consumers who can be expected to acquire the information they need for what they buy. This outlook is reflected in how Friedman treats occupational licensure in *Capitalism and Freedom.*[25] He devotes most of a chapter to an analysis and denunciation of occupational licensing as a kind of public monopoly in which those practicing a particular profession or trade restrict entry into the practice to ensure high fees. As such, licensing interferes with an individual's right to contract with whomever he pleases for a service. Consumers ought to be able to decide for themselves whomever they want to fix their sinks, audit their books, file suits on their behalf, or remove their appendixes. Including medical doctors in his analysis dramatizes Friedman's point, since concern about the competence of someone with control over life and death would seem essential to most of us. Friedman thinks we can rely on malpractice suits to weed out incompetence and, therefore, have no need for licensing physicians.[26] Or, even without any licensing, identifying competent physicians would be made easy, as they would join together in group practices that would develop their own reputations, presumably by establishing a brand of some sort, for "reliability and quality."[27] Private "licensing" through these group practices is desirable in this libertarian world, while public surveillance of competence is not. That, absent government oversight, some of these group practices might be run by unscrupulous individuals seeking to misrepresent their "reliability and quality" through misleading advertising, covering up mistakes, or cutting corners to reduce costs escapes Friedman's notice. Nor does Friedman seem concerned that a malpractice suit after a failed open heart surgery may not be an attractive method of revealing an unqualified doctor. Most of us would prefer some mechanism for assuring the qualifications of a surgeon prior to going under the knife!

Finally, market failure involving externalities again requires no government intervention in the libertarian world but can be handled by private market transactions. As noted earlier, from an economic point of view, the problem with negative externalities is that the producer of a good imposes social costs on others rather than including those costs in the price of whatever is being produced. This results in an inefficient allocation of resources, specifically an overproduction of the good, more than what an efficient market would have produced. The point of government regulation in this case, say a requirement that a factory install equipment to eliminate pollution, is to require the producer to pay the true cost of production thereby making the allocation of resources more efficient. In a famous 1960 article, "The Problem of Social Cost," Ronald H. Coase argued that, in some cases, with appropriate assignment of property rights, voluntary exchanges in the marketplace could correct the market inefficiencies of externalities without government intervention.[28] Coase imagined an ideal market world in which individuals could automatically communicate with one another regarding their preferences, one without what economists call "transaction costs"—the time and effort usually needed to communicate such preferences. In such a world, he reasoned, optimal efficiency even when externalities were involved would be achieved if those damaged by, say, the smoke of a polluting factory could either receive payment from the polluter for the cost of the damage done to her property or pay the polluter not to cause the damage. The advantage, for Coase and libertarians, would be that this could be accomplished through a voluntary bargain among the parties that reflected the true market value to them of the goods involved and in which they would share. The result would be as efficient as any government regulation could produce and, thus, such regulation was unnecessary.

Economist Joseph Stiglitz suggests a simple example of smokers and nonsmokers sharing an office to illustrate the point.[29] Imagine an office in which smokers possess a "property right" to smoke and nonsmokers also have a "property right" not to have to inhale secondhand smoke. In this scenario, the pleasure smokers derive from their smoking imposes an external cost on the nonsmokers, but banning smoking, while advantageous to nonsmokers, would impose a social cost on the smokers. Coase would suggest that an ideal solution could be reached if the smokers and nonsmokers worked out a bargain in which the nonsmokers, assuming their loss from inhaling smoke exceeded the smokers' pleasure from smoking, paid the smokers not to smoke. Alternatively, the smokers might compensate the nonsmokers for the harm their smoking does to them. In either case, they would agree on a deal that reflected both how much nonsmokers valued working smoke free and how much the smokers valued their nasty habit. Either way, an efficient (from an economic point of view) result would be attained without regulation. While Coase's point was that private voluntary market bargains could produce an outcome as efficient as any government regulation, libertarians, given their disdain for government, would expect such a private bargain always to be more efficient than what government could produce. They would expect a bargain between smokers and nonsmokers to reflect the true value smokers place on their ability to smoke compared to the value nonsmokers place on the discomfort of secondhand smoke. Nevertheless, the significance of the Coase theorem is that it reinforces a libertarian view that even externalities do not require government regulation.

This analysis, of course, depended greatly on the assumption of no transaction costs. People might be able to reach economically optimal bargains regarding the externality of cigarette smoke in a small office, but organizing market bargains involving millions of people over a large territory would be a different matter. The transaction costs involved in determining the optimal compensation to be given to each New England resident for the damage incurred as a result of acid rain from Midwest power plants would be enormous. Organizing such bargains becomes impossible if we consider the environmental harms from global warming. How can the market spontaneously bring together those of us currently injecting carbon dioxide into the atmosphere with the future generations who global warming will harm? Many if not most externality problems involve enormous transaction costs, meaning government regulation likely will be the most efficient means of handling the problem. Coase himself acknowledges this to be so in pointing out that regulation is needed "when, as normally the case with the smoke nuisance, a large number of people is involved and when therefore the costs of handling the problem through the market . . . may be high."[30]

Despite this qualification, the point of Coase's analysis was to show that "direct governmental regulations will not necessarily give better results than leaving the problem to be solved by the market."[31] This conclusion served as a mantra to the "law and economics" movement, centered at the University of Chicago, which burgeoned in the years following the publication of his article and became influential in promoting the deregulation movement two decades later. Distinguished economists including Noble laureates such as Coase, Milton Friedman, and George Stigler, along with legal scholars such as Richard Posner and Richard Epstein, wrote influential books and articles arguing how common law jurisprudence attentive to free market principles could achieve superior economic results than economic regulation through government agencies.[32] These scholars and others have produced an enormous body of work analyzing the negative effects of regulation in a wide variety of areas and promoting the value of applying microeconomic analysis to nearly every aspect of human life. By the 1970s, libertarian pundits and think tanks were translating this work into a wide range of practical policy proposals, all justifying reducing the amount of government regulation in American life.

At the same time, while the economics and law movement was promoting the virtues of the market for solving policy problems, another intellectual movement in political science, called Public Choice, or Rational Choice, aimed to demonstrate how government regulation could never produce the public interest. Regulatory agencies ostensibly created to serve the public interest were, in fact, captive of the special interests they were supposed to regulate. Public choice theorists were not the first to formulate the regulatory capture argument. In 1955 Marver H. Bernstein, in *Regulating Business by Independent Commission,* developed a life cycle theory of independent regulatory commissions.[33] Although a public majority concerned with industry abuses provides the impetus for established regulatory agencies, over time the broader public loses interest in regulatory issues while the regulated industry retains an intense interest in the process that determines its profits. Soon the regulated industry manages to exercise major influence over the regulatory process to ensure that its interest rather than the broader public interest is served. Bernstein argued that the commission structure, insulating agencies from elected officials who might be responsive to popular majorities, and the legal and technical complexity of most regulation worked to the advantage of regulated industries who could mobilize experts most effectively to get their way. By the 1950s, he argued, the ICC was captive of the railroad and trucking industries, the FCC by the broadcast and telephone industries, and the CAB by the airline industry. All used the regulatory process to protect themselves from competition and maintain profits, often at the expense of the consumer, who regulation was supposed to serve. Unlike the later arguments of public choice theorists, Bernstein did not favor deregulation of these industries but thought that more direct oversight by the political branches, especially the presidency, could restore them to their original public mission.

Unlike Bernstein, who saw regulatory capture as the result of a reversible historic process, George Stigler, in his famous essay "The Theory of Economic Regulation," proclaimed capture as an immutable law. In his words, "regulation is acquired by the industry and is designed and operated primarily for its benefit."[34] All business regulation, according to Stigler, can be explained as industry efforts to use government to obtain one or more of the following benefits: a direct subsidy, control over market entry, suppression of substitute products, and direct price fixing. Industries obtain regulation through funding the campaigns of self-interested politicians and political parties seeking regulation. Public choice theorists would elaborate on this thesis, arguing that regulated industries, even though their benefits come at the expense of the majority, can obtain them because they are highly organized and easily mobilized while the majority is usually unorganized and inactive.[35] Moreover, regulated industries receive concentrated benefits, in the form of higher profits, giving them incentive to seek regulation, while the costs are distributed diffusely to the public, who may not notice the degree to which a slightly higher price on the product it buys results from regulation.

Eventually, the public choice theorists would generalize Stigler's thesis to all of government, arguing that self-interested bureaucrats, politicians, and special interests all behave as "rent-seekers."[36] A rent in economic theory is an excess profit beyond what a truly competitive market would return. Described in these terms, regulation (and even all of politics and government) represents collusion between government policymakers and special interests to extract "rents" they could not earn in a free market. If we conceptualize government as a rent distributor, we can begin to understand both why government regulation grows and why it is inevitably destructive of economic productivity. Just as the prospect for high profits attracts investments in the free market, the high returns available from government regulation also will attract investment. Unlike high returns in the market that are subject to competition from alternative investments, government rents are guaranteed through the coercive power of the state. Yet, as public choice theorists point out, when rent-seekers invest in seeking regulation they are wasting resources that, from a social point of view, would be allocated more efficiently in the free market. As a leading public choice theorist argues, "As the expansion of modern governments offers more opportunities for rents, we must expect the utility-maximizing behavior of individuals will lead them to waste more resources in trying to secure 'rents' . . . promised by government."[37] So regulation is doubly wasteful—it provides beneficiaries of regulation undeserved rents and it undermines the productivity of the market by distorting investment. Where self-interested behavior—utility-maximizing—in the market leads, thanks to the invisible hand, to the social good of ever-expanding productivity, the same behavior in government and politics will be destructive. For the public choice theorist, this leads to an obvious conclusion: all regulation is bad and we would be better off without it.

While the deductive logic of the public choice theorists seems persuasive, if the beginning assumptions of self-interested rent-seekers are accepted, empirical support for their claims seems weak. The most powerful refutation of their view of regulation is the deregulation movement itself.[38] If only self-interested rent-seekers influence government, how can one explain the reduction in government regulation over the past thirty years denying, according to their model, industry after industry its "rents"? Moreover, how can one explain, if they were the instigators of regulation, the enthusiastic support of most formerly regulated businesses for deregulation? In the late 1970s, prior to deregulation, political scientists found little evidence that regulatory agencies were captive of regulated industry; instead, most studies found that, with some exceptions, agencies vigorously regulated, based on the professionalism of their staffs and support from advocacy groups.[39] Once deregulation took hold, as we shall see, regulated industries tended to lead the way in arguing for the elimination of regulation. Even industries such as airlines and trucking that initially opposed deregulation soon dropped their resistance and embraced the new competitive market environment. Somehow many businesses seemed to see more profit opportunities in the deregulated marketplace than in extracting rents from government. The public choice view of politics was much more persuasive when government was expanding and new regulation was being added, but public choice theories cannot explain the era of smaller government and less regulation that we have lived in for the last thirty years.

The public choice school's assumption of purely self-interested action on the part of political actors ignores the role of other motivations such as ideology and principled commitment to the public good. Paradoxically, the willingness of politicians to embrace their conclusions on the inefficiency of regulation seems to prove that, if deregulation truly was in the public interest, something other than "utility-maximization" can succeed in politics. The claim that regulation only serves selfish rent-seekers, while superficially plausible in the case of some business regulation, cannot account for the new social regulation of the late 1960s and 1970s. First, in the case of environmental, consumer, and workplace safety regulation, those being regulated vociferously resisted the imposition of regulations and continue to do so today. The self-interested behavior of regulated business under this form of regulation seemed to lead them to favor deregulation, not regulation. Second, it also is difficult to see how rent-seeking can explain the behavior of environmental, consumer, and workplace safety groups that promoted the new social regulation. Ideology and a public-spirited concern for protecting the environment or consumer safety can account in a much more straight forward way for such activism.

This entire libertarian critique of government regulation can be summed up in a single proposition: government regulation always will fail to benefit society in general because powerful special interests will use regulation to enrich themselves at the expense of everyone else. While this view recognizes how the powerful might use government to further their interests, libertarians seem to be blind to the possibility that powerful actors can manipulate markets to advantage themselves at the expense of the common good. The exercise of market power has traditionally been why government regulation has been deemed necessary. Preventing anticompetitive, private monopolies and public oversight of natural monopolies is meant to prevent monopolists from using their dominant position in a market to coerce either potential competitors or consumers. If we assume, as libertarians do, that people act in a self-interested manner in markets, then we should expect some individuals to take advantage of opportunities of their market power to benefit themselves. The Enron electricity traders who induced California blackouts to squeeze more money from Grandma Millie also were extracting "rents," but they were doing so using their market power rather than regulation.

Aside from complaining that regulation always provides undeserved benefits to special interests, libertarians claim the costs businesses pay to comply with regulation and the administrative costs of enforcement undermine our economy. Libertarian David Boaz, for example, claims regulation costs the economy $600 billion per year in lost economic output.[40] Boaz assumes those costs are a loss to society and does not consider what benefits might have been derived from safer products and workplaces or a cleaner environment; since libertarians assume that regulation cannot work, Boaz does not find it necessary to address this issue. Because libertarians are so confident that regulation's benefits can never justify its cost, some advocate using cost-benefit analysis as a method of undermining regulation. Many such studies evaluate the benefits of consumer and worker safety programs with estimates of the monetary value of lives saved based on estimates of worker lifetime earning power. These estimates lead to bizarre conclusions, such as very low benefits from fewer occupational deaths and injuries because those saved typically earn very low incomes, zero benefits from retirees and homemakers saved because they earn no wages, and negative benefits for the survival of the severely disabled because their lives are a "cost" to society.[41] Basing regulatory decisions on attempts to value a human life place a price on something most of us would consider priceless. Critics of regulation frequently cite one analyst's finding that preventing the sale of flammable children's clothing cost $1.5 million per life saved as proof of out-of-control regulation costs, but many would consider that a small price if it were their own baby's life saved.[42] Even using these ghoulish methods for measuring the value of a life do not always lead to the conclusion that regulation is not worth the cost. A 1996 study found that the direct and indirect costs of regulation per life-year saved came to about $36,100, but in our affluent country that is about half the value Americans in surveys place on the value of a year of their lives.[43] In other words, according to this study, rather than being a burdensome cost, regulation provides a 100 percent return on investment!

No matter how the public might perceive the benefits of regulation relative to costs, libertarians can never accept the value of regulation because of their dogmatic faith in free markets. For example, much of the libertarian literature labels the Occupational Safety and Health Administration (OSHA) as a total waste and a violation of workers' freedom of contract because it interferes with their right to choose hazardous work. Supposedly, workers who take risky or hazardous jobs do so voluntarily for the higher wages those jobs must provide, according to market dogma, to attract workers! This bit of perverse logic, of course, is at odds with the reality of hazards in the textile industry, from cotton dust and toxic dyes, or the poultry industry, from repetitive motion injury and severe cuts—two of the lowest-paid industries in the country.[44] Sometimes relatively high wages in mining are cited as proof that workers are compensated for hazardous work, but good mining wages are thanks to the United Mine Workers union. Prior to unionization in the 1940s, mining paid very low wages. Workers find themselves in hazardous jobs not because of the attraction of nonexistent high wages but because many unskilled workers have no alternatives. Yet again, libertarian criticisms ignore hard facts about benefits from OSHA, which since its creation has cut workplace deaths in half.[45]

Similar dogmatic faith in markets has led another researcher to conclude that auto safety regulation, imposed in the 1960s, requiring seat belts, padded dashboards, and other safety features, actually increased highway fatalities.[46] These features only increased the "moral hazard" of driving, leading people to drive more recklessly. How does one account, then, for the declining auto death rate since the introduction of these safety features? According to the study, rising living standards already were producing safer drivers before the 1960s because, as people became richer, they valued their life more. Safety features supposedly ran counter to this trend! I doubt that many of us will stop fastening our seat belts or buying cars with air bags based merely on the logic of this analysis.

Even if we accept the claim of Friedman and other libertarians that pure monopolies cannot last forever or market competition eventually exposes defective products or incompetent service providers, they can do tremendous damage while they exist. Lax FDA regulation of imports from China allowed tainted pet food, children's toys, and toothpaste to enter the U.S. market in early 2007.[47] In response, U.S. corporations tightened up oversight of their Chinese production facilities and the Chinese government, worried about losses in the U.S. market, increased regulatory oversight, but in the meantime tens of thousands of pets died, thousands of children were exposed to lead poisoning from toy trains, and thousands of Americans brushed their teeth with a chemical damaging to their kidneys. Even with the market responses to supposedly correct these problems, we should not complacently assume that some future foreign or U.S. producer might seek some market advantage by lax production methods. When we depend on the market to produce the food we eat and the quality of products we consume, we empower those market producers to determine whether those products are safe. Regulation provides a way to ensure that those producers use that power properly and do not put us at risk seeking market advantage by cutting corners in their production methods.

The libertarian critique of regulation also ignores completely the need for regulation in the name of nonmarket values. Since libertarians value only individual liberty and economic efficiency, they dismiss regulations that promote greater equality and social justice, ensure standards of fairness, or encourage moral behavior as violations of property rights—as in redistribution or paternalism. Even in their critiques of regulation, libertarians believe that if they show that regulation fails to increase economic efficiency, they have won the argument against regulation. Coase's analysis of externalities reflects this bias. The notion that social costs disappear and an economically optimal result occurs when individuals negotiate a bargain about their distribution assumes that the preferences of all parties are legitimate and moral. This assumption reflects the libertarian premise that individuals are the sole judge of the morality of their actions and these actions need be constrained only if costs are imposed on others. The point of Coase's analysis is to show how the market-pricing mechanism alone can allocate appropriate compensation for those costs.

Consider the smoking example discussed earlier. No differentiation is made regarding the preferences of the smokers and nonsmokers. The only concern is reaching the correct price to compensate non-smokers for the costs they incur from the action of the smokers or avoid this cost through a payment to smokers to compensate them for the cost of not smoking. The right to smoke or to be free of smoke is considered morally equivalent. Given what we know about the insidious health effects of smoking, nonlibertarians would question this moral equivalence. The problem with resolving the "cost" of smoking through a private market bargain rather than an outright ban, from a communitarian point of view, is that it allows a behavior to continue that undermines the well-being of everyone, including those who wish to engage in it. Regulation to discourage smoking, such as bans in bars, restaurants, and workplaces, are intended to reduce or eliminate the practice altogether by making it inconvenient and undesirable.

Proponents of smoking regulation who emphasize the costs of secondhand smoke as the rationale for nonsmoking actually undermine the goal of preventing smoking. They implicitly accept the libertarian assumption that the only issue regarding smoking is the cost smokers impose on nonsmokers rather than the inherent harm of smoking to the common good. If secondhand smoke were the only rationale for smoking bans, then a Coasian bargain to allocate the cost of secondhand smoke (if transaction costs were low) would be a reasonable solution. If enforcing standards of appropriate behavior for the common good, as agreed upon by a democratic citizenry, is the aim, then only regulation, not the market, can produce this result. Besides smoking, this is a justification for regulation communitarians would accept in a wide variety of areas, including discouraging prostitution, pornography, racial discrimination, and the broadcast of prurient images or foul language. Libertarians would label such regulation as paternalistic, but a communitarian would see such measures as necessary to enhance the common good.

Libertarians reject any regulation that promotes equality or redistribution as vehemently as those it regards as paternalistic. But concern for the common good leads to many ways one might justify regulation to ensure all equal access or benefits from a service. For example, utility regulators traditionally have promoted *universal access* as a key nonmarket obligation of utility providers. Everyone, according to this principle, ought to have the opportunity to access some level of utility service regardless of ability to pay. In the past, telephone companies have been obliged to offer minimally priced services than are affordable to people with low incomes. Universal access rules also required telephone and electrical utilities to provide service connections to remote and small communities, even though potential revenues derived could never cover the costs of stringing wires to them. Urban consumers were expected to subsidize such access through a small increment in their own rates to ensure that people who live in rural areas were connected to the larger community. More recently, the Telecommunications Act of 1996, despite its deregulation thrust, included provisions to ensure free access to the Internet in public libraries, schools, and other public facilities, including offering access to people with disabilities. Neither the market nor voluntary charity can be relied upon to provide such access.[48] All these mandates for universal access recognize the need for everyone to be able to communicate and connect to basic utilities to participate fully in community life. A society in which the market alone offered access to making a telephone call, using the Internet, or receiving electricity might please libertarians, but it would deny millions of low-income and rural Americans these basic amenities of modern life.

In spite of the limitations of the libertarian critique of regulation, their arguments provided much of the justification for the deregulation movement of the past three decades. Libertarian ideology alone, of course, did not cause the movement. Weak economic performance during the 1970s opened the door to claims that overregulation might be undermining economic efficiency. Many observers across the political spectrum, as we shall see, were concerned that older regulatory agencies served the interests of those they regulated more than the public interest. Certainly, big business mobilization against regulation provided much of the impetus and the resources to support deregulation. Finally, the rise to power of Republican conservatives after nearly fifty years of liberal Democratic dominance placed deregulation firmly on the policy agenda as a part of the policy revolution they intended to put in place. Libertarians, however, gave the movement its intellectual heft and established the overall ethos that made deregulation plausible to policymakers. Beginning in the early 1980s, the notion that all of us would be better off with less government regulation dominated political discourse. Soon a new deregulated economy and society would emerge. The next section looks at deregulation and its effects.

The Deregulation Movement: The 1970s to Today

The deregulation era began thirty years ago when Democratic president Jimmy Carter, with full-throated support from liberal senators such as Edward Kennedy of Massachusetts, persuaded Congress to pass the Airline Deregulation Act of 1978. Although many liberal Democrats would later regret their early embrace of deregulation, in the 1970s they too succumbed to the libertarian illusion that encouraging more free market competition, at least in some industries, would benefit the average citizen. In the 1960s, liberal activists such as Ralph Nader adopted the "capture theory" of regulation in strong critiques of how big businesses used regulation to exploit consumers. The best-selling *The Interstate Commerce Omission,* by a Nader associate, lambasted the ICC for setting rates in the interests of the trucking, bus, and railroad industries while imposing high prices on consumers.[49] No libertarian, Nader derived his position more from his consumer activist ideology and general distrust of big business rather than faith in deregulation across the board. In fact, he, like many liberals at the time, promoted expanded government regulation in areas like environmental and consumer protection while criticizing big business dominance of independent regulatory commissions. They sought regulatory reform, rather than across-the-board deregulation, to return it to the original Progressive vision of regulation in the public interest. In some cases, such as the transportation industries, this reform included allowing more market competition and less government oversight.

In the mid-1970s, Nader, Senator Kennedy, and President Carter's newly appointed Civil Aeronautics Board chair, Alfred Kahn, joined forces to bring more competition to the airline industry. Airline regulation and the CAB dated from the beginnings of the passenger airline industry in the 1930s. At the time, most countries around the world saw developing a strong airline industry as essential for national prestige and economic growth. Limitations in the quality and capacity of existing aircraft plus the reluctance of consumers to embrace this new and seemingly risky form of travel prevented the emergence of investor-owned, private airlines. In most European countries, government stepped in to invest government funds in national airlines such as British Airways, Air France, and Lufthansa. The U.S. government took a more indirect approach, first encouraging and subsidizing U.S. private airline companies with contracts to carry U.S. airmail and then, with regulating entry into the industry, assigning routes to the restricted number of carriers, and setting prices through the CAB. This regulatory regime proved quite successful, as air passenger travel expanded steadily over the next thirty years and the major airlines, such as Eastern, TWA, Pan American, Delta, American, and United, earned steady profits for their investors. By the 1970s advocates of airline deregulation argued that the initial rationale for nurturing a nascent industry that justified regulation in the 1930s no longer existed and the now muscular industry should be set free to compete in an unregulated market.

Airline deregulation advocates promised a new world of more numerous competitor airlines offering consumers a wider choice of services and travel destinations with lower fares; at the same time this new, more competitive industry would offer enhanced profit opportunities to investors because of greater efficiency. This vision was based on three assumptions that experience proved to be dubious.[50] First, unlike the typical natural monopoly, there were no significant economies of scale in the airline industry. A small airline with a few planes could fly passengers on routes from point A to point B as cheaply as a large airline could. Second, there were no significant barriers to entry into the market—capital to buy a single airplane and hire a crew could put one into the passenger airline business. And third, unlike the railroad lines serving small farm towns in the nineteenth century, even if an airline were the sole carrier serving a certain city, it would keep fares low because, if it tried to use its monopoly position to raise fares, a competitor could easily enter the market simply by showing up with an airplane and taking away its business with low fares. Deregulators knew that the most intense competition would happen where demand was highest—between large cities—and that a single airline might end up meeting all the demand in smaller cities. In the early years, this vision and these assumptions seemed to prove true—new airline companies formed offering new service at lower prices and average fares in the industry dropped precipitously. In only a few years, however, the rosy expectations of the deregulators proved wrong.

It turned out there were economies of scale in the new, deregulated indus-try. Larger carriers developed "hub and spoke" routing systems that con-nected multiple routes to a single city hub, such as United's Chicago O'Hare Airport hub, that allowed routing thousands of passengers to multiple desti-nations at extremely low cost per passenger.[51] Airlines were able to establish minimonopolies within their hubs and spoke connections through selectively underpricing any competitors that dared intrude. In addition, investments in computer reservation systems allowed "yield management" systems the large airlines could use to alter the price of tickets based on demand for particular flights. As these systems developed, ease of entry into the industry declined as new airlines had to invest in similar infrastructure to compete effectively. Within a few years the many low-cost airlines, such as People Express, that entered the market after deregulation had either been forced into bankruptcy or merged with other airlines. Within a decade of deregulation the industry seemed headed for more consolidation into a small number of large airlines.

Rather than lower fares across the board, airline deregulation has led to lower prices for some travelers and higher prices for others, depending on whether there is competition on the particular route one is flying and when one's ticket is bought. Rather than keep fares low everywhere for fear of the entry of a competitor, airlines establish monopolies on certain less-traveled routes where they can charge high prices. Under deregulation, airlines soon learned they could easily prevent competitors from encroaching on these routes with the threat of underpricing if the competitor would dare enter the market. Low fares can be had on those routes, usually from large cities or to popular vacation destinations such as Orlando, Florida or Las Vegas, where airlines are forced to underprice competitors—often charging below cost—a factor in the financial troubles of the industry over the years. So if you live in a big city or in a hot travel destination, flying has become much cheaper under deregulation; but if you inhabit a small or medium-sized city, taking wing costs significantly more, as Sen. Bryon L. Dorgan, D-N.D., knows from per-sonal experience. In a Senate hearing in 2007 he bemoaned the fact that the cost of returning to his home state from the District was twice as much as a trip to Los Angeles, a journey of twice the length.[52] Individual fares also vary due to the airlines' discriminatory pricing. Using their yield management systems, airlines charge different fares to different customers depending on estimated demand for the flight at a given time. These lead to a bewildering variety of fares charged on each flight, with differences charged passengers reaching into hundreds of dollars. Discriminatory pricing is a far cry from deregulation's promise of low, unrestricted fares on all routes.[53]

An unexpected casualty of deregulation has been massive financial instability in the industry. In spite of hub and spoke systems, mergers and consolidations, yield management, and discriminatory pricing, airline companies have lost money most years since deregulation.[54] Cut-throat competition on big-city routes has forced airlines to fly planes below cost that they have not been able to make up on those routes where they have monopolies. The result has been multiple airline bankruptcies since the 1980s and government subsidization of the industry. Bankruptcy or bankruptcy protection allowed giant carriers such as United, US Airways, and Delta to abrogate union contracts, slash employment, and turn over their pension obligations to the federal Pension Benefit Guarantee Corporation. Retired employees from these companies now collect only a portion of their promised benefits and from the federal government rather than from airline funds. To stay afloat, airlines are continually searching for ways to cut costs, including slashing jobs—140,000 were lost in the industry between 2002 and 2007, paying reductions, managing seat capacity through reducing flights and using smaller planes, dropping service on unprofitable routes, and providing passengers fewer amenities.[55] After September 11, 2001, Congress voted direct subsidies to the industry to make up for business losses in the wake of the tragedy.

A consequence of the financial turmoil has been increasing consolidation in the industry, even as new carriers sometimes emerge to exploit competitive opportunities along certain routes—such as Jet Blue or AirTran recently—they eventually are absorbed by a larger carrier. In early 2007, US Airways, itself having recently emerged from bankruptcy, attempted to acquire the bankrupt Delta to create the world's biggest airline. The deal fell through, but had US Airways succeeded analysts predicted that the remaining four competitor airlines—American, Northwest, United, and Continental—would have merged into two larger companies. The three behemoth airlines would have controlled over 75 percent of the market. Although this has not yet happened, experts believe such consolidations in the future will allow the industry to reduce capacity further and prop up fares.[56] If this consolidation were to come about, deregulation will have produced a national oligopoly that is unlikely to deliver any of the benefits the 1978 deregulators intended.

Defenders of deregulation argue that lower-than-average air fares and the growth of the number of people flying make it a success despite some negative consequences.[57] Yet other observers assess the trade-offs differently. A former

AIRLINE DEREGULATION HAS PRODUCED A CHAOTIC SYSTEM LEAVING STRANDED TRAVELERS TO COPE WITH FREQUENT DELAYS AND CANCELLATIONS, MAKING THIS SCENE FROM SUMMER 2007 A COMMON ONE.

Senate staffer who helped write the 1978 deregulation act now says: "Deregulation cut airline salaries, slashed retirement benefits, forced job cuts despite rises in the frequency of airline services, bankrupted many formerly great airlines or forced them into bankruptcy protection, ruined standards of airline service, raised fares on most non-mainline services, and made life miserable for travelers and airline employees."[58] The currently crowded skies, in terms of both numbers of flights and people traveling, that deregulators routinely cite as a sign of its success also imposes costs on harried travelers and the economy as a whole. Airline practices, encouraged in a deregulated environment, of clustering flights during the most profitable times of the day, yield management to ensure packed planes, use of smaller planes, and increase of the numbers of flights, create a taut system prone to massive delays systemwide whenever something goes wrong. Bad weather in just a few cities often sends the system reeling, causing millions of harried passengers to face delayed and cancelled flights, even when flying between cities unaffected by the weather disturbances. Mere congestion often causes millions to sit on airline tarmacs for hours with inadequate food, water, and restroom facilities. One cannot travel by air today in the United States without at some time being subject to these conditions. While these situations are often cited as mere "inconveniences" that travelers are willing to put up with in exchange for low fares, the country's dependence on modes of transportation for rapid intercity mass transit, given our inadequate passenger rail structure, suggests that most of us simply have no alternative. In addition, while low average fares may characterize the system, price discrimination means tremendous inequities in the actual fares passengers pay depending on where they live and access to opportunities to benefit from discount fares. The realities of air travel in a deregulated environment clearly do not live up to the promises made thirty years ago.

Market failure may be an inevitable attribute of passenger air travel that can only be corrected through regulation. The airline deregulators seem to have bought the libertarian illusion that potential government failures in regulation trump any worries about markets not functioning as promised in economics textbooks. The experience with deregulation suggests a deregulated market provides two options for organizing the system, neither of which offers the prospect of long-term industry stability or low-cost, satisfactory service to passengers. One option is hypercompetition among multiple carriers that delivers low fares, along with system crowding, but does not seem to deliver the stable profits airlines need. The U.S. economy has paid a high price over the last thirty years from the costs of airline bankruptcy, shifts of pension obligations to taxpayers, and direct bailouts of the industry. The other option, one industry leaders claim is imperative for financial stability, is to accept consolidation of major airlines, giving them monopolistic control over parts of the system. Only in this way can airlines push up fares sufficiently overall to cover their costs and deliver an adequate profit to satisfy investors. This option clearly defeats the central purpose of deregulation—low fares—and subjects consumers to the market power of the big airlines. Over the past thirty years, market forces have produced oscillation between these two options along with periods when both seem to operate simultaneously. Market failure seems an inevitable characteristic of the system that only effective regulation can correct.

Deregulation of air travel in 1978 initiated a mania for deregulation over the next thirty years that involved nearly every corner of the economy. Deregulators triumphed in trucking, banking, telecommunications, electricity production, and securities trading, to name a few. Although the experience has varied somewhat in different industries, as in airlines, deregulation promising marvelous benefits from free markets has produced market failures and market abuses and failed to deliver the level of benefits promised. In banking, for instance, a whole series of settled rules governing the industry dating to both the Progressive Era and the New Deal have been abandoned in the last few decades. For example, since the 1930s, savings and loan associations had been restricted to loaning their depositors money for home mortgages—the purpose for which they had originally been created. In the early 1980s Congress, in one of its early stabs at deregulating financial services, freed the S&Ls to diversify into other types of loans; it also loosened rules regarding S&L

ownership. Entrepreneurs, some of them unscrupulous, anxious to get their hands on the deposits of millions of S&L members, bought up S&Ls and began to make risky loans in commercial real estate and other endeavors. Soon S&Ls across the country were in bankruptcy and some of their owners, such as Charles Keating, owner of an S&L empire in the Southwest, were under indictment for fraudulently looting their companies.[59] Eventually, in 1988 Congress had to bail out a fractured industry at the cost of $500 billion in tax-payer money.[60] Despite this early failure in banking deregulation, Congress continued to drop regulatory restrictions left and right, including limits of credit card interest, restrictions on interstate banking, oversight of mortgage lending, and Glass-Steagall restrictions on commercial bank involvement in investment banking and stock brokerage.

Predictably, in this new deregulated environment, a few large banks such as Bank of America, Citicorp, and Chase Manhattan have consolidated the industry into one a few large institutions dominate and returned high profits to their investors and astronomical compensation to executives. Thanks to deregulation, Citigroup CEO Sanford I. Weill saw his personal wealth rise to $1.5 billion, a figure reminiscent of the tycoons of the Gilded Age.[61] Ordinary consumers have not fared as well, as banking services have deteriorated and consumer debt has risen. Today, instead of seeking loans or making deposits at a locally owned bank, local businesses and consumers must work with employees of a nationwide conglomerate—often through customer service representatives manning phones overseas. With reductions in regulation of loan rates and marketing practices, consumer debt has risen astronomically, with many people paying double-digit credit card interest and burdened with high-mortgage payments from variable-rate mortgages.[62] In 2007, deregula-tion in the home mortgage industry precipitated a national financial crisis as low-income borrowers with "subprime" mortgages, many who had been sold loans beyond what their incomes allowed, began to default on their loans when housing prices sagged. Working out loan modifications with lenders to avoid foreclosure was difficult for most borrowers because, in the deregulated mortgage market, the typical mortgage had been resold to multiple investors.[63] The days of working out a repayment plan at your friendly local bank are long gone. As with airline deregulation, promises that freeing banks to free market competition would benefit ordinary consumers have not been fulfilled.

Deregulation in the telecommunications industry has produced similar unfulfilled promises. Clearly, the emergence of new communications tech-nologies in recent decades such as cable and satellite TV, cell phones, broad-band networks, and the Internet required reform of a regulatory framework that dated to 1934. Early in the 1980s, AT&T's Ma Bell monopoly of the long-distance and local telephone service industry was broken up into a deregulated long-distance market and locally regulated "Baby Bells" for pro-viding local service. By the 1990s, however, the cable TV industry, telephone companies, broadcasters, and Internet service providers were clamoring for a new telecommunications environment where free market competition would rule. They got their wish with the 1996 Telecommunications Act, which opened up the industry to a competitive free-for-all. Although corporate lobbyists claimed that technological innovation would ensure continuing competition and low consumer prices, in reality they sought unregulated competition in order to gain market dominance to raise consumer prices. As Joseph Stiglitz, Clinton's chief economic advisor at the time, recalled, "Although deregulation advocates argued that with the new technologies . . . competition would ensure low prices, they knew that that was not the case: they believed that there were huge profits to be made, and they wanted to make sure that the new regulations were written to enable them to grab them."[64] The cable industry expected to earn $4 to 5 billion per year as a result of deregulation.[65] What followed was a trillion-dollar scramble of investors to take advantage of the potential profits from telecom deregulation and firm-seeking to become dominant in the expected "winner-take-all" markets. When the telecom boom collapsed in 2002, twenty-three companies had gone bankrupt, five hundred thousand employees had lost their jobs, and investors lost about $59 billion.[66] Deregulation had produced, in Stiglitz's words, "a tremendous amount of excess capacity and a marketplace that in some areas was more concentrated than before."[67] What did not materialize were the low cable TV rates and the bargain basement phone service promised consumers. Nor did deregulation stimulate technological innovation and better service. As of 2007, the United States was lagging behind Japan and most of Europe, where regulation was designed to stimulate both competition and innovation, in broadband access, speed of Internet connection, and consumer choice among competing providers.[68] Yet nowhere have the limitations of deregulation and the need to retain regulatory oversight to ensure adequate service been more apparent than with the United States' experience with electricity deregulation.

Electricity Deregulation: Undependable Power at Rising Prices

For decades, economic texts described electrical utilities as the classic case of natural monopoly. The technical attributes of electricity generation and service delivery over an electrical transmission grid contained all the economies of scale making a single provider much more efficient for electricity production than multiple competing providers would be.[69] Whether a publicly owned municipal power company or a regulated private one, the standard model involved "vertical integration" within a single company from energy generation at a large local power plant, high-voltage transmission to the communities served, and distribution to individual homes and businesses. Because electrical transmission involved some loss of power, electrical utilities had to be local businesses generating power close to the customers who received power. For private utilities, prices were regulated to keep prices to the consumer as low as possible while also generating sufficient revenue to provide a fair rate of return to investors and ensure sufficient investment in future capacity. This was the regulatory model that electrified the country in the twentieth century and supported its enormous industrial expansion.

By the 1970s, new technologies began to raise questions, at least in the minds of deregulation advocates, of the long-term efficiency of this model. While electrical generation plants traditionally had been huge coal-fired, hydroelectric, or, beginning in the 1950s, nuclear-powered affairs, in the 1970s and 1980s new, smaller, more efficient, natural gas generators began to come online and interest increased in alternative electricity generation such as solar and wind power. It now seemed possible to draw on power from a multitude of these smaller power sources rather than a few huge plants to light up a community. New transmission technologies also made it possible to transmit power a thousand miles, allowing a single local utility to acquire power from multiple sites spread over a large area.[70] Deregulators claimed these technological changes undermined the character of electricity production as a natural monopoly and the logic of the vertical integration model of electricity generation and distribution. Although the local electrical grid retained its natural monopoly characteristics, there was now no reason why the utility that retailed electricity over its local grid also had to be the power supplier. They pushed for requiring utilities to obtain their power from competing private power suppliers and simply charge a fee for the use of their grid for transmitting power to customers. Under this new model, power generators would compete to sell their power to local utilities or even directly to customers. Supposedly, the market competition, under this new model, would produce efficiencies in power generation, stimulate further technological innovation, and deliver lower electricity prices to consumers. Deregulation would transform electricity from a commodity produced under an arcane set of regulations into one bought and sold in the marketplace. In the ultimate deregulatory visions, utilities would become like farmer's markets displaying the competing wares of power producers for their customers to choose from, just as they pick apples from competing farms.

In describing the new market for electrical power, deregulators implied the familiar work of supply and demand achieving an efficient, low equilibrium price characteristic of all competitive markets. This vision, however, failed to account for how even the best electricity markets differ from those for most commodities. In a normal commodity market, demand and supply rarely match precisely at any one time and need not. When demand for automobiles falls, auto dealers can let their inventory of cars accumulate in their lots while they formulate a new sales campaign to get sales moving again. Also, keeping some inventory on hand allows responding quickly to a sudden increase in demand. The supply and demand for automobiles, lettuce, or MP3 players can all be coordinated in a decentralized way in a market, through individual voluntary exchanges, without any central coordinator. Unlike these commodities, there is no way to store electricity in inventory in response to fluctuations in demand and supply. For an electrical system to function smoothly, the amount of electricity generated and flowing through the system always must match precisely the amount consumed.[71] This means that even if multiple power suppliers are competing to supply electricity into a grid, someone must centrally control the flow of power through the grid to manage supply and demand. Even "deregulated" electricity markets demand substantial regulation from a neutral supply coordinator (called an Independent System Operator [ISO]) to function. This complex task of balancing supply and demand through an electrical grid includes accounting for constant fluctuations throughout the day and in different seasons. Failure to control properly will produce both blackouts due to insufficient supply and physical damage to the power grid.

Because demand for electrical power can increase rapidly in response to the weather—both extreme heat and cold raise demand or overall supply might fall if low rainfall diminishes hydroelectrical power, surplus generating capacity has to be present to satisfy both spikes in demand and unforeseen supply shortages. This creates a particular challenge for a deregulated electrical power market. In a regulated system, provisions are made to compensate utilities for building in excess capacity in their generating systems that can be brought online in times of need. The cost of letting the capacity sit idle is covered in the regulated price. Under a system of competition, where competition among suppliers is supposed to determine the price, ensuring sufficient capacity at times of high demand poses significant problems. Deregulators assumed sufficient supply could be found from private generators when demand increased, but there is no incentive in a market system for competing suppliers to pay for capacity that is going to sit idle most of the time. In fact, to do so would place a company at a disadvantage with competitors that maintained just the generating capacity needed that could be sold at a given time. In fact, one of the standard ways markets are supposed to encourage efficiency and reduce costs is to encourage producers to trim excess capacity. The outcome of this market logic is tight supply with minimal excess capacity. Such an outcome is disastrous in an electricity market, as Californians discovered to their regret in 2001.

California's 1998 deregulation of electricity made it one of the first states in the nation to do so. Although passed because legislators thought deregulation would produce lower prices for consumers, prices, in fact, began to rise rapidly as deregulation was implemented. By 2000, two years after deregulation, average wholesale prices were four times what they had been in 1998.[72] More ominously, there were growing signs of restrictions in supply that culminated, eventually, in the 2001 crisis described at the beginning of this chapter. At the time, as mentioned in the introduction, electricity deregulation advocates blamed the crisis on environmental regulations for impeding

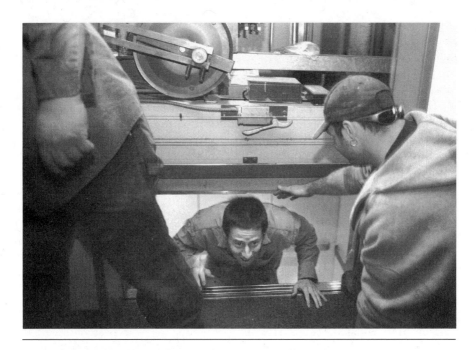

THE ROLLING BLACKOUTS THROUGHOUT CALIFORNIA IN 2001 CAUSED BY ELECTRICITY DEREGULA-
TION DISRUPTED THE LIVES OF HUNDREDS OF THOUSANDS LIKE THIS UNIVERSITY OF CALIFORNIA–
BERKELEY STUDENT TRAPPED IN AN ELEVATOR.

expansion of generation capacity, flaws in the way California deregulated, and
high natural gas prices. Claims that environmental regulations caused the situation ignored the fact that power companies had not sought to build new
plants after 1998. Further proof came when ample supply of electricity sud-
denly became available when the Federal Energy Regulatory Commission
reimposed regulation of interstate wholesale prices after the crisis.[73] Deregulators saw the 6.5 percent cap on retail electricity prices as the key flaw in the
California deregulation design. It certainly can be blamed for the immediate
financial crisis: the utilities could not recover their wholesale costs from consumers when wholesale prices skyrocketed. But this argument ignores the reason the caps were imposed in 1996—as reassurance from deregulators that
lower prices would result. The cap also intended to serve as more of a floor
rather than a cap on retail prices sanctioning prices up to that level so utilities
could recover their "stranded costs" for previous investments in generation
capacity. Moreover, even without the caps, there still would have been a
crisis—not resulting in utility bankruptcies, perhaps, but sky-high prices for
consumers (and lots of individual bankruptcies). When San Diego Electric, the
first utility to recover its "stranded costs" under the law in 2000, passed on

the higher wholesale costs to its consumers, prices tripled and a panicked legislature reimposed the cap.

Deregulators also criticized other provisions in the law, such as the prohibition on utilities negotiating long-term contracts for electricity, but in the end the true cause of the crisis proved to be the market manipulation of Enron and other energy traders.[74] Even the claim that higher natural gas prices caused the higher prices also proved to be an artifact of market manipulation. El Paso Natural Gas eventually revealed it had restricted the flow of natural gas through its pipeline to California in order to gain higher prices for the gas that, thanks to natural gas deregulation, it also sold.[75] Prior to deregulation, natural gas producers were not allowed to own gas pipelines precisely to avoid this conflict of interest. The California crisis simply illustrated the potential for market failure when an industry like electrical power production is opened up to market forces without adequate regulatory oversight. Given the profit potential to generators when supply is tight, it was naïve to think that some would not find ways to manipulate supplies to produce that result. Deregulation also neglects the need for sufficient capacity to cope with the fluctuations inherent in electricity markets.

Beyond the California crisis, the national experience demonstrates the limitations of electricity deregulation. The lower prices promised in the 1990s have materialized nowhere. In fact, in the twelve states that have experimented with deregulation electricity prices have increased more rapidly on average than in the states that did not deregulate.[76] None of the consumers in regulated states have had the opportunity to choose among rival electricity-generating companies that have not found marketing directly to retail consumers to be profitable. Under deregulation, households still must purchase their power from a local monopoly, but one now permitted to pass on directly the cost of unregulated wholesale prices.[77] Even those sympathetic to introducing more free market competition into electricity generation these days are apt to call for "restructuring" of the industry rather than deregulation. As one such report admits, "even small amounts of market power [in the electricity industry] imply large transfers from consumers."[78] Now for these market advocates, the best that can be hoped for are long-term benefits that may offset higher short-term prices for consumers. In sum, the experience with electricity deregulation has shown the ongoing value of regulation in the industry and suggests market forces are unlikely to offer significant benefits to consumers. Some might continue to argue that new generation and transmission technologies still make potential benefits from market competition in the future, but experience thus far shows such competition has to occur within a regulated framework. Yet skeptics might see this once again as simply succumbing to the libertarian illusion that market forces always work better than regulation. Many Californians as well as consumers in other states where deregulation has been tried have been the guinea pigs who have suffered from this massive experiment. Some may look with envy on those who are lucky enough to rely on old-fashioned electricity regulation, like the citizens of Los Angeles whose municipal power system pumped out electricity steadily in 2001 while the rest of the state went dark.

The fate of Enron Corporation provides the final cautionary tale of the downside of the libertarian era of deregulation. As we have seen, Enron was a major participant in electricity deregulation, but this was only a portion of how it benefited from the era of deregulation. In the 1990s, Enron's CEO, Ken Lay, billed the growth of his corporation as a model for a deregulated future America. Enron began as a small natural gas pipeline company that took advantage of deregulation in that industry to branch out into other endeavors. Over a decade or so, it transformed itself into a corporation that traded energy and commodities, taking advantage of deregulation in securities trading, banking, and accounting as it became one of the country's richest companies. It prided itself on being the go-between that moved assets around to enhance economic value rather than produce a particular product. Enron executives such as Lay and Jeffrey Skilling used their political connections to powerful politicians such as George W. Bush to promote deregulation policies. Before its demise, Enron was a large contributor to the campaigns of Bush and other, primarily Republican, politicians.[79]

When the corporation spectacularly collapsed in 2002, revelations showed how lax regulation had allowed company executives to engage in a variety of deceptive behaviors to manipulate its balance sheets. For example, in their electricity trades, Enron execs would arrange a future electricity trade and record the sale immediately on its books as incoming revenue but delay recording the cost Enron would have to pay for the sale until the trade occurred.[80] The result was to push continually corporate expenditures into the future and inflate revenues. This allowed Enron to give to its Wall Street investors the appearance of greater profits than it actually was earning. Eventually more elaborate schemes were developed, such as making fictional trades with subsidiaries its executives created for the sole purpose of generating positive accounting entries. Operating in the spirit of the new era of deregulation, neither its own outside accounting firm, Arthur Anderson, nor SEC investigators looked too closely at the details of these arrangements. Both Enron and its accounts also were in the forefront of those resisting efforts by SEC chair Arthur Leavitt in 2000 to devise new corporate disclosure rules that might have revealed what was going on.[81] Thirty years earlier, the banks that loaned Enron money might have inquired more earnestly into the corporation's real value, but with the repeal of Glass-Steagall these banks also sold Enron stock and invested in the corporation. This financial conflict of interest, just as the Glass-Steagall Act had anticipated, diminished the incentive to ask hard questions before the banks loaned money. When Enron collapsed, its banks' reputations would be put in question and its accounting firm destroyed.[82] Enron executives eventually would be sentenced to long jail terms for their crimes. The worst victims, however, would be Enron's employees, who lost $1 billion in pension benefits from the firm's bankruptcy. Most of these losses came from their investments in Enron stock, which top executives were encouraging its employees to continue to buy in order to prop up stock value while they themselves sold $1.1 billion of their own shares.[83] When riding high in the 1990s, Enron had symbolized the swagger and arrogance of the new deregulated economy, but in its demise in 2002 vindicated the Progressive and New Deal suspicion of big business that demanded their regulation.

Conclusion

Like the libertarian illusion in general, the deregulation promises of the last few decades were based on an illusory understanding of the relationship between regulation and markets. Deregulators claimed that removing regulations would allow the market free reign and its "invisible hand" would deliver all the wonderful efficiencies promised in economics textbooks. This ideological, almost theological faith in the market ignores the reality of market failure, at times, to produce the efficiency that is its hallmark. It also fails to recognize values other than efficiency—nonmarket values—as worthy collective goals that markets alone are incapable of achieving. A communitarian understanding of regulation sees it as both a corrective for market failures and as a means of achieving nonmarket values. We cannot achieve the common good without recognizing why deregulated markets alone fail to achieve it.

Deregulation foundered on a failure to recognize markets as arenas of power. The idealized market model, embraced by libertarians, consisting of spontaneous voluntary exchanges ignores how market power at times can force exchanges. Market manipulations that forced Californians to pay sky-high electricity prices were about as voluntary as a thief asking for "your money or your life." Airline passengers forced to pay the exorbitant fare to the sole airline serving their town on a particular route also are victims of market power. In the nineteenth century, farmers who mobilized to insist on railroad regulation understood the power those railroads wielded against them. They turned to the only power capable of taking on those powerful interests, the federal government, through the power of their democratic voice. In the 1980s and 1990s, many U.S. politicians either forgot or chose to ignore this reality of markets. Embracing a vision of the ideal, self-regulating, competitive market of libertarian lore, they merely freed markets of regulatory restraint in multiple economic sectors. Not surprisingly, self-interested, as they must be to succeed in free markets, actors organized to acquire market power and wield it to enrich themselves. The Enron debacle was a logical consequence of this naïve view that only good would come from unsupervised market activity. The United States' experience with deregulation should lead the country to relearn the lesson of those nineteenth-century farmers and rebuild a reasonable regulatory framework to prevent businesses from abusing their market power to harm the common good.

In the 1970s, there was ample reason to reexamine the regulatory structures that had been put in place over a seventy-year period. Changing technology, an increasingly globalized economy, a life cycle of regulation that
seemed to have made some independent regulatory commissions captive of
industry, all suggested a need for regulatory reform. But rather than reform
regulation, policymakers opted to deregulate. As Stiglitz has pointed out,
"for the market economy to function well, there is a need for laws and
regulations—to ensure fair competition, to protect the environment, to make
sure that consumers and investors are not cheated. What was needed was not
deregulation, but *reformed* regulation. . . ."[84] The failure of the deregulation
experiment now requires Americans to pursue this task of reregulating the
economy to meet the challenges of a global economy while ensuring that the
common good is achieved.

In reforming regulation we may need to reinvent traditional ways and
methods of a century ago to address modern conditions, but in doing so, we
need to recapture the Progressive faith of that time when regulation in the
public interest (or in the language of this book—for the common good) could
be achieved. Deregulators and libertarians play on cynicism about government
incapacity and special interests' ability to manipulate it. Much of the success
of the deregulation movement derived, I believe, from the ease with which
many of us accept the argument that government serves as a means powerful
interests exploit to capture, in public choice terms, "rents" for themselves.
Government can become captive of special interests, but the solution to such
a problem cannot be found in sapping government of regulatory authority;
that simply allows special interests to work their will through market power.
As the Progressives recognized, the better solution to special interest government (and market power) is a vigorous democracy using government for the
ends of a democratic community.

A vigorous democracy would demand that government regulation super-
vise our capitalist market economy to ensure that it serves the common
good. Citizens are right to demand an economy that preserves the environment; protects workers from avoidable injury; ensures the safety of the
products we consume; and does not discriminate on the basis of race, religion,
gender, or disability. They also must be protected from market monopoly and
market manipulations that enrich a wealthy few at the expense of the average
consumer. And citizens must turn to regulation to see that markets serve the
interests of all and provide some equity in the distribution of essential services.
Regulation may not always work perfectly on behalf of these ends; but when
government regulation fails, the solution does not lie in its abandonment and
reliance on market forces. Deregulated markets simply open citizens to further exploitation over which they have no collective control. The better
solution comes from the use of democratic processes to make sure that
government gets regulation right. A vigilant, democratically responsive

government provides our best means to balance power in the market with the power of the common good.

SUGGESTIONS FOR FURTHER READING

Dibadj, Reza R. *Rescuing Regulation*. Albany: State University of New York Press, 2006. A critique of deregulation with proposals for regulatory reform.

Kuttner, Robert. *Everything for Sale: The Virtues and Limits of Markets*. New York: Knopf, 1996. A leading liberal public intellectual analyzes the failures of deregulation.

Nelson, Richard R. *The Limits of Market Organization*. New York: Russell Sage Foundation, 2005. A balanced analysis of regulation, including case studies of several industries.

Stigler, George J. *Chicago Studies in Political Economy*. Chicago: University of Chicago Press, 1988. A compendium of classics of the law and economics movement.

Stiglitz, Joseph E. *The Roaring Nineties: A New History of the World's Most Prosperous Decade*. New York: W. W. Norton, 2003. An administration insider's account of how deregulation prospered in the Clinton years and the effects on economic problems today.

SELECTED WEB SITES

www.aei.brookings.org. Two think tanks, the American Enterprise Institute and the Brookings Institution, joined in debating regulation from a range of ideological perspectives.

www.cato.org/pubs/regulation/index.html. Web site of *Regulation Magazine,* a Cato Institute publication, whose articles, not surprisingly, usually advocate deregulation, but not always.

www.ferc.gov/default.asp. Web site of the Federal Energy Regulatory Commission.

NOTES

1. The account of the California electricity crisis is drawn from Peter Schrag, "Blackout," *The American Prospect,* February 26, 2001; and Newsbatch Internet Guide to Public Policy Issues, www.newsbatch.com/electric.htm.

2. Federal Energy Regulatory Commission, Final Report on Price Manipulation in Western Markets, Staff Report (March 2003), www.ferc.gov/industries/electric/indus-act/wec/enron/summary-findings.pdf.

3. Dale Kasler, "State's an Enron Subplot; Houston Trial May Shed Light on How California Got Burned on Energy," *Sacramento Bee,* February 15, 2006, A1.

4. Robert Kuttner, "Electrical Storm," *The American Prospect*—Web Edition, August 21, 2003, www.prospect.org/cs/articles?article=electrical_storm.

5. Marianne Lavelle, "Deregulation Heats Up Power Bills," *U.S. News and World Report,* July 11, 2007.

6. Roger L. Ransom, *Coping with Capitalism* (Englewood Cliffs, N.J.: Prentice Hall, 1981), 61–62.

7. Quoted in ibid., 73.
8. Alan Stone, *Regulation and Its Alternatives* (Washington, D.C.: CQ Press, 1982), 32.
9. Ransom, *Coping with Capitalism,* 96.
10. The classic analysis is William Lilley III and James C. Miller III, "The New Social Regulation," *The Public Interest* (Spring 1977): 51.
11. Ralph Nader, *Unsafe at Any Speed: The Designed-in Dangers of the American Automobile* (New York: Grossman, 1965).
12. The best account of the business mobilization is still Thomas Edsall, *The New Politics of Inequality* (New York: Norton, 1984).
13. William E. Hudson, *American Democracy in Peril: Eight Challenges to America's Future,* 5th ed. (Washington, D.C.: CQ Press, 2006), 228–233.
14. Joseph Stiglitz, *Economics of the Public Sector,* 3d ed. (New York: Norton, 2000), 78.
15. Ransom, *Coping with Capitalism,* 50–82.
16. Woodrow Wilson, "The Study of Administration," *Political Science Quarterly* 2 (June 1887); reprinted in Jay M. Shafritz and Albert C. Hyde, *Classics in Public Administration,* 3d ed. (Belmont, Calif.: Brooks/Cole, 1992), 13.
17. Hudson, *American Democracy in Peril,* 204.
18. Richard R. Nelson, *The Limits of Market Organization* (New York: Russell Sage Foundation, 2005), 62.
19. Milton Friedman, *Capitalism and Freedom* (Chicago: University of Chicago Press, 1962), 28, 128.
20. Robert Kuttner, *Everything for Sale* (New York: Knopf, 1996), 251.
21. Yochi Dreazen et al., "Why the Sudden Rise in the Urge to Merge and Form Oligopolies?" *Wall Street Journal,* February 25, 2003, A1.
22. Cited in Kuttner, *Everything for Sale,* 276–277.
23. Reza R. Dibadj, *Rescuing Regulation* (Albany: University of New York Press, 2006), 18–19.
24. Ibid., 27.
25. Friedman, *Capitalism and Freedom,* 137–160.
26. Ibid., 157.
27. Ibid., 159.
28. Ronald H. Coase, "The Problem of Social Cost," *The Journal of Law and Economics* 3 (October 1960): 1–44; reprinted in Ronald H. Coase, *The Firm, the Market, and the Law* (Chicago: University of Chicago Press, 1988), 118.
29. This is a modification of an example found in Joseph Stiglitz, *Economics of the Public Sector,* 3d ed., 219.
30. Coase, "The Problem of Social Cost."
31. Ibid.
32. George J. Stigler, *Chicago Studies in Political Economy* (Chicago: University of Chicago Press, 1988).
33. Marver H. Bernstein, *Regulating Business by Independent Commission* (Princeton: Princeton University Press, 1955).
34. George J. Stigler, "The Theory of Economic Regulation," in George J. Stigler, ed., *Chicago Studies in Political Economy* (Chicago: University of Chicago Press, 1988), 209.

35. Mansur Olson, *The Logic of Collective Action* (Cambridge: Harvard University Press, 1965), 128.
36. Kuttner, *Everything for Sale*, 335.
37. James Buchanan quoted in ibid., 335.
38. Ibid., 339.
39. Kenneth Meier, *Regulation: Politics, Bureaucracy, and Economics* (New York: St. Martins, 1985), 19.
40. David Boaz, *Libertarianism: A Primer* (New York: The Free Press, 1997), 173–174.
41. Kuttner, *Everything for Sale*, 301.
42. John E. Schwarz, *Freedom Reclaimed: Rediscovering the American Vision* (Baltimore: Johns Hopkins University Press, 2005), 90.
43. Ibid., 90.
44. Kuttner, *Everything for Sale*, 294.
45. Ibid., 294.
46. Ibid., 304–305.
47. Christian Warren, "The Little Engine That Could Poison," *New York Times*, June 22, 2007, A19; David Goldstein, "Poison for Profit," *The Nation*, July 30, 2007.
48. Arturo Gandara, chair, Public Policy Committee, Alliance for Public Technology, Testimony before the Federal Communications Commission, July 14, 2004.
49. Robert C. Fellmuth, *The Interstate Commerce Omission* (New York: Grossman, 1970).
50. Paul Stephen Dempsey and Andrew R. Goetz, *Airline Deregulation and Laissez-faire Mythology* (Westport, Conn.: Quorum Books, 1992), 335.
51. Mark S. Kahan, "Confessions of an Airline Deregulator," *The American Prospect*, November 30, 2002.
52. Chris Isidore, "Senators Fly Idea of Airline Re-regulation," CNNMoney, CNNMoney.com, January 24, 2007.
53. Kahan, "Confessions of an Airline Deregulator."
54. Robert Kuttner, "Chaos in the Skies," *Boston Globe*, May 4, 2007, A19.
55. John D. Rockefeller IV, Chairman, Subcommittee on Aviation, Statement: Hearing on the State of the Airline Industry: The Potential Impact of Airline Mergers and Industry Consolidation, *U.S. Federal News*, January 24, 2007.
56. Martin Zimmerman, "Talk of Airline Consolidation Quiets Down," *Los Angeles Times*, February 1, 2007, C3.
57. Alfred Kahn, *Lessons from Deregulation* (Washington, D.C.: AEI-Brookings Joint Center for Regulatory Studies, 2004), 3–4.
58. William Pfaff, "Airlines' Experience Proves Deregulation Wrong," *Charleston Gazette*, April 2, 2006, P3E.
59. Donald L. Bartlett and James B. Steele, *America: What Went Wrong?* (Kansas City: Andrews and McMeel, 1992), 180–182.
60. Joseph Stiglitz, *The Roaring Nineties: A New History of the World's Most Prosperous Decade* (New York: W. W. Norton, 2003), 38–39, 103; L. J. Davis, "Chronicle of a Debacle: How Deregulation Begat the S&L Scandal," *Atlantic Monthly*, September 1990, 50–66.
61. Louis Uchitelle, "The Richest of the Rich," *New York Times*, July 15, 2007, A1.

62. G. M. Filisko, "Subprime Lending Fallout," *National Real Estate Investor,* July 1, 2007, 93.
63. E. Scott Reckard, "Giving Borrowers a Break," *Los Angeles Times,* October 4, 2007, A1.
64. Stiglitz, *The Roaring Nineties,* 94.
65. Ibid., 96.
66. Ibid., 92.
67. Ibid., 101.
68. Paul Krugman, "The French Connections," *New York Times,* July 22, 2007, A23.
69. James M. Griffin and Steven L. Puller, *Electricity Deregulation: Choices and Challenges* (Chicago: University of Chicago Press, 2005), 2–4.
70. Ibid., 3.
71. Ibid., 5.
72. Stiglitz, *The Roaring Nineties,* 250.
73. Ibid., 254.
74. Ibid., 256.
75. Ibid., 257.
76. Jim Snyder, "Consumer Groups Call for More Oversight of Energy Regulation," *The Hill,* March 1, 2007, 12.
77. Richard Rosen, Marjorie Kelly, and John Stutz, "A Failed Experiment: Why Electricity Deregulation Did Not Work and Could Not Work," (Boston: Tellus Institute, March 2007), www.tellus.org/Publications/Tellus_Electric_report%20final.pdf.
78. Severin Borenstein and James Bushnell, "Electricity Restructuring: Deregulation or Re-regulation," *Regulation* 23, no. 2, 52.
79. Hudson, *American Democracy in Peril,* 47–48, 191–192.
80. Stiglitz, *The Roaring Nineties,* 242.
81. Ibid., 262.
82. Ibid., 242–243.
83. Ibid., 242.
84. Ibid., 91.

Chapter 4   Social Security: The Battle over Privatization

The day after his narrow but decisive victory in the 2004 presidential election, President George W. Bush held a nationally televised press conference to outline how he would spend the "political capital" he felt he had earned from his reelection. To the assembled reporters, he revealed that reform of Social Security would be a central priority of his second term. His plan involved changing the politically popular pension program from a government-centered system providing guaranteed retirement benefits to one centered on private investment accounts under individual control. This shift, he argued, would be the centerpiece of his plan for a new "ownership society" that would transform the relationship between government and citizens. Drawing largely on libertarian ideals, the ownership society, in the words of one of its supporters, would free individuals from "dependence on government and make them owners, instead, in control of their own destiny."[1] Reflecting this philosophy, Bush's partially privatized Social Security system would give workers "ownership" of a portion of their Social Security contributions that they could invest as they saw fit and reap the benefits of their investments when they retired.

An impending crisis in the financing of Social Security, Bush argued, required its transformation according to libertarian principles. For many years, reports of the trustees of the Social Security program, the group responsible for overseeing its fiscal integrity, had projected that in about the third decade of the twenty-first century, Social Security would not have sufficient revenues to pay all its benefit obligations. The reason was the impending retirements of the "baby boom" generation, that demographic bulge of people born as birth rates soared at the end of World War II. Because the existing Social Security program depends on payroll tax payments from current workers to finance current benefits, the "pay as you go" financing method described in more detail later in this chapter, the smaller post–baby boom generational cohorts would be responsible for paying for the benefits of the huge number of baby boomer retirees. In short, according to the Social Security trustee projections, eventually too few workers would be paying into the program to cover its obligations to the retired baby boomers. Adapting the rhetoric of his libertarian supporters, Bush characterized this future moment as the impending "bankruptcy" of the Social Security system. In order to avert this fiscal disaster,

PRESIDENT GEORGE W. BUSH FAILED TO SELL HIS PLAN FOR PRIVATE SOCIAL SECURITY ACCOUNTS IN 2005, DESPITE RALLIES ORGANIZED AROUND THE COUNTRY, LIKE THIS EVENT IN FLORIDA.

in the view of the libertarians, a fundamental change in the design of the Social Security system was required.

Placing Social Security reform at the center of his second-term domestic agenda was a politically risky decision for President Bush. Earlier politicians had been wary of proposing any change in this politically popular program for fear of adverse voter reaction. Thirty years earlier, another conservative Republican, Ronald Reagan—who also was inclined to alter the program along libertarian lines—had described it as the "third rail" of U.S. politics: "Touch it and you will die." The program's elderly beneficiaries tended to regard any proposed changes in Social Security as a threat to their benefits, prompting an adverse reaction at the polls to those promoting change. At the dawn of Bush's second term, the president's advisers thought that Social Security's impending fiscal difficulties, along with an electorate more sympathetic to libertarian ideas, had diminished the current flowing through the "third rail." This new context would allow Bush to survive and even prosper by touching it. In the end, the current in the third rail proved as powerful as ever. Bush's proposal for private Social Security accounts failed to gain traction in Congress and, as his popularity waned in 2005, Bush quietly dropped his proposal.

Although this most recent attempt to revamp Social Security along libertarian lines has not succeeded, recasting the program as a system of private accounts remains a key part of the libertarian agenda. As will be shown below, libertarians have been laying the groundwork for this shift for over thirty years, and they will continue to push for it in the years to come. As the fiscal day of reckoning for Social Security grows closer, renewed calls for establishing private accounts, as in the Bush plan, are likely. Students of public policy, as well as citizens, need to be aware of the advantages and disadvantages of such proposals. I believe careful consideration of the libertarian alternative to retirement security will lead to a greater appreciation for the *social insurance* principles underlying the existing Social Security program.

The History of Social Security: Social Insurance for Retirement Security

The Social Security Act of 1935, a key part of President Franklin D. Roosevelt's New Deal, created and established the design of the Social Security program. Enacted in the midst of the Great Depression, the new legislation aimed to alleviate the severe poverty produced in this massive failure of the economy. A key indicator of this fiasco was the high unemployment rate that reached a height of 25 percent of the workforce in 1933 but remained at about 20 percent in 1935.[2] Yet unemployment captured only a part of the deprivation of the period, as even employed workers worked intermittently and had to accept falling wages. By some estimates, over one half of all Americans were living in poverty in 1935.[3] Among those who suffered most from this economic deprivation were the elderly. As the first fired and last hired, they were most likely to be unemployed and, given the general economic distress, could not count on much support from their families.[4]

Despite the plight of the poor, Roosevelt initially resisted establishing any permanent structure of social welfare benefits. His plan was to rely solely on temporary relief through public works projects and new economic regulations to revive the economy. But political pressure from two different sources, both focused on the elderly, pushed Roosevelt to consider the new programs created in the Social Security Act. The first came from Louisiana senator Huey Long, whose Share Our Wealth proposal seemed to be the centerpiece of a possible challenge for the presidency. Long proposed spending $3.6 billion to pay for pensions for everyone over age 60.[5] The other source of pressure came from the Townsend movement, organized around a plan by Dr. Francis Townsend, a retired California physician, to pay $200 a month to all persons over age 60. The Townsend Plan was portrayed not only as assistance to the elderly but a means of reviving the entire depressed economy. Under the plan, elderly recipients would be forbidden to work, releasing their jobs to younger workers; they were also required to expend all of their grants in one month, thereby stimulating the economy. Townsend's plan had enormous appeal. Within a few months of its unveiling in January 1934, there were 1,200 Townsend clubs across the nation and over twenty-five million people had signed petitions favoring the proposal.

Both Long's Share Our Wealth campaign and the Townsend Plan sought to assist the elderly poor through direct systems of economic redistribution. Both envisioned free grants of funds to elderly recipients financed from general tax revenues and saw their plans as drawing on the total economic resources of the national community. Long's plan called for paying for his plan through a tax on millionaires. Long claimed such a redistributive transfer would simply share "our," meaning the country's, wealth—wealth the rich had taken from the poor. Townsend proposed financing his plan through a national sales tax. He also explicitly tied his proposal to the general economic prosperity, claiming, "The old people are simply to be used as a means by which prosperity will be restored to all of us."[6]

Responding to pressure from both Long and Townsend, Roosevelt moved quickly in 1935 on a plan for a structure of social welfare benefits. Roosevelt's advisers, however, rejected the idea of "sharing the wealth" through direct redistribution from general tax revenues. Instead, they proposed social welfare benefits based on the idea of social insurance as existed in many European countries and in some American states at the time. The basic idea of social insurance is to protect individuals from certain risks to the ability to earn income in a capitalist market economy. These risks result from unavoidable circumstances individuals might find themselves in that prevent them from working, such as unemployment, a work injury, a permanent disability, or old age. In a capitalist economy in which individuals normally are expected to provide for themselves through the market, either from wages or profits from a business, the possibility that one might be unable for some reason to derive income from the market poses a universal risk to economic security. Social insurance systems require citizens to make mandatory contributions (usually in the form of taxes) to the social insurance program to generate the revenue needed to provide benefits for those individuals in times of need.

Just as ordinary insurance, say fire insurance, spreads the risk of loss from fire among the pool of all those who buy the insurance, social insurance spreads the risk of what FDR called the "hazards and vicissitudes of life" among all citizens. And, just like fire insurance, although not everyone will experience a "fire," the loss insured against, the fact that millions of other citizens have contributed to support the social insurance program will guarantee that resources are available to those who do experience a loss. Because individuals cannot predict with certainty whether they might lose their ability to earn a living in the marketplace due to unforeseeable circumstances, all are served by participating in the system, although some individuals ultimately will derive more benefits from the system than others. In the case of social insurance pensions, the loss insured against is the possibility that an individual will outlive both the ability to work and one's life savings. Contributions to a social insurance pension system guarantee that those who live to a ripe old age will receive at least some income until the end of their lives. While in such a system those who die young will receive less in pension payments than those who live longer, all benefit, since none of us know for sure how long we might live.

For social insurance to work best it needs to be universal and mandatory; that is, all citizens must participate and none can be allowed to opt out. Allowing voluntary participation in social insurance programs leads to a phenomenon economists call "adverse selection." This is a problem that bedevils private insurance as well. Insurance works best if the pool of individuals paying insurance premiums is large and if many who pay premiums never experience a loss. If, for example, there is a large pool of people who buy fire insurance, most of whom never collect on their policies, then the fire insurance company will have ample funds to cover the losses of those who do have fires, and premiums can be kept low. If, however, the only people who buy insurance are those who are careless with matches, then the insurance company will have to charge very high premiums to generate enough funds for the large number of policyholders who will need to collect on their policies. Adverse selection problems arise when purchasing insurance is voluntary, because those individuals who guess that they are most likely to need the insurance—people who are careless with matches—are most likely to buy it, while those who know they are careful with fire—those not likely to need the insurance—will opt not to buy it. Although individuals cannot predict with certainty whether they will need to collect on any type of insurance, they are good enough at estimating the probability of such a need to make adverse selection a real problem for the insurance business. In the case of social insurance, voluntary participation would allow individuals who expected to die young, to have a small chance to be unemployed, or to be wealthy enough to handle misfortune on their own to opt out, leaving only the poor, the long lived, and the marginally employed in the program. Universal mandatory participation prevents adverse selection and generates ample revenue to provide benefits without imposing exorbitant contributions on individuals.

But why is social insurance needed to protect individuals from failure in the marketplace? Should not people be expected to protect themselves, either through private insurance or saving for a "rainy day"? Proponents of social insurance give two basic reasons why individuals are unlikely to protect themselves from "the hazards and vicissitudes" of life on their own. First, many workers fail to earn sufficient income to save an adequate cushion against misfortune. While good public policy ought to encourage citizens to save for their individual needs, in practice, given the unequal distribution of incomes, some will be unable to save enough. The pooled savings available in a social insurance program compensate for the unequal distribution of the ability to save. Second, even for those with higher incomes and a larger capacity to save, a catastrophic loss might exhaust even a large pool of individual savings. The experience of many well-off individuals who lost their fortunes in the stock market crash of 1929 or high-paying jobs when the factories closed proved that no one is immune to economic catastrophe. This might have been why

Roosevelt found ample support for the idea of social insurance proposed in the Social Security Act of 1935.

The Old Age Assistance title of this act, creating what came to be known as the Social Security program, reflected the essential elements of this social insurance model. First, Social Security pensions were to be financed from payroll tax "contributions" (initially 2 percent of the first $3,000 of income—half paid by the employee and half by the employer) to create accumulations in a trust fund to cover eventual benefits. Covered employees would begin paying taxes in 1937 and no benefits would be paid until 1942, allowing a substantial reserve fund, invested in Treasury bonds, to finance the initial benefits. Because the number of beneficiaries in the early years would be small in relation to tax-paying contributors, and because the legislation provided for gradual tax increases as the number of beneficiaries grew, the fund would easily accumulate reserves needed to cover all benefits far into the future. The legislation projected accumulating a reserve fund of $47 billion by 1980—a fantastically large sum in 1935.[7] Second, access to Social Security benefits was limited to those workers who contributed to the system and this, as envisioned in 1935, would be only a portion of the workforce. While falling short of the social insurance ideal of universal mandatory coverage, the half of the

IDA FULLER, WHO RECEIVED THE FIRST SOCIAL SECURITY CHECK IN THE EARLY 1940S—BASED ON A CONTRIBUTION OF $22—RECEIVED BENEFITS UNTIL SHE DIED, AT AGE 100, IN 1975.

workforce that was covered provided a large enough pool to allow good benefits based on very low contributions. Current retirees before 1937 who had not paid into the system would not be eligible; those retiring in 1942 and collecting the first benefits would have built up five years of contributions. The agricultural workers, domestics, and the self-employed excluded in the initial legislation would be incorporated into it in later years. Importantly, participation was compulsory for covered workers and their employers, avoiding any adverse selection issues.[8]

Finally, the program created a legal entitlement to a Social Security pension for covered workers with benefits defined independently of contributions built up by individual workers. Unlike private insurance annuities, which calculate benefits based on balances in individual accounts, Social Security would pay benefits based on a congressionally determined formula. Although this formula related pension benefit levels to wages at retirement—higher-paid workers received higher dollar benefits—it actually benefited, as it still does, lower-wage workers, who could receive a higher proportion of their preretirement wage than their more affluent counterparts. This commitment to "benefit adequacy" ensured that Social Security would have a mildly redistributive impact on the overall income of beneficiaries.[9]

As enacted in 1935, the Old Age Assistance program possessed the central elements that would ensure its popularity in later years. Its social insurance structure guaranteed that it would never be equated with welfare. In making their payroll contributions to the program, workers gained a sense of justified entitlement to their subsequent Social Security retirement checks. Roosevelt, consummate politician that he was, realized the political importance of the social insurance structure from the beginning. As he said to a reporter questioning the regressive nature of the payroll tax in 1935:

> I guess you're right on the economics, but those taxes were never a problem of economics. They are politics all the way through. We put those payroll contributions there so as to give the contributors a legal, moral, and political right to collect their pensions. . . . With those taxes in there, no damn politician can ever scrap my social security program.[10]

And "no damn politician" in the following seventy-plus years dared try, until President George W. Bush proposed his privatization scheme in 2005.

While the basic structure of Social Security was already in place in 1935, Congress found itself revisiting the program's financing even before any benefits were paid. The problem was the rapid accumulation of reserves in the Social Security Trust Fund as payroll contributions began in 1937. Originally the fund had been conceived like any other pension fund—a prudent reserve in anticipation of future obligations. Yet with millions of workers and their employers contributing to the fund, it soon became large enough to cause anxiety among both liberal Democrats and conservative Republicans. Democrats worried about the negative impact of the fund on economic expansion, as billions of dollars were pulled out of the economy into the Social Security Trust Fund. Some economists would attribute the start of Social Security tax payments as a contributing factor to the severe economic recession of 1938. For their part, Republicans grew alarmed about the federal government accumulating such a large pool of financial capital and its implications for government control of the private economy or as a spur to wasteful government spending. For both parties the solution to the problem lay in switching from a system of benefits financed from accumulated reserves in the Social Security Trust Fund to a "pay as you go" system.

In 1939, Congress amended the Social Security Act to eliminate the reserve fund. The way to do this was to accelerate disbursements from the fund through moving forward the start of benefit payments and expanding the number of beneficiaries. The changes included distributing the first checks in 1940 rather than 1942 and creating a new entitlement for "survivors," the children and spouses of Social Security contributors.[11] Henceforth, Social Security would be financed on a "pay as you go" basis, with most Social Security revenues collected in a given year being paid out immediately to existing beneficiaries. Not until the 1980s would the idea of accumulations in a trust fund return as a part of the program.

For the next three decades, Congress found expanding the number of eligible beneficiaries and raising benefit levels as pleasant solutions to the "problem" of excess revenues for existing beneficiaries. Favorable demographics—a large number of paying workers for each beneficiary—plus robust economic growth facilitated the process. Throughout the 1950s and 1960s, biennial increases in Social Security benefits just prior to congressional elections became routine. By the 1960s, Congress was able to raise retirement benefit levels sufficiently to protect even the lowest elderly wage earners from poverty in retirement. With only very small increases in the Social Security tax, Social Security benefits easily outpaced inflation and reflected seniors' rising expectations about the living standards of their retirement.[12]

Social Security's happy days came to a screeching halt amid the economic slowdown of the 1970s. The severe recessions and high inflation of the decade had the combined effect of both reducing revenues and increasing costs to the program. With slow economic growth, workers were paying less into the program. At the same time, the introduction of an annual "cost of living adjustment" (COLA) in the program in the late 1960s, intended to keep benefits from eroding with inflation, caused program costs to skyrocket as inflation rose dramatically in the 1970s. (Flaws in the COLA formula actually caused Social Security benefits to rise faster than inflation.) Compounding these economic woes was the natural erosion of the favorable demographic conditions in the program. There were now only about four workers paying into the program for each beneficiary, compared to the comfortable 14:1 ratio of the 1950s.[13] By the end of the decade, Social Security experts projected that, without substantial tax increases and benefit reductions, Social Security revenues would be insufficient to pay all benefit obligations early in the 1980s. As Ronald Reagan assumed the presidency in 1980, a real Social Security crisis was at hand.

In 1982, nervous about the "third rail" reputation of Social Security, President Reagan reached an agreement with Democratic congressional leaders to appoint a Social Security Commission, chaired by Alan Greenspan, to formulate a solution to the existing crisis. After complex and difficult negotiations, the commission produced recommendations substantially enacted by Congress in 1983.[14] This reform constituted the most substantial changes in Social Security in three decades, but they produced primarily incremental adjustments without any substantial alteration in the structure of the program. On the benefit side, future costs were reduced through modifications in the COLA formula and a gradual increase in the retirement age from 65 to 67 in the next century. The most meaningful changes came on the revenue side, as a formula for gradual but large increases in both tax rates and the minimal taxable income were provided for into the next century. These latter increases were substantial enough to significantly modify the "pay as you go" structure that had prevailed since the 1940s. For the first time since 1939, Social Security contributions would exceed benefit payments into the twenty-first century. The purpose was to build up large trust fund assets that could be drawn upon, beginning around 2013, to cover the projected costs of the retirement of the baby boom generation. The commission reforms provided, in effect, for baby boomers to "save," through higher Social Security contributions, for their own retirements.

Current Status of Social Security

Social Security has more than fulfilled the vision of its founders in the 1930s. Thanks to the program, most elderly Americans have the security in retirement envisioned in the original legislation. Due to the expansions in program eligibility enacted in the 1950s, about 91 percent of Americans over age 65 receive a monthly Social Security check.[15] In addition to these thirty-three million elderly Social Security recipients, another fourteen million people, disabled workers and the survivors of deceased workers, receive benefits. Social Security provides substantial income support to Americans over age 65 with about two-thirds receiving half their income from the program.[16] For lower-income seniors, those in the bottom two-fifths of the income distribution, Social Security supplies closer to two-thirds of total income. Yet despite its size, the program operates quite efficiently spending only 1 percent of its total budget on administration, compared to the 10 to 15 percent administrative costs of most private insurance companies.[17]

As mentioned in the previous section, Social Security has been financed on a "pay as you go" basis since it first began paying benefits, meaning that most payroll taxes collected from current workers are spent immediately to cover benefit costs. In 2005, workers paid a 6.2 percent flat tax on up to $90,000 of their wages, with their employers paying an equal amount.[18] Since the mid-1980s, these payroll tax receipts have provided more than needed to cover immediate costs, allowing the surplus to be put in the trust fund. Moneys in this fund are invested in U.S. government securities to prepare for the higher costs of baby boomer retirements in the first half of the twenty-first century.

The amount of monthly benefits a worker earns in retirement is calculated from an average of the highest thirty-five years' wages. Workers receiving a higher wage during this period get a higher monthly check. For example, in 2003, low-earning workers received $701 per month upon retiring at age 65, while maximum earners received $1,721.[19] (Workers who opt to begin receiving benefits when first eligible at age 62 receive a slightly smaller amount.) Unlike most private annuities, these payments are adjusted annually to keep pace with inflation thanks to the COLA mentioned above. Although higher lifetime earners receive larger monthly checks, the Social Security benefit formula replaces a much higher percentage of preretirement income for lower-wage workers than high earners. In 2004, Social Security replaced 84.8 percent of a low-wage earner's income, compared to only 44.6 percent for a maximum-wage earner.[20] The higher replacement rate for lower-wage workers modestly redistributes income from the rich to the poor, reducing income inequality among elderly Americans. This redistribution has made Social Security the United States' most effective antipoverty program to date. Thanks to Social Security, poverty among Americans over age 65, a group most likely to be poor in the 1930s, has become relatively rare. As recently as 1959, over one-third of elderly Americans earned incomes below the poverty level; today less than 10 percent do so.[21] The Social Security Administration estimates that the program keeps about 40 percent of seniors out of poverty.

Is Social Security Going Bankrupt? Despite the historic success of Social Security, recent years' media reports on the program have focused less on its past success and more on anxiety about its future. Headlines referring to impending "insolvency" or "bankruptcy" create the impression that Social Security cannot be sustained as currently constituted. Scholarly and popular books fuel this perception through references to an impending "generational crisis" or the dangers of the "graying" of America.[22] Libertarians, who (as we shall see) want to replace Social Security with a privatized pension system, have fueled this discussion with numerous publications describing the program's impending doom.[23] President Bush played on this perception of a Social Security crisis in his own proposal in 2005 to introduce private accounts into the program. Not surprisingly, many Americans view Social Security's future to be "insecure," and young people worry that the program's benefits will "not be there for them."

The perceptions of financial difficulty in Social Security's future stem from the reality of an aging U.S. population. Under the "pay as you go" design, as

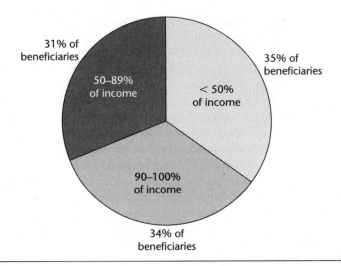

Figure 4-1 PERCENT OF ELDERLY BENEFICIARY INCOME FROM SOCIAL SECURITY BENEFITS, 2005

SOURCE: "Fiscal Year 2006 Performance and Accountability Report: Overview of the Social Security Administration," November 7, 2006, www.ssa.gov/finance/2006/Overview.pdf (accessed July 6, 2007).

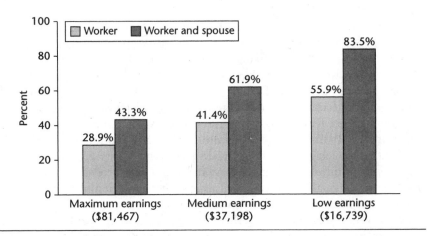

Figure 4-2 PRERETIREMENT EARNINGS REPLACED (WORKERS AGE 65 ENTITLED IN JANUARY 2006)

SOURCE: "Fiscal Year 2006 Performance and Accountability Report: Overview of the Social Security Administration," November 7, 2006, www.ssa.gov/finance/2006/Overview.pdf (accessed July 6, 2007).

the number of workers paying into the system relative to retirees collecting benefits declines, financing the program becomes more difficult. As pointed out earlier, in the early years of Social Security there were many more workers paying into the system than receiving benefits, allowing ample revenue to pay generous benefits at a relatively low cost to each tax payer. Over time this ratio became less favorable. In recent years, about three workers have paid into the system for each beneficiary. According to the Social Security trustees, by about 2030 there will be only about two workers for each beneficiary.[24] It was in anticipation of this demographic reality that the 1983 reform raised taxes to fund the Social Security Trust Fund. How adequate is this fund to cover future Social Security benefits?

Each year the trustees of the Social Security Trust Fund issue a report projecting the future financial health of the Social Security program for the next seventy-five years. Media coverage of these reports focus on the trustees' findings regarding two future dates: the year Social Security will need to draw on the trust fund to cover all its obligations and the year the trust fund will be exhausted. For example, in 2006 the trustees estimated 2017 to be the first year payments from the trust fund would be needed to cover a shortfall in the tax revenues collected that year.[25] Over the next twenty-three years, the trust fund would continue to be drawn upon until it is exhausted in 2040. Although this latter date is often portrayed as the moment of Social Security "bankruptcy," the reality is less dramatic. What the trustees are saying is that in that year, without any more trust fund revenues, projected tax payments will cover only about 75 percent of projected benefit obligations. A 25 percent shortfall in revenues surely suggests a future financial problem, but it does not seem to constitute the crisis suggested in words like "bankruptcy" and "insolvency."

Projecting the future financial health of Social Security over the next seventy-five years requires looking into a very cloudy crystal ball. The trustees' vision depends on educated guesses about the large number of demographic and economic factors that will determine Social Security's financial future. Future revenues depend on the number of workers paying into the system, a function of both fertility rates and immigration, and economic factors such as productivity, average wages, and unemployment. Costs depend on the life expectancy of future beneficiaries and inflation rates. Predictions about what will happen with all these variables over such a long period require gifts of prophecy as much as sound statistical analysis.

Because of the uncertainty of these projections, the trustees make three different projections of Social Security's future based on three different sets of assumptions about future demographic and economic trends. In 2006, for example, under the most optimistic assumptions, the trust fund would never be exhausted and it would easily cover all of Social Security's obligations for the next century. Under its most pessimistic assumptions, the trust fund would be depleted ten years earlier in 2030. The figures normally reported from the reports come from trustee estimates based on their intermediate projections.

Table 4-1 Trustee Estimates of Social Security Trust Fund, 1997–2007

Year of Report	Year Costs Exceed Revenues	Year Trust Fund Exhausted
1997	2012	2029
1998	2013	2032
1999	2014	2034
2000	2015	2037
2001	2016	2038
2002	2017	2041
2003	2018	2042
2004	2018	2042
2005	2017	2041
2006	2017	2040
2007	2017	2041

SOURCE: Annual Reports of the Social Security Trustees 1997–2007, Social Security Administration, http://www.socialsecurity.gov/OACT/TR.

The history of the variation over time in this intermediate projection only underscores the uncertainty of these projections. In the mid-1990s, for example, the trustees' intermediate projection painted a more dire future than today. In 1996, they predicted a need to draw on the trust fund in 2012 and that it would be exhausted in 2029 (see Table 4-1). Better than expected economic performance in the late 1990s dramatically improved Social Security's economic prospects, adding thirteen years to the projected lifetime of the trust fund by 2003. Slower wage growth shaved off two years from that projection by 2006.

Given the uncertainty regarding the assumptions underlying the trustee projections, we must be cautious in using them as justifications for changes in Social Security. Prudent policymakers need to pay attention to the projected future of the trust fund in devising ways to shore up Social Security's financial future. But the projections need to be evaluated in light of the assumptions on which they are based. There will likely come a time sometime in the next four to five decades when Social Security as currently designed will fail to raise sufficient revenue to meet its obligations. No one can say for sure when this will happen and exactly how far revenues will fall short of obligations. To prevent that from happening, policy changes today to modestly increase future program revenues and reduce future obligations are in order. Later in this chapter, I will suggest some modest reforms that should ensure Social Security's future financial health. The financial projections of the trustees, however, do not justify the full-scale privatization of Social Security that libertarians advocate.

Before examining such libertarian proposals, however, one other alarmist doubt about Social Security's financial health relates to the character of the Social Security Trust Fund. The assets in the fund are in the form of Treasury bonds, that is, loans to the federal government. Looked at another way, the Social Security Trust Fund represents the program's ownership of a sizeable portion of the national debt. As is the case with anyone who buys a U.S.

Treasury bond or savings bond, the Social Security Administration depends on the faith and credit of the U.S. government to repay its loan with interest when it comes due. Monies coming into the trust fund are not saved in a piggy bank somewhere; under the unified federal budget, they allow a reduction in the annual deficit (that is, less money needs to be borrowed to cover spending from the financial markets) equal to the size of Social Security payments. Because the federal government has spent this borrowed money to fund its activities, alarmist critics of this arrangement characterize the trust fund as merely a pile of "IOUs" that will never be repaid. In effect, they claim that Congress might repudiate its debt to Social Security when the day comes when the program needs to draw on the trust fund to cover a portion of its obligations.

Such repudiation is not credible. The United States of America has never defaulted on any of its debt obligations in its entire history. If Congress took such a step in regard to its legal obligation to Social Security, it would call into question the entire fiscal integrity of the government, constituting a declaration that U.S. Treasury bonds are worthless. If this happened, individuals and foreign governments holding Treasury bonds would demand immediate payment. Such a declaration of bankruptcy would be unimaginable save in the face of the total collapse of the U.S. economy. Future Social Security beneficiaries need not fear the integrity of the Social Security Trust Fund.

Nor should one regard the use of the trust fund balances to reduce past deficits as somehow a waste of Social Security assets. Social Security surpluses have helped to finance spending that Congress and the president deemed to be in the national interest. Without the trust fund, the federal government would have borrowed more money from the private financial markets by selling its Treasury bonds there and would be obligated to pay that much more principal and interest on those bonds. Instead, the trust funds constitute an overall savings in the government balance sheets that make the federal government's future fiscal capacity.[26] This means that interest costs for future citizens will be lower than they would have been without the trust fund.

Although its integrity can be relied upon, drawing on the trust fund to pay Social Security obligations will place fiscal pressure on the federal government. To cover trust fund obligations, a future Congress and president will need either to borrow additional money, reduce funding from other programs, or raise taxes. Its ability to do so easily will relate to the federal government's overall fiscal soundness. As discussed in chapter 2, overcoming the structural deficit, induced by libertarian-inspired tax cuts, will be critical for the financial stability of Social Security. Future Social Security obligations do represent a claim on future government resources and on U.S. society. Sensible measures to ensure the federal government's future fiscal integrity will be needed to cover Social Security obligations. But obligations to Social Security need to be put into perspective. Those obligations are smaller than other fiscal commitments the federal government has made. For example, projections of Social

Security trustees of currently unfunded obligations to the program over the next seventy-five years amount to about $3.7 trillion. That seems a formidable amount to make up, but it compares favorably to the estimated $11.6 trillion cost of President Bush's tax cuts over the same period, or the $8.1 trillion cost of the recently enacted Medicare prescription drug benefit.[27] Meeting Social Security's obligations will involve policy choices, but these must be made with a mind to other policy obligations and priorities.

The Libertarian Alternative to Social Security: Private Accounts

If libertarians had their way, there would never be anything like Social Security. Any governmentally sponsored pension program contradicts the philosophical commitment to granting individuals control of their own destiny. For purist libertarians, like Milton Friedman, individuals should be free to choose whether to save for retirement or spend their money on more immediate gratification. As he wrote in *Capitalism and Freedom:* "If a man knowingly prefers to live for today, to use his resources for current enjoyment, deliberately choosing a penurious old age, by what right do we prevent him from doing so?"[28] Government-mandated savings for retirement, in whatever form, violate the fundamental libertarian commitment to individual freedom to dispose of one's resources as one sees fit.

Keep in mind that the libertarian commitment to individual liberty to dispose freely of one's assets also assumes that individuals, not government, are the best judge of how to use their resources. Requiring people to save for retirement might prevent some individuals from making use of that income in a way that better serves their individual needs. That might not just involve immediate consumption, as implied in the Friedman quote; it could mean investing in a new business or spending on additional education that might even create more individual wealth than any retirement investment. According to a purist libertarian view, those individuals concerned about retirement security should be free to buy a private insurance policy or annuity, but those with other priorities should not be forced to do so. Coping with Roosevelt's "hazards and vicissitudes of life" should be a matter of personal choice and responsibility, not a shared collective obligation, as the social insurance model assumes. A government pension program, then, violates the libertarian commitment to the free market as well as individual liberty. Government pension programs end up distorting the market and, given the libertarian belief in the superiority of markets, produce a less-efficient economic outcome than letting people freely choose how to use their incomes.

Therefore, the libertarian ideal policy regarding Social Security would be its abolition. Yet more practical-minded libertarians realized years ago that, given the historic success of Social Security, advocating its abolition is a nonstarter. The experience of libertarian-minded politicians, such as Barry Goldwater and

Ronald Reagan, in the 1960s and 1970s with simply suggesting that Social Security be made voluntary made this clear. Goldwater's disastrous presidential campaign in 1964 had suffered from his stance on Social Security. In 1976 Ronald Reagan, running for the Republican presidential nomination, saw his campaign collapse when he made a similar proposal. After nearly half a century of experience with government-guaranteed retirement security, Americans were not about to embrace any policy proposals that seemed to take away that security. By the late 1970s, many libertarians had ceased to advocate their preferred solution but switched to a second-best alternative: changing Social Security from a social insurance program into a program of government-mandated private retirement accounts. The challenge was to convince Americans that such a change was a good idea.

This first step toward meeting this challenge required convincing the public and, more particularly, political elites that the existing Social Security system was in crisis. Beginning in the 1980s and proceeding up to the present, a wave of books and articles has sounded this theme. Dire prognostications about the "graying of America," the "demographic tsunami of the baby boom," and the looming "entitlement" monster claim that future obligations to Social Security beneficiaries cannot be met or can only be met at catastrophic cost to the economy.[29] These analyses find the declining ratio of workers to beneficiaries an insurmountable barrier to the future of the "pay as you go" social insurance model. Besides sounding the alarm about demographic trends, proponents of the Social Security "crisis" interpret the predictions found in annual reports of the Social Security trustees as solid proof of the unsustainability of the program's financing. Both the relatively short-term need to draw on the trust fund to pay benefit obligations and the long-term shortfall in system revenues to meet projected obligations are characterized as predictions of future program "bankruptcy" and "insolvency." Libertarians claim that abandoning the social insurance model in favor of a privatized system of personal accounts is the only way to meet the demographic challenge of entitlement obligations and future financial challenges of the Social Security Trust Fund.

In addition to solving the Social Security "crisis," libertarians claim a system of mandatory private accounts would provide future retirees with a better return on their investment.[30] They point out that Social Security recipients in the past received relatively high benefits while having paid relatively low Social Security taxes. Many paid Social Security taxes only part of their working careers but collected full benefits. Even more recent retirees who paid into the system their whole working lives benefited from the past favorable worker-to-beneficiary ratios allowing high benefits with low tax rates. Now that the system has matured, however, workers can expect an individual return equivalent only to the increase in value of what they paid into the system produced by the growth in real wages and the rate of increase in the working population. One study estimates this rate to be, at best, about 1 to 2 percent annually.[31]

(Because the value of real wages has stagnated since 1973, the real individual rate of return for some wage earners may be negative.) This means today's workers could receive a much better deal investing their Social Security contributions in stocks and bonds. Libertarians make much of historic average annual rate of return on U.S. stocks. For example, between 1926 and 1996, this return, adjusted for inflation, was 7.56 percent.[32] Why not, libertarians ask, allow the young workers of today benefit from this high rate of return through investments in private accounts?

Not only are libertarians concerned about the generational inequity of a declining rate of return in a maturing social insurance system, they object to the many other inequities inherent in social insurance. Because individual benefits are not related directly to contributions, the life circumstances of different individuals result in higher benefits relative to contributions for some than for others. The most obvious relevant life circumstance is longevity; those who die young receive much less in benefits than those who die at a ripe old age. Considered in this light, Social Security redistributes wealth from those unfortunates who either die before they collect any benefits or those who live only a few years after qualifying for benefits to those who live long enough to collect many years of benefits. Libertarians claim this aspect of the system is especially unfair to poor and minority workers who have lower life expectancies on average than more affluent and white workers.[33] At the same time, the benefit formula redistributes from wealthier workers to poorer ones because the preretirement replacement rate is greater for lower-income workers. Libertarians regard these many redistributions as "perverse" deviations from individual equity—treating all individuals the same.[34] A system of private accounts would end these inequities by providing each individual with the full benefit from her individual contributions.

Finally, the most significant flaw in the existing Social Security system from a libertarian perspective is its failure to give workers ownership rights over their future benefits. Since Congress establishes benefit levels through legislation, individuals have no direct legal control over future benefits. Libertarians often cite a 1960 Supreme Court decision, *Fleming v. Nestor,* which ruled that Americans have no individual property right to their Social Security benefits based on their payroll tax contributions.[35] Future benefits depend on the political will of Congress and the president to continue to provide them. Unlike President Roosevelt, libertarians do not trust that the political obligation inherent in Social Security contributions will bind future politicians. Rather than depend on a communal commitment to support the incomes of retirees, libertarians would prefer individual ownership of a private investment account. Moreover, ownership of such an account would permit individuals to bequeath it to their heirs rather than lose their investment at their death as they do under social insurance. Managing an account that they own also would permit individuals to control the adequacy of their own benefit in light of their own individual circumstances.

By the 1990s, this critique of the Social Security system had produced a wide variety of privatization proposals from academics, think tanks, journalists, and politicians.[36] A few of these advocated replacement of the entire existing system with private accounts, but a "transition cost" problem led most privatization proponents to recommend only partial replacement of the current system. Under the "pay as you go" structure of Social Security, shifting current payroll contributions into private accounts would deny the revenue to fund existing benefits. If benefits to current recipients were to be maintained, additional revenue would have to be found to fund those benefits to replace Social Security taxes diverted to private accounts. Even libertarian privatizers were not prepared to eliminate benefits to existing beneficiaries. In fact, libertarian activists always have realized that success of privatization requires guaranteeing the full benefits of existing beneficiaries and soon-to-retire workers who would not be able to accumulate balances in private accounts.[37] This was not just a matter of keeping faith with the commitment of the program, but recognition of the political clout of senior citizens dependent on the existing system. In addition to commitments to retirees, Social Security provides benefits to millions of survivors of contributors and the disabled. To privatize the entire system would require, in effect, doubling its costs for the near future until current retirees and those nearing retirement passed on. To make these transition costs more manageable, privatizers have shifted, in recent years, toward a strategy of partial privatization.

Michael Tanner of the Cato Institute has proposed such a partial privatization, which he calls the "6.2 percent solution."[38] Under his plan, workers would have the option of investing their half, 6.2 percent of covered payroll (employers pay the other 6.2 percent for a total contribution of 12.4 percent), in a private investment account. Those exercising this option would give up any benefits under the existing Social Security program. Current retirees and persons born prior to 1950 would receive full benefits as guaranteed under the current system. The 6.2 percent employer contribution would fund most of the transition cost, according to Tanner, but he recognizes additional monies are likely to be needed—including support from general revenues.[39] Eligible workers opting not to participate in the 6.2 percent plan would pay their full 12.4 percent into the system and receive benefits under current law. However, the formula used to calculate their benefits would not be adjusted, as is presently the case, to reflect increases in average wages over time but adjusted according to price inflation. Since increases in average wages reflect increases in the standard of living, the real value of Social Security benefits for these workers would decline over time. (This would erode over time the adequacy of Social Security benefits to replace as much of preretirement income—see below for a more complete discussion of similar proposals in the Bush plan.) In addition, benefits for younger workers "would gradually be adjusted to a level sustainable under the current level of payroll taxation," suggesting further erosion of future benefits to those remaining in the Social Security program as workers opting into the 6.2 plan denied the system their taxes.[40] Eventually, however, existing Social Security would be phased out as new workers entering the workforce would be required to join the 6.2 percent plan.[41] (Tanner does not detail the devastating impact this last measure will have on those current workers who opt to stay in conventional Social Security. If no new workers are allowed to enter Social Security, then their 6.2 percent contributions are not available, under the "pay as you go" system to support benefits of existing retirees. This suggests that benefits in the existing system, if it must operate, as Tanner says, out of available revenues, would be reduced drastically. From this perspective, the 6.2 percent option does not seem voluntary even for current workers who can look forward to only a very meager Social Security benefit if they do not opt for the private account.)

Individuals participating in the 6.2 percent plan would have a variety of investment options with various levels of risk—although workers would need to accumulate assets up to some "trigger" level before being allowed to participate in riskier options. Upon retirement, workers would have three options for disposing of the account assets. First, they could purchase a lifetime annuity with the entire amount. Second, they could take programmed withdrawals over a period of time based on twice their average life expectancy. Any funds remaining at death could be left to heirs. Finally, they could take a portion of their account in a lump sum, to be used any way they wished, but only after purchasing an annuity equal to at least 120 percent of poverty level. This latter requirement presumably was intended to prevent anyone from becoming destitute through exhausting their retirement nest egg before death. Of course, Tanner realizes that under his plan there might be some individuals whose retirement account, because of poor investment performance, may be insufficient to purchase an annuity at 120 percent of the poverty level. For those unfortunates, he recommends a "safety net" funded from general revenues to allow the purchase of the annuity.[42]

Tanner claims that his plan would correct all the defects of the current Social Security system. It would provide workers ownership of a retirement fund to ensure the most security in old age. Most workers, according to Tanner, would realize benefits greater than under the current system due to the superior rate of return of market investments. Inequities linked to the different life expectancies of different individuals would be eliminated because everyone would realize individually all the benefits of their own individual contributions. Finally, he claims that his plan would "restore Social Security to long-term and sustainable solvency."[43]

George W. Bush's proposal for private accounts in Social Security, like the Tanner proposal, aims to divert a portion of Social Security contributions from current workers into private accounts while maintaining some benefits from the existing system.[44] Like the Tanner proposal, only workers born after 1950 would be eligible to invest in private accounts; existing retirees and those born prior to 1950 would continue in the existing system. Rather than diverting 6.2 percent, the Bush plan calls for only 4 percent of the total 12.4 percent of payroll contributions being used to set up a private account. Participation in the plan would also be voluntary; workers could opt to continue paying their full contribution into the current system and receive their full, legally entitled benefit upon retirement (although, as we shall see below, that benefit would be lower than under existing law).

Unlike the Tanner proposal, the Bush plan provides a more explicit account of how the future Social Security benefits of someone opting to join the plan would be affected.[45] To join, one would agree to forego a portion of the future legally defined benefit equivalent to the value of the funds invested in the account assuming a 3 percent (inflation-adjusted) rate of return. The reduction in each month's Social Security check would be based on the monthly income this amount would earn over an individual's expected lifetime (as determined from average life expectancy data). An illustration can clarify how this would work. Suppose Jane Jones, under the existing Social Security system, is entitled to a $2,000 per month benefit upon retirement. Over her working life she has contributed enough money that if, at a 3 percent rate of return, she purchased a lifetime annuity it would provide $1,000 per month. Under the Bush plan, her Social Security benefit would then be reduced by $1,000 and replaced with the funds from her private account. As this example shows, participants in the Bush plan would break even, that is, earn no more than under the existing Social Security program, if they earned only a 3 percent return. (The plan design picks the 3 percent figure because that is the average future return the Social Security trustees project for the Treasury bond investments in the trust fund. Private account participants are required, in effect, to pay back in the form of reduced benefits the cost to the trust fund of the withdrawals for their private accounts.)

The attraction of private accounts is the possibility that some participants will earn higher rates of return, so that, even covering the reduction in their Social Security benefit, they would have funds left over from their account. Participants could use these left-over funds, not needed to make up the reduction in the Social Security benefit, in any way they pleased—including leaving them to heirs. The amount left over would depend on the success of their investments. Bush administration supporters have claimed that the average rate of return for participants is likely to be at least 4.6 percent, implying that workers "on average" would end up with more cash than under the existing program.[46] No matter how workers fared on average, however, there undoubtedly would be some whose private account would earn less than a 3 percent return and, in that case, they end up receiving a lower benefit than they would have under the existing system. This is the risk inherent in the Bush plan, as in any privatization plan. Unlike the social insurance model of Social Security, which guarantees individuals a specific benefit upon retirement, the Bush plan, even though it only partially privatizes the program,

"IF HE SAYS WE'LL BE WELCOMED WITH CANDY
AND FLOWERS, I'M OUTTA HERE!"

Source: © 2005, R. J. Matson. All Rights Reserved.

removes that guarantee and links future benefits to the investment perfor-mance of private accounts.

Concerned that this increased risk might prove politically unpalatable, the Bush administration has promised to restrict investment choices for those par-ticipating in the program to a small number of well-regulated funds. These funds would minimize investment risk in order to ensure that most workers would avoid major losses in their investments. While this approach is under-standable as a means of preventing participants from suffering from the con-sequence of unwise investments, it is at odds with the promises of ownership and control that are supposed to be the advantages of a privatized system.

Unlike Tanner, who admits that his partial privatization plan is a step toward eliminating Social Security altogether, the Bush administration has taken pains to emphasize the voluntary and supplementary character of its plan. Afraid of being seen as undermining Social Security, it calls its plan Social Security reform and a way to save the program. Despite these claims, adopt-ing Bush's plan would create a political dynamic leading to the long-term "unraveling" of Social Security.[47] As we have seen, although participation in private accounts is voluntary, the reduction in future benefits for those who would opt not to participate creates an incentive to open a private account in hopes of recouping the lost future income. Those participants, probably more affluent, savvy investors, will see their private accounts grow and seek to expand the proportion of their contribution available for the private accounts. They would probably have sufficient influence with future politicians to succeed. With even more funds diverted from Social Security, additional reduction in planned benefits would be needed, only increasing dependence of workers on their private accounts. Soon, those workers looking more to their private accounts than the ever-diminishing Social Security benefit would come to resent paying taxes to cover "transition costs" or to support the existing system in any way. More affluent workers would want to withdraw from the system altogether, leaving it a program for the poor and bringing an end to the existence of Social Security as a universal system of social insurance. In evaluating the merits of even partial privatization of Social Security, we must consider the real stakes. Do the promises of libertarians merit abandoning a social insurance system that has worked well for a new world of government-mandated private retirement accounts?

Do Private Accounts Achieve the Goals Libertarians Seek?

As we have seen, libertarians claim that we need to privatize Social Security in order to solve the Social Security "crisis," provide retirees a better rate of return on their Social Security contributions, eliminate "perverse" inequities in the system that provide differential benefits based on life circumstances, and provide retirees ownership of their retirement assets. Would a shift to private retirement accounts achieve these goals?

Those who claim Social Security is in crisis typically cite the reports on the status of the trust fund described above to justify their claim. If the impact of Social Security privatization on the "solvency" of Social Security over the seventy-five-year period tracked in these reports is the measure, then creating private accounts makes the problem worse, not better. Diverting a portion of Social Security contributions to private accounts makes them unavailable to pay obligations to current beneficiaries. But since under the "pay as you go" system these contributions are needed to finance the system, unless you substantially reduce benefits to current retirees—something both the Bush and Tanner plans vow not to do—the shortfalls to the trust fund come sooner than under the current system. This transition cost problem increases financial pressure on the trust fund and creates a huge fiscal headache for the federal budget rather than provides relief. For example, according to the Center for Budget and Policy Priorities, if workers diverted 4 percent of their Social Security contributions to private accounts, using the assumptions contained in the 2005 Trustees Report, the trust fund would be exhausted in 2030, not 2047.[48] For those concerned about the fiscal impact of meeting trust fund obligations to beneficiaries when they are needed, that day of reckoning comes sooner— 2011 instead of 2017, under the Bush plan—and the problem is greater, as funds will have to be found to cover both existing trust fund obligations and the increased losses from the diversion of contributions to private accounts. Creating private accounts alone, as even the Bush administration admitted, would do nothing to solve the financial problems facing the trust fund.[49]

Because private accounts alone do not solve the financial problems of Social Security, privatization proposals tend to insert future benefit reductions in Social Security as a means of "solving" the problem. In the Tanner proposal described above, substantial reductions in promised benefits are presumed that may or may not be made up by private account investments. In the initial version of its private account proposal released in February 2005, the Bush administration offered no real solution to the Social Security financing problem, but under pressure to show some impact, by spring, had linked its proposal to the idea of "progressive price indexing."[50] Rather than benefits being adjusted to increases in average wages in calculating a worker's initial benefit, as is done under the current system, future benefits would be linked to price inflation. No longer would calculation of workers' initial benefits aim to replace a certain portion of preretirement earnings—ensuring an adequate income in retirement. The practical impact of this proposal is to gradually reduce future Social Security benefits on a sliding scale, with the benefits of wealthier workers shrinking faster than those of lower-wage workers. This would make up about a quarter of the projected seventy-five-year shortfall in Social Security, but at the cost of preventing the Social Security checks of future retirees from keeping up with improvements in the standard of living.[51] The rate of return on private accounts would have to be very good indeed to make up for these reductions in guaranteed Social Security benefits.

This, of course, is the second promise of private account proponents—that workers will realize such a better rate of return from private accounts that they will have no need for a guaranteed Social Security benefit. It is certainly true that some individuals might earn much more through market investments of their Social Security contributions than from the benefits they will receive from the program. Also, the average rate of return from Social Security has declined over time as the program has matured. (Mrs. Ida Fuller, Social Security's first beneficiary, earned $20,000 in benefits over her lifetime, after paying only $22 in contributions—that is a remarkable rate of return!) Workers in this century, when there will be a 2:1 worker-to-beneficiary ratio, can never match the average rate of return from Social Security that their grandparents earned. Proponents of privatization, however, exaggerate when they imply that everyone would earn a higher rate of return investing in private accounts. Risks inherent in market investments guarantee that there will be great variation in the rate of investment return among different individuals. Unlike the children of Lake Wobegon, not all private accounts will perform "above average" or even "average."

In promoting private accounts, libertarians trumpet the higher average historical returns from stock markets and downplay the risks associated with stock investing. Even if the "average" rate of return in private investment accounts over the next seventy-five years matched or exceeded past stock performance, there is no guarantee that every private account, or even most, would earn this average. Keep in mind that averages are the sum of many individual measurements that can vary among themselves radically and can be influenced dramatically by very high or low amounts at the extremes of the distribution. Bill Gates walks into any room and the *average* income in the room grows astronomically! Variations in individual returns in stock investing are quite high. Even if future average rates of return in private retirement accounts are very high, there will still be many individuals who earn well below that average.

We can imagine various specific ways that some individuals might earn well below average returns. First, some individuals will make poor or unlucky investment choices, no matter what safeguards are provided in privatization programs. Even the most knowledgeable and experienced investors often incur large losses because of bad investment decisions. We can safely assume that among the millions who would invest in private retirement accounts, there will be many bad choices that produce investment losses. Second, the eventual rate of return realized from investments in private accounts depends greatly on the timing of individual retirements. The value of stocks and bonds fluctuate over time, sometimes market prices can rise rapidly and at other times they can crash—that is what references to "bull" and "bear" markets mean. Those account holders who are lucky enough to retire when the bulls are running in the markets are quite likely to earn a high rate of return and will be able to purchase a large annuity for a comfortable retirement. Unfortunates who retire in a bear market will earn a below average market return and have to accept lower incomes. Third, real rates of return from private accounts must take into account the transition cost problem. The same workers who presumably in the libertarian vision will be earning good rates of return in their private accounts will have to pay the taxes to cover the transition costs of shifting from the current system. The costs to individuals of this transition subtracted from any gains in the return to private accounts constitute the real rate of return individuals will receive.[52] Finally, administrative costs associated with managing private accounts can consume a large percentage of the accounts, particularly for smaller accounts. In both Chile and Great Britain, two countries that have experience with private retirement accounts, these costs have been a factor in reducing significantly the rate of return earned by low-wage workers.[53]

Because of concern for these risks of market investments, privatization proposals often include restrictions on investment choices and regulation of administrative costs to lower individual risk. The Bush plan, as described above, is replete with assurances that account regulation will reduce risk. For example, the plan calls for placing most accounts in "lifecycle portfolios" that shift account allocations from riskier stock investments to safer bond investments as workers approach retirement. While such a strategy can reduce risk, it cannot eliminate it (investments in bonds carry risks too). No matter how market investments are structured, they cannot guarantee the average rate of return libertarians promise as a reward for shifting from social insurance to a system of private retirement accounts. Paradoxically, in trying to compensate for market risk, libertarian plans end up undermining one of the virtues they claim for privatization—individual control over personal accounts!

The citation of average market rate of return during the last half of the twentieth century as proof that most workers would gain such returns from privatization assumes past performance predicts future performance. Many economists doubt this will be the case over the next several decades.[54] Slower economic growth in the first half of the twenty-first century, which causes the Social Security trustees to project shortfalls in trust fund financing, also would have a negative impact on stock market performance. Libertarians seem to be claiming that Social Security must be privatized because of inadequate financing stemming from a slowdown in growth, but that same slowdown would adversely affect private markets. If this were to happen, the promised average high rate of return could never be realized. Some analysts believe that the creation of millions of private accounts invested in stocks itself would depress future returns. Millions of new investors entering the markets would bid up stock prices, requiring these investors to buy at inflated prices. Those owning stocks at the time would realize windfall returns, but those buying stocks to invest in their retirements would realize lower returns because they entered the market when its prices were inflated. Of course, no one knows for sure how stock markets will perform in the future (just as no one knows for sure whether the Social Security Trust Fund will ever be exhausted), but prudent people should not count on future market returns to equal past returns. This is the view of Bush's former chief economic adviser, N. Gregory Mankiw, who wrote in 1999: "We live in the world's richest country, at the end of the most prosperous century ever, it should come as no surprise that the market has done so well. The future may give us a similarly lucky draw, but let's not count on it."[55]

Even if we were to believe libertarian claims of high average rates of return in private investment accounts, we should reject this argument as a rationale for Social Security privatization. To evaluate Social Security in comparison to private retirement accounts in terms of rate of return involves what logicians call a category mistake: it places Social Security in the category of "personal retirement investment," where it clearly does not belong. Contributions to Social Security are not investments in a retirement account; they are insurance premiums. I make them not to realize future wealth, but to guarantee a minimal level of income no matter how long I might live, in case I become disabled, and for my survivors if I die. To contribute to Social Security in expectation of high rates of return would be as foolish as expecting a high rate of return from my homeowner's insurance. Although I have realized "returns" occasionally from my homeowner's insurance premiums, my rate of return is thankfully quite low: I have never experienced a disaster that would deliver a better return. Likewise, I hope never to collect on the Social Security disability benefit or that my survivors collect my survivors' benefit, even though if such collections were made my "rate of return" on contributions would go up.

And, although I do expect to collect a retirement benefit one day, I am happy for a benefit that will be much lower than income I might have earned investing my contributions in the stock market. That is because the Social Security benefit is guaranteed while my stock market investments, no matter how potentially lucrative, are not. (This is something my retirement financial adviser points out continually. My "three-legged stool" in my retirement portfolio includes two potentially large but unstable legs: my savings and my retirement pension investments and one small but solid Social Security leg.) This Social Security guarantee to a minimal income in retirement may be quite valuable if I live to a ripe old age and outlive the income from my investments with high rates of return. Because Social Security benefits are adjusted to inflation, I can be sure they will remain adequate to meet my minimal needs no matter how long I live, something no private annuity can promise. If we keep in mind that Social Security is insurance, not a retirement investment account, it is a "good deal," even if it has a low "rate of return."

The libertarian complaint that Social Security treats individuals inequitably, by which they mean individuals in different circumstances benefit differently from the program, collapses if we think of the Social Security as insurance rather than as a retirement investment. Groups with lower-than-average life spans such as lower-income workers and minorities (or smokers, those with high cholesterol or a family history of heart disease, couch potatoes, and people who ride motorcycles without helmets) will realize, as a group, fewer Social Security benefits than those with greater life expectancies. But even within these high mortality groups, there are particular individuals who will defy the odds and live to a ripe old age. Because life expectancy is uncertain at the individual level, insuring against the "hazard" of outliving one's assets makes sense even for members of groups with lower life expectancies. The same argument applies to high-income earners who reap a lower return on their Social Security contributions than lower-income workers. When I join the Social Security system, I cannot be sure what my income level will be at retirement, so the redistribution in the system insures everyone against the "hazard" of ending up poor. (Libertarian hand-wringing over Social Security's discrimination against minorities and the poor seems perverse, since they tend to oppose any government-sponsored efforts to improve the access of these groups to better health care that might extend their life expectancies. (See the next chapter.))

Finally, the libertarian argument about ownership and control of one's retirement assets also reflects a fundamental misunderstanding and distrust of social insurance. Changing Social Security from a social insurance program into a system of private retirement accounts would give individuals ownership of their future retirement, yet it also shifts all the risks of that future retirement to individuals instead of allowing them to share that risk with their fellow citizens. (The extent to which individuals actually would *control* their retirement accounts depends on the extent of investment choice regulation to lessen risk.) Because they distrust government and the outcomes of democratic processes, libertarians prefer individual ownership to dependency on the collective choices of future political leaders. They are correct when they say that future Social Security beneficiaries depend on the willingness of future political leaders to continue to provide their benefits.

The future of the program does require confidence that the political commitment to provide benefits will be fulfilled. Yet there is every reason to expect that commitment to be maintained as it has been for the past sixty years. As long as the United States remains a democracy, politicians are likely to be quite responsive to citizen demands to protect Social Security. Because the program is the special concern of senior citizens, one can expect political support for it to increase as the size of this most politically active group of citizens as a proportion of the population increases over the next few years. Of course, as will be discussed in more detail below, modifications to Social Security may be required so that its commitments can be met. But these can occur while protecting the basic social insurance framework upon which it rests. Furthermore, while libertarians voice distrust at relying on a political commitment to Social Security, they fail to recognize that even the ownership of private accounts would have to rely on such a commitment. If U.S. politicians would ever take such drastic steps as repudiating promised benefits to Social Security recipients or to fulfilling the financial obligations of the Social Security Trust Fund, then other fundamental political commitments would be at risk. Only a severe political, economic, and social crisis could threaten the integrity of Social Security. If a crisis that severe were to occur, even commitments libertarians hold dear, such as the protection of private property ownership, likely would be called into question. Libertarian distrust of the political commitment to uphold Social Security stems from their inability to recognize, as was discussed in this book's introduction, how the entire political order relies on a collective political commitment.

Why Americans Especially Need Social Insurance for Retirement Today

Changing Social Security from a social insurance program to a system of individual retirement accounts would shift the risks of life to individuals at a time when Americans already bear increasing uncertainty and risk in their lives.[56] In a globalizing economy, most Americans find their jobs less secure and their incomes increasingly unstable. The time of single-family breadwinner keeping a good, well-paying job for a lifetime seems as quaint as reruns of *Leave It to Beaver*. In an era of stagnant wages, two wage earners often working multiple jobs has become the method most families employ to maintain a middle-class standard of living. As factories close or move off-shore, many workers must retool and find employment in new jobs. A contemporary cliché is the admonition to young people that they must prepare to change careers multiple times over their working lives. Amidst all this employment uncertainty, employment benefits, such as health insurance or a company pension, that once were the hallmark of a good job are no longer guaranteed. The costs of employer-provided benefits, for those workers lucky enough to retain them, have been shifted more and more to the workers themselves.

This shift in cost and risk characterizes the transformation in employer-provided retirement pensions over the last three decades. During World War II, many of the country's largest employers began offering their employees retirement pension benefits.[57] This meant that workers in these firms could expect in retirement, not only their guaranteed Social Security pension, but also a check from their employer's pension fund. While never more than about one half of all U.S. workers benefited from employer pensions, they did represent a significant national commitment to enhanced retirement security for millions of Americans. A good job with a good pension remained a realizable goal for many working-class people well into the 1980s.

These employer pensions provided secure retirement incomes because they were *defined-benefit* pensions. That is, upon retirement, based upon participation in an employer's retirement plan, retiring workers were provided a fixed monthly income as defined by their plan. Most plans covered workers until their death, and many included coverage for surviving spouses. Beginning in the late 1970s, employers began to change the character of their pensions.[58] In 1978, Congress added a new section 401(k) to the tax code authorizing employers to allow their employees to contribute untaxed dollars, along with employer-matching funds, into a retirement investment fund; thus the *defined-contribution* pension was born. Under this type of retirement plan, employers would no longer be responsible for supporting retirees' incomes upon retirement as in defined-benefit plans. At retirement, employees realize whatever income they have accumulated in their individual 401(k) account; they now bear the full risk of their employer-provided pension. Throughout the 1980s and 1990s, in order to escape themselves the burden and risk of defined-benefit pensions, most corporations substituted defined-contribution 401(k) plans for defined-benefit plans. Today, only about 20 percent of private sector workers continue to participate in traditional defined-benefits, and these are scheduled to disappear over the next decade.[59]

Unlike the pensions of their fathers and grandfathers, a good employer-based pension for a young worker today means an opportunity to invest in a private retirement account. As with the promised private Social Security accounts described above, this young worker owns her 401(k) account, has the ability—dependent on the rules of the employer's plan—to direct how it is invested, and realize all the income it earns for her retirement. She also bears the risk of her investments and the possibility they will fail to provide adequate income in retirement. Given the risks they face in their employer-based pensions, keeping Social Security's structure as a social insurance program providing a guaranteed minimal income would seem a good idea. The changes libertarians advocate in Social Security would replicate what has already happened in the private sector. Shifting retirement income risk from the Social Security system to individuals in private retirement accounts seems an especially bad deal for young workers already shouldering the individual risk of their 401(k) retirement plans.

Conclusion: Ensuring Social Insurance Protection for Future Retirees

Americans should reject the libertarian illusion that a system of government-mandated private retirement accounts would provide a better deal than Social Security. Social insurance protection in retirement, in cases of disability, and for survivors has been the country's most successful domestic policy initiative of the past century. Today the elderly in the United States have more income security, less poverty, and more fulfilling lives than would be possible without Social Security. These benefits should not be abandoned on the basis of libertarian promises about the superiority of individual ownership or higher rates of return. As we have seen, the promise of higher rates of return for some in a privatized system requires workers to assume individually the total risk of earning an adequate income in retirement. The only guarantee in this system is that millions of workers will end up with too little to provide a minimally adequate income in retirement. Private accounts do offer the chance that some individuals will earn substantial incomes from their accounts but at the risk that poor market performance will leave them with too little money for a comfortable retirement.

The most important reason for rejecting this libertarian illusion is that the Social Security "crisis" that they conjure as the reason for abandoning social insurance is itself an illusion. Even if we make the rather pessimistic assumptions about economic and population growth in trustee estimates of the seventy-five-year financial future of the program, the "crisis" turns out to come down to a manageable shortfall in program financing thirty or forty years from now. The trustees themselves estimate that this shortfall amounts to a bit less than 2 percent of taxable earnings under current law over the next seventy-five years.[60] This means that raising the Social Security tax from the current 12.4 percent of taxable earnings to about 14 percent would solve any future financial problems. This illustration provides some perspective on the real extent of Social Security's potential financial problems.

Even though such a hike in Social Security taxes would meet future financial needs, no serious analyst would expect to solve the problem by placing the entire burden on the payroll tax. Many experts have developed plans for ensuring Social Security's financial future through a mix of both modest tax increases and benefit cuts.[61] For example, continued increases in the proportion of income taxable under the program would bring in substantial amounts of new revenue. This was one approach adopted in the 1983 reforms—the goal to ensure that about 90 percent of wage and salary income overall were taxable. Because the salaries of the most affluent U.S. workers have outpaced average wages for the last two decades, the current ceiling on taxable payroll captures much less than this 90 percent goal. Raising the ceiling sufficiently to return to the 1983 plan would both seem fair and generate much additional revenue. Other proposals for helping Social Security financing include continuing increases in the retirement age to keep up with longer life expectancies in the future, changing benefit formulas to reduce the income replacement rate for the most affluent workers, bringing into the system some state and local employees who remain in their own retirement plans, and adjusting the inflation calculation in the annual cost of living adjustment to reflect more accurately the real price increases senior citizens face. Addressing future Social Security financial needs through a variety of measures shares the burden throughout the population and does not place undue responsibility on any one group. Furthermore, incremental adjustments phased in over time, as political scientist Joseph White has pointed out, takes into account the uncertainty inherent in trustee projections of future financial problems.[62] Their assumptions about future productivity growth or the future growth of the workforce may turn out to be overly pessimistic or, perhaps, too optimistic. Preventing problems far in the future based on hazy crystal-ball gazing calls for incrementalism, not radical policy surgery.

Prudent attention to the real financial concerns in the Social Security system can ensure that future generations of U.S. workers have the same social insurance guarantees of past generations. In a capitalist market economy, future Americans will continue to need the protection from the "hazards and vicissitudes" of life that FDR promised in the 1930s. Libertarian proposals to privatize Social Security are blind to this fundamental reality of modern life. Their philosophical premises prevent them from seeing how collective arrangements can ensure greater security than abandoning individuals to their own devices. Even in the face of threatening icebergs, staying with the ship and making sure it successfully steers clear of them is a better solution than everyone fleeing in their individual lifeboat. Social Security has provided a safe and comfortable voyage to several generations of Americans. With careful steering it can continue to do so for generations to come.

SUGGESTIONS FOR FURTHER READING

Diamond, Peter A., and Peter Orzag. *Saving Social Security: A Balanced Approach.* Washington, D.C.: Brookings Institution, 2004. Two Brookings Institution experts offer a clear and moderate proposal for maintaining Social Security's social insurance character while ensuring its future fiscal integrity.

Ferrara, Peter J., and Michael Tanner. *A New Deal for Social Security*. Washington, D.C.: Cato Institute, 1996. The Cato Institute plan for privatizing Social Security.

Hacker, Jacob S. *The Great Risk Shift*. New York: Oxford University Press, 2006. A thorough analysis of how individuals in the United States have come to bear more of the risks of the "hazards and vicissitudes" of life.

Hiltzik, Michael A. *The Plot against Social Security: How the Bush Plan Is Endangering Our Financial Future*. New York: HarperCollins, 2005. The title says it all; an entertainingly written book.

Korlikoff, Laurence J., and Scott Burns. *The Coming Generational Storm: What You Need to Know about America's Economic Future*. Cambridge: MIT Press, 2005. The best of the many books trumpeting the dire dangers resulting from future baby boom retirements.

SELECTED WEB SITES

www.socialsecurity.org. The Cato Institute's comprehensive site advocating privatization of Social Security.

www.socsec.org. The Social Security Network, a project of the Century Foundation, advocates retaining the social insurance character of the program.

www.ssa.gov. The official site of the Social Security Administration, offering plenty of facts and figures about the program.

NOTES

1. David Boaz, "Defining an Ownership Society," www.cato.org/cgibin/scripts/printtech.cgi/special/ownership_society/boaz.html.
2. James T. Patterson, *America's Struggle against Poverty, 1900–1994* (Cambridge: Harvard University Press, 1994), 42.
3. Ibid.
4. Ibid., 37.
5. Edward D. Berkowitz, *America's Welfare State: From Roosevelt to Reagan* (Baltimore: Johns Hopkins University Press, 1991), 18–19.
6. Ibid., 19.
7. Martha Derthick, *Policymaking for Social Security* (Washington, D.C.: Brookings Institution, 1979), 232.
8. Berkowitz, *America's Welfare State*, 28.
9. Derthick, *Policymaking for Social Security*, 214.
10. Quoted in ibid., 230.
11. Berkowitz, *America's Welfare State*, 46–48.
12. Derthick, *Policymaking for Social Security*, 213–216.
13. Ibid., 268.
14. For a detailed analysis of the 1983 reforms, see Paul Light, *Still Artful Work: The Continuing Politics of Social Security Reform* (New York: McGraw Hill, 1995).
15. Social Security Administration, Office of the Chief Actuary, *Fact Sheet on the Old-Age, Survivors, and Disability Insurance Program*, January 3, 2006.

16. Benjamin I. Page and James R. Simmons, *What Government Can Do: Dealing with Poverty and Inequality* (Chicago: University of Chicago Press, 2000), 79.
17. Ibid., 78.
18. The Century Foundation, *The Basics: Social Security Reform: Revised 2005 Edition* (New York: The Century Foundation Press, 2005), 7.
19. Ibid., 9.
20. Social Security Administration, *Performance and Accountability Report for Fiscal Year 2004* (Baltimore: Social Security Administration, 2004), 9.
21. The Century Foundation, *The Basics*, 11.
22. Peter B. Peterson, *Gray Dawn: How the Coming Age Wave Will Transform America—and the World* (New York: Three Rivers Press, 2000); Laurence J. Korlikoff and Scott Burns, *The Coming Generational Storm: What You Need to Know about America's Economic Future* (Cambridge: MIT Press, 2005).
23. Peter J. Ferrara and Michael Tanner, *A New Deal for Social Security* (Washington, D.C.: Cato Institute, 1996).
24. Social Security Trustees 2006 Annual Report, U.S. Government Printing Office, May 1, 2006, 9.
25. Ibid., 2–16.
26. Joseph White, *False Alarm: Why the Greatest Threat to Social Security and Medicare Is the Campaign to Save Them* (Baltimore: Johns Hopkins University Press, 2001), 43–49.
27. Charles R. Morris, "Just the Facts: The Truth about Social Security," *Commonweal*, February 11, 2005, 14.
28. Milton Friedman, *Capitalism and Freedom* (Chicago: University of Chicago Press, 1962), 183.
29. For a good description of the hysterical language of Social Security critics, see White, *False Alarm*, 2–4; investment banker Peter G. Peterson has been a primary proponent of the "graying of America" theme; see his *Will America Grow Up Before It Grows Old?* (New York: Random House, 1996) and *Gray Dawn*. See also Korlikoff and Burns, *The Coming Generational Storm*.
30. Ferrara and Tanner *A New Deal for Social Security*, 59–91.
31. Ibid., 63.
32. Ibid., 73.
33. Michael Tanner, "The 6.2 Percent Solution: A Plan for Reforming Social Security," Cato Institute, SSP no. 32, February 17, 2004, 4.
34. Edward P. Lazear, "The Virtues of Personal Accounts for Social Security," *The Economists Voice* 2, no. 1, 2005, 2, 7.
35. David C. John, "Why Americans Should Own Their Social Security Retirement Benefits," Heritage Foundation Executive Memorandum, no. 562, Heritage Foundation, Washington, D.C., December 11, 1998.
36. For a detailed analysis of a variety of Social Security reform proposals, including privatization proposals, see Sylvester J. Schieber and John B. Shoven, *The Real Deal: The History and Future of Social Security* (New Haven: Yale University Press, 1999), 317–327; White, *False Alarm*, 143–169.
37. Stuart Butler and Peter Germanis, "Achieving a 'Leninist' Strategy," *Cato Journal* 3, no. 2 (Fall 1983): 549.
38. Tanner, "The 6.2 Percent Solution."

39. Ibid., 9. Tanner never admits that general revenues will be needed, but he implies the possibility by including reductions in "corporate welfare" as a revenue source. This means general revenues currently spent on the corporate welfare would be redirected to pay existing Social Security costs. Presumably, if corporate welfare reductions were inadequate to cover costs, reductions in other programs or higher taxes would be needed.

40. Ibid., 7.

41. Ibid., 9.

42. Ibid., 9.

43. See summary: ibid., 1.

44. White House, "Strengthening Social Security for the Twenty-first Century," February 2005, www.whitehouse.gov/infocus/social-security/200501/strengthening-socialsecurity.html.

45. Jason Furman, "How the Individual Accounts in the President's New Plan Would Work," Center on Budget and Policy Priorities, February 4, 2005.

46. David C. John, "Bold and Responsible: The President's Plan to Improve Retirement Security," WebMemo#650, February 3, 2005, www.heritage.org/Research/SocialSecurity/wm650.cfm.

47. Page and Simmons, *What Government Can Do* (Chicago: University of Chicago Press, 2000), 91–92.

48. Jason Furman, "The Impact of the President's Proposal on Social Security Solvency and the Budget," Center for Budget and Policy Priorities, July 22, 2005.

49. Jonathan Weisman, "Competing Visions for Social Security," *Washington Post*, February 24, 2005, A1.

50. Furman, "The Impact of the President's Proposal on Social Security Solvency and the Budget," 8.

51. Ibid.

52. Furman, "Would Private Accounts Provide a Higher Rate of Return Than Social Security?", 8.

53. Greg Anrig Jr. and Bernard Wasow, "Twelve Reasons Why Privatizing Social Security Is a Bad Idea," TCF Issue Brief (New York: The Century Foundation, February 14, 2005), 8.

54. Jason Furman, "Would Private Accounts Provide a Higher Rate of Return Than Social Security?" Center for Budget and Policy Priorities, June 2, 2005, 8; see also White, *False Alarm*, 146–149.

55. Quoted in Furman, "Would Private Accounts Provide a Higher Rate of Return Than Social Security?", 8.

56. Jacob S. Hacker, "Privatizing Risk without Privatizing the Welfare State: The Hidden Politics of Social Policy Retrenchment in the United States," *American Political Science Review* 98, no. 2 (May 2004): 243–260.

57. For a history of such plans, see Jacob S. Hacker, *The Divided Welfare State: The Battle over Public and Private Social Benefits in the United States* (Cambridge: Cambridge University Press, 2002), 29–178.

58. Ibid., 164–166.

59. Charles Morris, *Apart at the Seams: The Collapse of Private Pension and Health Care Protections* (New York: Century Foundation Press, 2006), 22.

60. Page and Simmons, *What Government Can Do*, 87; Alice H. Munnell, "Social Security's Financial Outlook: The 2006 Update in Perspective," Boston College, Center for Retirement Research, *Issue in Brief* 46, May 2006, 3.
61. There are many sound proposals for solving Social Security's financial problems while maintaining its social insurance structure. For one example, see Peter A. Diamond and Peter R. Orszag, *Saving Social Security: A Balanced Approach* (Washington D.C.: Brookings Institution Press, 2004).
62. White, *False Alarm*, 234–240.

Chapter 5 Health Care: The Limits of Markets

Several years ago, political scientist Michael D. Reagan described the "trilemma" of health care policy.[1] In the ideal, all of us would want health care policy to achieve three worthy goals: highest *quality* care, widespread *access* to that care, and all provided at the lowest possible *cost*. Achieving these goals poses a trilemma because they are mutually contradictory—maximizing any one usually comes at the cost of the other two. Providing the widest possible access to health care inevitably increases health care costs. It also may come at the expense of quality, as some elective care may need to be rationed so sufficient resources are available for essential medical needs. Maximizing quality means investing in expensive procedures and technologies, and driving up overall health costs; access to the very highest quality may not be accessible to all. Based on experience in all parts of the world, cost reduction in health care routinely comes at the expense of both access and quality. Health care, Reagan argues, inherently requires public policy trade-offs between these three goals, hence the trilemma. Balancing and negotiating these trade-offs define the central task of health care policymakers.

In all industrialized nations, with the exception of the United States, negotiating the trilemma takes place in the context of a system of universal health insurance coverage. The United States is the only industrialized nation in the world today that does not provide universal health insurance. In all other industrial countries, all citizens have access to health insurance coverage as a part of the mix of social insurance coverage provided in their welfare states. Health insurance programs vary widely in the details of how they are organized: Britain has National Health Service, through which citizens receive medical care from government-salaried medical personnel; Canada has a "single-payer" health insurance system that reimburses private and nonprofit medical providers; and Germany provides health insurance through local nonprofit "sickness funds." What these countries' health programs have in common, that the United States lacks, is a guarantee that the programs will pay the cost of a basic package of health care services to all citizens. Systems of universal health insurance place a high priority on access to basic quality care within governmentally determined cost constraints.

During the past century, when most other industrial democracies were crafting their system of universal government health insurance, Americans devised a hybrid system of private and public health insurance coverage for most citizens, but one that leaves about 16 percent (forty-five million people) of the population uninsured and with limited access to health care. Most Americans receive health insurance coverage through their employers, who contract with private or nonprofit health insurers for group coverage. This unique system of employer-based coverage expanded after World War II to make health insurance coverage a standard employee benefit for most workers. While some praise this system as a positive alternative to "government control of health care," two groups, the elderly and the eligible poor, are covered under two essentially single-payer government plans, Medicare and Medicaid. In addition, military personnel and veterans receive medical care through a network of government-run medical facilities. Consequently, although Americans normally think of their health care system as nongovernmental, the federal government pays close to 50 percent of the total cost of health care.[2]

When many of my students learn of the United States' unique stance as a country that does not provide universal government insurance, they assume that health consumers are better off in quality and cost as a result. Even if some people do not have health insurance, aren't the majority of Americans who do better off without government control of health care? And wouldn't any new government program to provide universal coverage only make health care more costly and introduce bureaucratic complexities to undermine the quality of health overall? Being patriotic Americans, these students assume that things are better organized in their country than elsewhere, and, having absorbed a libertarian like distrust of government, believe that more government involvement in health care should be avoided and feared.

Contrary to my students' assumptions, comparisons with other nations do not support the proposition that our hybrid health insurance system negotiates Reagan's trilemma better than systems of universal insurance. In addition to leaving a large proportion of its population without any health coverage, the United States does worse than countries providing universal care in terms of both costs and some measures of good health. Total health care expenditures in the United States are the highest in the world. In 2002, Americans spent nearly 15 percent of GDP on health care, while most other industrial democracies spent less than 10 percent.[3] In 2004, health care spending per person in the United States was $6,102, while France, Canada, Britain, and Australia spent around $3,000 per person or less in their universal health insurance systems.[4] Much of this additional cost comes as a result of the higher administrative costs of the complex reimbursement systems and regulatory oversight of private insurers. A recent study by the McKinsey consulting firm found that a major factor in American health care costs was the administrative overhead of private insurers.[5] Despite these higher costs, infant mortality is higher and average life expectancy lower in the United States than in industrial democracies with universal health care.[6] Americans live about three years less on average than Canadians, Australians, or the French and while nearly seven babies per thousand die in childbirth in the United States, only four per thousand do in France.[7]

Rather than look on the United States' health care system as a model, as my students do, recent observers have characterized our health care system as a system in crisis.[8] Not only is the cost of health care high, it has risen dramatically as a percentage of GDP over the past three decades and is projected to continue to rise in the future. For these critics, the rising percentage of Americans without health insurance coverage represents not only a massive moral failure but a gross inefficiency in the system. Because so many Americans cannot easily obtain care, especially preventive care, they tend to be sicker than they otherwise would be, contributing to the poor statistics on infant mortality and life expectancy cited earlier. The uninsured also increase health care costs, because when they typically access the health care system through hospital emergency rooms, a setting where treatment costs are high, their illnesses tend to be severe and much more expensive to treat than they would be if they had been treated earlier in a doctor's office.

Nor does the system serve those with health insurance well. When ill, many Americans find themselves at the mercy of a complex set of insurance plan regulations that limit their choice of health care providers, control physician decisions regarding treatment, and undermine quality care. Since employers—not individual employees—choose health insurers, most of us are relatively powerless to influence the conditions under which we will receive care. With more and more health insurers and hospitals becoming investor-owned enterprises, earning profits seems to take precedence over delivering quality care. The surest way to profitability in the health care business is cutting costs by limiting hospital stays, trimming medical staff, and avoiding responsibility for the health of the sickest patients. Increasingly, despite phenomenal advances in medical technology and procedures, many experts worry about the overall quality of medical care in the United States. Hospital mistakes have become so routine that, according to one study, they are now a leading cause of death in this country.[9]

Libertarians are among the most vociferous critics of the existing system of health care in the United States. For them, the root of the problems discussed is the failure to allow free market forces to work their magic in providing health "consumer" access to efficient, low-cost, quality health care. Rather than point to successes abroad in providing universal health care through government programs, libertarians study the logic of the market. If only health consumers could meet their particular individual needs through direct purchases in the marketplace, just like when they buy automobiles, personal computers, or vacuum cleaners, then problems of quality, access, and cost would vanish. Their mantra is "consumer-driven" health care: empower consumers to control their health care purchases like any other market commodity. Through the power of the free market, in this view, the trilemma vanishes and we can have it all.

This chapter will examine this illusory "solution" to our current health care problems. In brief, its thesis is that the particular character of health care makes its provision through market mechanisms unworkable. Rather than eliminating the trilemma, market forces impose perverse and unjust trade-offs between access, cost, and quality. As we shall see, part of the reasons relate to the characteristic of good health as an economic "good," in contrast with market commodities like automobiles or apples, which prevent markets from providing it efficiently and equitably. But also, we will see the moral issues associated with making access to health dependent on purchasing it in a market.

Moreover, we shall see that many of the problems in our existing health care system derive from the illusory attempts, over the last several decades, to introduce market mechanisms into the health care system. Experience already has shown that the mismatch of markets and health care has failed to produce the more efficient and accessible system its advocates expected. The libertarian solution of "consumer-driven" health care will exacerbate the pathologies of the current system rather than correct them. Before we see why in detail, we need to review how the United States' unique hybrid health insurance and health care systems came to be.

Markets and Medical Care

Readers of this book should not be surprised that libertarians believe that the free market is the solution to the country's health care problems. As we have seen, libertarians assume markets are always the best way to produce and allocate any desirable good. But this assumption leads us dangerously astray when it comes to medicine. Health care is a good that has a number of attributes that prevent markets from working well to deliver health care services. For markets to work well, consumers must have some control over whether or when to purchase a particular good. This allows them to shop around and time their consumptions to take advantage of the best price in the marketplace. Anyone who has delayed buying something until it goes on sale is engaging in this typical market behavior. Consumers also must be able to make judgments about which competing products best satisfy their needs. This process includes an assessment of the affordability of various consumption options: wealthier consumers can shop at Whole Foods while less-wealthy shoppers can meet their needs at Wal-Mart. Shopping around and product comparison in markets send crucial signals to producers that prompt them to deliver precisely what consumers want, at the appropriate price, and at a high quality. Furthermore, only if producers are able to enter the market freely and set prices in relation to consumer demand will the market work efficiently to deliver the highest quality good at the lowest possible price. Competition among producers, over price and quality, to satisfy the preferences of knowledgeable consumers describes why markets work so well to efficiently produce so many things.

None of these attributes of efficient competitive markets applies to health care. Very often, especially when it comes to the most expensive and critical health care services, people have no control over the need for the service. Shopping around for the best price or the best medical facility is not an option for someone having a coronary or suffering from appendicitis. Also, people who are sick or physically impaired are not in a position to act like savvy shoppers and negotiate for the best deal. Rather than being able to enter the market or compete freely with the types of services they offer, doctors and other medical service providers are licensed to ensure that they are competent to provide the services they offer. The range of service options available to patients depends primarily on professional treatment standards and best practices. Especially in those cases where treatment is most effective, patients will find all providers offering similar treatment options and subject to the same professionally defined procedures. Medical consumers do not have the option of choosing between Whole Foods or a Wal-Mart heart bypass operation. These factors greatly restrict the amount of real competition that can occur among medical care providers.

Most important, inherent in medical care is what distinguished economist Kenneth J. Arrow labeled the "asymmetry of information" between doctors and patients concerning the need for and effectiveness of medical treatment.[10] In contrast to a decision to attend a movie or buy a pizza, when it comes to health care, most of us depend on the provider of the good desired to determine when or whether we need the good. We also depend on medical experts to judge what type and quality of medical procedure we need. This relationship is very different from market transactions where I pick what I need and the producer provides it. In medicine, the producer both determines the need for and provides the good—a far cry from the "consumer sovereignty" normally attributed to markets.

Finally, in markets, access to commodities depends on ability to pay the asking price. For most of us, unequal distribution according to differences in income of restaurant meals, in-ground swimming pools, health club memberships, and designer clothing seems perfectly appropriate. Even differentials according to income in the quality of necessities like housing or food (the rich live in big houses and eat caviar, the poor live in small apartments and eat rice and beans) are readily accepted characteristics of market economies. Linking access to basic and life-saving health care to income, in modern and affluent industrial democracies, is widely regarded as immoral. (This is the case, even though, as will be shown below, income differentials do influence health care access in modern America.) Even relatively affluent people would find access to critical medical care, such as chemotherapy or cardiac surgery, impossible if paid directly out of their incomes. Because medical care is not viewed, by most, as a normal market commodity to be bought and sold to the highest bidders, modern societies typically make provisions to provide medical care outside the marketplace, as in charity care or government programs for the indigent, and to insulate more affluent individuals from high medical costs through insurance.

Just as the market works poorly in delivering health care services, it fails by itself to adequately provide health insurance. Like all types of insurance, health insurance faces challenges from our friends from the last two chapters *moral hazard* and *adverse selection,* but the special characteristics of health care make these especially sticky problems when it comes to health insurance. Moral hazard, you may recall, is the label insurance specialists attach to people's perverse tendency to expose themselves more readily to the risk insured against when they have insurance than when they do not. In health care, the risk insured against is the need for health care, so moral hazard leads insured people to "overconsume" health care. If my insurance company pays the cost of my doctor visit, I have no incentive to wait a couple of days to see if my cold goes away by itself before visiting the doctor. Also, my doctor has an incentive to order that MRI today to see if my sore knee is the result of a torn ligament rather than delaying the test to see if it is really needed. Since a third party—the insurance company—and neither of the first two parties to the medical care transaction—the health consumer and health provider—pays the cost, there is no financial barrier for doctors and patients to opt for the highest level of treatment no matter what the cost or actual need. Medical insurance, then, can lead people to seek unnecessary care that drives up the overall cost of health care for all and, eventually, leads to higher insurance premiums.

Any system of health insurance, whether a universal government insurance or private insurance, must find ways to counter moral hazard. These usually take the form of regulations and rationing that limit when and how much treatment is provided. Health care is rationed when insurers impose regulations on what type of treatments they will pay for and impose conditions on treatment, such as refusing to pay for more than a certain number of days in the hospital for a particular medical condition. Most insurers also will exclude from coverage certain types of treatments such as cosmetic or LASIK surgery. Another approach requires patients to share in the cost of care, in the form of deductibles and co-pays, as an incentive not to seek unnecessary care. While rationing and regulation are justifiable as means of overcoming moral hazard, the uncertainties and complexities of health care make devising appropriate regulations quite difficult. Often, legitimate efforts to prevent overconsumption can lead to underconsumption of health services. Rules limiting hospital stays for people recovering from a certain type of operation can lead to premature discharge of a patient experiencing complications. Or a co-pay may lead some people, particularly patients with low incomes, to delay too long in seeking needed care until a condition becomes more expensive and difficult to treat. Combating moral hazard in health insurance is a difficult and morally risky enterprise if barriers to access needed care are to be prevented. A judicious balance must be struck between the need to prevent unnecessary care without preventing people from receiving the care they need.

A totally unregulated free market in health insurance is not likely to strike the right balance. When profit-making firms compete in a free market to provide health insurance, strong financial incentives exist to overcome moral hazard through limiting access to medical care for their customers, even if some receive less than adequate care. Both profits and competitiveness depend in health insurance markets on success in rationing patient care and shifting cost burdens to those insured. A company that succeeds best in reducing its customers' health care consumption will earn higher profits and be able to lower premiums to compete more effectively. Also, high co-pays that prevent overall overconsumption should be a profitable strategy in a health insurance market, even if lower-income patients fail to receive needed care on time. Business logic suggests tight regulation of access to care and high co-pays are profitable strategies in a health insurance free market, and, as we shall see in this chapter, have been characteristic of profit-driven health insurers in the United States.

The way adverse selection works in a free market health insurance system also leads to detrimental effects in providing adequate health care for all. As we saw in the last chapter, adverse selection, as applied to health care, is the tendency for those who expect to be sick to buy health insurance, while those who consider themselves healthy not to buy it. One way to counter this phenomenon would be to make health insurance universal and mandatory; that way healthier individuals share in the costs of insuring those prone to be sick. In a purely voluntary, free health insurance market, however, the key to profitability for a health insurance company is to avoid insuring the sick and seek to insure the healthy. Thus, in a free market, we should expect insurers to try to find ways of attracting healthier customers, through lower premiums and promises of better benefits, while providing insurance to the sick, if they are insured at all, at very high premiums. Free markets encourage insurers to develop different insurance products for different people based on calculations of their state of health. Good customer selection in a health insurance market is the winning business strategy. The logical result would be a system in which those least likely to be sick would most easily obtain insurance at the lowest cost, while the sick would either not be insurable or have to pay astronomical premiums to be insured. The only way to counter this tendency in an insurance market with competition would be regulations mandating broader insurance pools and requiring minimal packages of coverage for all.

Even though these limitations on the ability of free markets to provide adequate health services or health insurance are well understood, libertarians continue to advance market solutions to health care problems. For much of the past century, although the idea of universal health insurance was rejected, policymakers and health care professionals recognized the importance of extramarket factors in organizing health services. From about 1900 until the 1980s, the health care system in the United States included a substantial amount of regulated, nonmarket provision of health care. For the last couple of decades, however, the libertarian attitude has introduced more market-driven and for-profit care into the system. These developments have produced many of the perverse and detrimental effects on health care one should expect from introducing market values into the system. And, although their proponents promised that more market-driven health care would lower costs and improve quality, health care markets have failed to do so. Nevertheless, libertarians continue to promote market solutions that will only make American health care worse. Before looking at the latest illusory libertarian proposals for our health care system, the next section reviews how a largely nonprofit health care system evolved in the last century only to succumb more recently to a libertarian market ideology.

America's Unique Employer-Based System of Health Insurance: From 1920 to 1970

America's health care system toward the end of the nineteenth century well fit the libertarian image of a consumer-driven free market. Physicians were private entrepreneurs who offered their patients services in exchange for direct payments. Although a few states had begun to license physicians, one requirement of the economist's ideal market system—entry into the market—was relatively easy in most places. Just about anyone who hung up a shingle could become a physician. The cost of most medical care was relatively low; most patients could afford a doctor's services when needed, especially since many physicians adjusted their rates based upon a patient's ability to pay. Yet it was also a time when a physician had only a fifty-fifty chance of improving a patient's health.[11] Drugs also were freely available on the market, including narcotics such as heroin and cocaine, free of any government regulation. About the only government involvement at the time came in hospital care for the poor in public hospitals.[12] Wealthier people both underwent surgery and convalesced at home.

During the first two decades of the twentieth century, the ability of physicians to treat their patients effectively improved dramatically. Understanding of the role of germs in disease and spreading use of antiseptic procedures helped physicians diagnose, treat, and prevent the spread of infectious diseases. The use of X-rays and improvements in surgical procedures allowed them to operate more successfully. Contributing greatly to the effectiveness of medical care were improvements in medical schools that produced graduates well trained in the latest medical knowledge and procedures.

As medical interventions became more effective, medical professionals began to demand regulation of the free market in health care. Largely as a result of pressure from state medical societies, state legislatures restricted access to the medical profession through licensure of physicians. Physicians trained in scientifically based treatment methods argued that the public good required that they, who possessed the knowledge to adequately treat disease, and not the scientifically illiterate should have a monopoly of medical treatment.

In doing so, however, state licensure violated a key requisite of the free market—open entry by producers into the market. Now market entry was restricted to those trained in accredited medical schools. Not surprisingly, the number, size, and significance of medical schools expanded tremendously in this era, both in training and in medical research. With professional medical education and research, the treatments available to patients became standardized and based on professional knowledge. While this undoubtedly increased the quality of patient health, from a market point of view, it involved restricting consumer choice and sovereignty. Professionalization enhanced the power of physicians in relation to their patients in choosing both the nature and cost of their patients' medical care—the asymmetry of information described above. Physicians also gained control over the access to drugs through federal and state governments' regulation of the safety and effectiveness of drugs, restricting access for some through physician prescription.

The first two decades of the twentieth century also saw tremendous changes in the role of hospitals in delivering health care services. With improvements in hygiene, scientific understanding of disease, and surgical techniques, hospital treatment became desirable even for the more affluent, previously cared for at home. Instead of entrepreneurs investing in for-profit hospitals, the medical profession took the lead in forming nonprofit community hospitals, usually with boards dominated by physicians, which now became centers for care of rich and middle classes who could afford their charges. State charters for the nonprofit institutions typically required them to offer free care to the poor, spreading the costs of this charity care among the hospital's paying customers. This system paralleled the widespread professional norm among physicians of taking on a certain number of charity cases in their individual practices. Also, public charity hospitals continued to offer care for the poor, although now more effectively than before.

Yet even with deviations from a pure free market in health care brought on by licensing of physicians and professional self-regulation, the medical system in the 1920s still retained many free market features. Physicians continued to function as independent entrepreneurs, although pressure from professional associations curtailed any advertising and informally regulated fees. Through their state medical societies and the newly formed American Medical Association (AMA), physicians strongly opposed any introduction of public health insurance, by then common in Europe, and they frowned upon even private health insurance, both of which were seen as interfering with the doctor-patient relationship. The medical profession preferred a system in which patients paid doctors and hospitals out of pocket for their medical care. Nor was the private insurance industry interested in providing medical insurance. Because of adverse selection, private insurers found it difficult to sell insurance that was both affordable to consumers and profitable to themselves. The fundamentals of this system would begin to change as a consequence of the Great Depression.

Like all institutions after 1929, hospitals experienced a dramatic drop in revenues. In one year, average receipts per patient dropped from $236 to $59.[13] Given this financial crisis, ideological commitment to direct payment from patients evaporated as hospitals sought ways to shore up their finances. In Dallas, Baylor University Hospital devised an arrangement that soon spread to hospitals across the nation. Starting with 1,500 school teachers in the Dallas area, the hospital agreed to offer employees of those employers who agreed to join the plan, twenty-one days of hospital care a year in exchange for a prepaid premium of $6.[14] Soon community hospitals began cooperating in Blue Cross plans, organized as nonprofit corporations under boards of directors dominated by medical providers. To avoid adverse selection, Blue Cross contracted with employers to enroll employee groups, including both healthy and nonhealthy individuals; more importantly, most also charged insurance premiums at the same community rate for all subscribers. This process, *community rating,* spread total hospital costs among all subscribers in a community, keeping premiums relatively low for all while allowing healthier subscribers to subsidize the higher costs of the less healthy. In addition, instead of the indemnity model of cash reimbursement of a portion of costs typical in the private insurance industry, Blue Cross plans paid the full costs of hospital care services for a given period, as in the first Baylor University plan. Facilitating the expansion of Blue Cross plans were favorable state laws exempting the plans from taxation and state insurance regulation.[15] Perceiving the success of Blue Cross plans for hospital expenses, physicians began to organize associated Blue Shield plans to cover costs of physician office visits.

Although Blue Cross and Blue Shield plans grew slowly during the 1930s, only about 10 percent of workers were enrolled in a health insurance plan in 1940.[16] World War II would stimulate a rapid expansion of employer-based health insurance coverage. Under wartime wage and price controls, large manufacturers could not offer higher wages to attract good workers, but they could offer fringe benefits like pensions and health insurance. Also, unionization expanded in industrial firms with encouragement from the federal government and health insurance became a standard feature of union contracts with employers. These trends continued after the war so that by 1950, a majority of all workers were covered by employer-based health insurance plans. For those employed by large firms, about two-thirds had health coverage.[17]

As more employers began to provide health coverage, a market for health insurance had developed that held potential for commercial for-profit insurers. Now that the availability of nonprofit Blue Cross/Blue Shield plans had made employer-provided group insurance a standard benefit for many workers, commercial insurers found they could make profits competing in providing health insurance. During the late 1940s, commercial group health insurance more than doubled so that by 1949 commercial insurers covered nearly as many employees as the Blues. During this period and throughout the early 1950s, commercial insurers underbid the "community rated" Blue Cross/Blue Shield plans by offering lower premiums to firms whose employees had low health risks. This competitive strategy reflected the market logic that health insurance could be quite profitable if insurers could select the healthy and avoid the sick. The practice of "experience rating" substantially altered the health insurance system, as the Blues also shifted to experience rating in order to compete with the commercial insurers for firms with younger, healthier employees. By the late 1950s, a majority of health plans were experience rated, including the nonprofit Blue Cross plans, which in the face of competition from for-profit insurance companies also shifted to an indemnity model.[18] As health care costs rose dramatically in future decades, this shift to experience rating would lead those employers with less-healthy work forces to opt out of health coverage, a fact that contributed to the steady rise in the proportion of uninsured Americans after 1980.

During this period of expansion of employer-based insurance coverage, liberal activists tried and failed to enact a universal health care system. Some had advocated including universal health insurance as a part of the 1935 Social Security Act, but President Franklin D. Roosevelt rejected the idea. He worried that opposition to universal health insurance by the AMA would torpedo the entire legislation if it included health insurance. Later, President Harry S. Truman would propose universal health insurance, only to see his initiative largely ignored by a Congress responsive to opposition from the medical establishment. By the 1950s, opponents of universal health insurance began to argue that the United States' system of voluntary, employer-based health insurance made any government plan of universal coverage unnecessary. They could point to the steady increase in the proportion of the population covered by employer plans (coverage grew from 50 percent in 1950 to slightly over 80 percent by the late 1970s) as proof that eventually universal coverage would be achieved without a government plan.[19] Besides, the country's "voluntary way" was deemed superior to government control as a way of organizing health care. In the face of this opposition, liberals turned away from promoting universal health insurance to a focus on one group of Americans that failed to obtain employer-based coverage: the elderly.

The realities of the life cycle mean that as people age they become more prone to health problems and thus at risk of the need for costly medical care. The shift to experience rating made affordable insurance for the elderly impossible. Attempts by Blue Cross plans in some communities to enroll the elderly in community-rated plans failed to attract sufficient numbers of younger, low-risk individuals to be financially feasible.[20] In the face of this reality were pressures built in the early 1960s for federal government involvement in providing health insurance for senior citizens. Standing in the way were the AMA and other conservative groups who remained adamantly opposed to any type of government-sponsored health insurance. Enacting health insurance for the elderly only became possible after the 1964 elections, in which President

Lyndon Johnson's landslide victory brought strong Democratic Party majorities in both houses of Congress. In 1965, Johnson signed into law the new Medicare program providing federal health insurance to all citizens over age 65. The new program covered all hospital costs—the highest cost item for the elderly sick—in Part A, which was compulsory for all Social Security recipients. Part B, covering physicians' bills, was technically voluntary, based on payment of a small partial premium, but automatic deduction of the premium from Social Security checks resulted in high participation rates.[21] The legislation did not provide for coverage of prescription drugs, which, at the time, were only a small component of the health costs of most elderly patients. The discovery and increasing use of new drug therapies in the years to come, and their rising costs, would make this gap in coverage a major policy problem by century's end. Almost as an afterthought, Congress included a third component to the legislation—Medicaid, the health insurance for the indigent poor. Unlike Medicare, state governments would administer and partly finance the Medicaid program. In order to mollify AMA worries about government intrusion in medicine, the legislation forbade federal officials from "any supervision or control over the practice of medicine," which meant in practice not regulating doctor fees and hospital charges.[22] This feature would mean Medicare and Medicaid would adopt the "fee-for-service" model of the private insurance industry.

Under a fee-for-service system, doctors and hospitals bill the insurance carrier for each service performed, whether a vaccination or open-heart surgery. The more services providers give the more money they make, creating an incentive to encourage more services. In addition, health insurance involves a "third-party" payment, that is, patients do not pay a doctor directly for services provided but the insurance company pays, increasing the potential for moral hazard. Because the two parties who decide whether a medical service will be provided need not be concerned about the cost of the service when deciding upon it—the insurance company "third party" can be counted on to pay the cost—there is an incentive for both patients and medical providers to seek more services, even if they may not be absolutely medically necessary. Economists see the moral hazard inherent in the third-party payer, fee-for-service system as a perfect guarantee for medical price inflation. Compounding the tendency toward rising health costs was Medicare's practice of reimbursing health care providers according to "reasonable and customary" rates in a community, a practice Blue Cross/Blue Shield and commercial carriers also followed. Very soon after Medicare's passage, what was considered "reasonable and customary" began to increase rapidly. In the five years after Medicare's passage, medical cost inflation doubled as per capita health costs grew from $198 per capita to $336 per capita.[23] With the federal government now insuring those Americans with the greatest health care needs, rising health care expenditures became the fastest-growing component of the federal budget. After 1970, reining in ever-rising health care expenditures became a major public policy concern.

Crisis of Coverage and Costs: From 1970 to Today

Only a portion of the rise in health care expenditures could be blamed on moral hazard through the third-party/fee-for-service system. Dramatic improvements in medical care procedures involving new technology, such as CAT scans and MRIs; new surgical techniques, such as open-heart surgery and organ transplantation; and improved cancer treatments proved successful in treating disease, but were costly. Increased life expectancy also meant that more people were living into old age, when need for costly medical services increased. Nevertheless, the Nixon administration focused most of its attention on addressing moral hazard through replacing the fee-for-service system with the introduction of health maintenance organizations (HMOs). Dr. Paul M. Ellwood, a Minneapolis physician, coined the term to refer to a form of prepaid group practice that had existed in several parts of the country since the 1930s. The most famous prepaid group practice was the Kaiser-Permanente plan in California, first established for the employees of the Kaiser Corporation.[24] Under a prepaid group, insurance subscribers received care from a group of salaried physicians, both general practitioners and specialists, who took responsibility for their subscribers' total health care needs. The economic incentives of prepaid group plans were the reverse of those of the fee-for-service/third-party payment. Instead of making more money for each service provided, prepaid practices succeeded financially when they kept their subscribers healthy and minimized the number and costs of medical interventions. Emphasis on preventative care, careful diagnosis, and avoidance of unnecessary procedures was the hallmark of these plans. Ellwood assumed these plans would be organized on a nonprofit model and would require government subsidies for startup capital. Following this logic, during the 1970s the federal government promoted through a federal grant program the development of nonprofit HMOs as a solution to rising health care costs.

Although federal policy encouraged HMO formation, both the medical professionals and consumers, accustomed to the fee-for-service model, resisted the idea of prepaid practice. Consumers worried that joining an HMO would restrict their choice of physicians, and physicians preferred to operate as independent entrepreneurs rather than salaried employees of an HMO organization. Despite this resistance, and with the help of the federal subsidies, HMOs achieved a substantial presence in the Northeast, upper Midwest, and California, and they did seem to restrain health costs. By the end of the decade about 4 percent of the population belonged to nonprofit HMOs.[25]

At the end of the 1970s, the U.S. health care system could be described as one that combined both market and nonmarket values in the provision of health care, but in which nonmarket values tended to predominate. Most physicians continued to act as individual entrepreneurs selling their services on a fee-for-service basis, but professional norms emphasized viewing health care as a social good and not a commodity. Many practices normal in most areas of business such as advertising or investing in health care businesses were discouraged.[26] Despite a growing presence of for-profit commercial insurers and more investor-owned hospitals, nursing homes, and health clinics, nonprofit institutions continued to predominate the hospital and health insurance industries. Hospitals and health clinics, in particular, regarded their mission as public service, not earning profits, and felt obligated to serve all, regardless of income. Substantial philanthropic contributions were seen as a critical revenue source, so they were not totally dependent on payments from patients. Although rooted in trends going back to the early 1960s, the 1980s would be a period when for-profit corporate medicine, driven by market values, would begin to make major inroads. The next two decades would represent a transformation of the U.S. health care system into one in which profitability and market success would drive health care decision making.

Ironically, especially from a libertarian perspective, the expansion of government insurance through Medicare and Medicaid was a major factor in making health care an attractive investment on Wall Street.[27] The large flow of revenue from these programs guaranteed, especially in the prevailing fee-for-service system, substantial profits to those providing health services. Investors soon began pouring money into for-profit hospital corporations, many of which developed national chains in sharp contrast to the single-community orientation of the traditional nonprofit community hospital. Despite traditional professional norms discouraging such investments, physicians themselves became major players in this development. Former Republican Senate majority leader and doctor Bill Frist, for example, made a fortune through ownership, along with his physician father and brother, of HCA, Inc., one of the country's largest hospital chains.[28] Much of this entrepreneurial activity involved buying up, reorganizing, and squeezing previously nonprofit hospitals, nursing homes, and community health clinics for maximum profit.

At the same time, for-profit commercial insurers began to adapt the HMO model for profitability and market success. As described earlier, the nonprofit HMO model usually involved salaried physicians providing health care services to subscribers in clinics offering a full range of primary and specialty care. Rather than set up single clinics, the for-profit "managed care" HMOs involved insurance companies writing contracts with a network of physicians, including primary caregivers and specialists, who agreed to provide services at a fixed cost and in conformity with the regulations of the insurer. These arrangements gave the managed care insurer leverage over moral hazard, allowing them to limit care and costs to maximize profits. In this way, insurers could offer coverage to employers at a lower premium cost than fee-for-service insurance. A drawback to managed care for some of those insured was restrictions on choice of physicians. Subscribers enrolled in a managed care plan, unlike the typical fee-for-service arrangement, could only receive care from those physicians in a particular insurer's network. By the end of the 1980s, many employers were offering participation in these managed care plans as an option to their employees. Within a decade, they would dominate the private health insurance field.

In sharp contrast to this movement toward privatization and market values, one of the more significant changes in health care came in the form of increased government regulation. Since its inception in 1965, Medicare had avoided regulating prices charged by medical providers. Although there were some rather ineffectual attempts to restrain charges, the program basically paid whatever medical providers billed. As health care costs continued to escalate and became an ever-larger component of the federal budget, the Reagan administration decided in 1984 to rein in Medicare costs directly through a change in how hospitals and physicians were reimbursed.[29] Under the fee-for-service model, Medicare had always paid hospitals based on the number of days a patient received care. This meant that the longer patients stayed and the more beds hospitals filled the more money they made. Also under this system, hospitals made more money from healthier patients who needed less care but who filled hospital beds; they thus had an incentive to avoid the sickest patients. To attempt to correct this situation, Medicare began to reimburse on the basis of the average cost of treating a patient diagnosed with a particular condition. Payment through this rating system of diagnosis related groups (DRGs) was intended to force medical providers to find the most cost-effective way of treating patients. While seeking greater efficiency, however, the use of DRGs had some potential dangers, such as the risk of undertreatment of seriously ill patients whose actual cost of treatment exceeded the DRG reimbursement rate. Just like under the previous reimbursement system, hospitals still had an incentive to avoid the sickest patients, this time to reduce costs rather than increase incoming revenue. Following Medicare's lead, the private insurance industry soon adopted DRG-based reimbursement systems, typically using the Medicare ratings in their own reimbursements. In the 1990s, the DRG reimbursement system would assist private insurers in regulating their costs and boosting profits.

The continued rise in health care costs and insurance premiums made the cost of health insurance a major business concern in the 1980s. In response, many employers began to require their employees to pay a larger share of the health care premiums, and some opted no longer to provide a health insurance benefit. In addition, changes in the economy, such as a decline in manufacturing and unionized jobs, contributed to the increase in the number of the uninsured. Nonunion service-sector jobs, which were the source of job growth in the era, often failed to provide health benefits, or did so only with extremely high employee premium co-pays and deductibles that low-wage workers in particular could not afford. As a consequence, for the first time in forty years, the proportion of the population with employer-based coverage began to decline and the number of Americans without health insurance coverage steadily increased. The number of uninsured Americans increased by about two million per year beginning in 1988 and, by 1992, the total had reached a then-record of about forty million uninsured.[30] The vision of earlier years that the U.S. system of voluntary employer-based coverage would eventually cover all workers was proving illusory. With businesses worried about ever-expanding health insurance costs and the rapid rise in the number of uninsured Americans, establishing some form of universal national health insurance was once more moved onto the public policy agenda.

During the 1992 presidential campaign, Democratic candidate Bill Clinton made achieving the goal of universal national health insurance a key plank in his platform. Encouraged by favorable public opinion polls, support from some key business groups, and even an historic shift in position of the AMA (traditionally an adamant opponent of national health insurance) in support of universal insurance, Clinton and his advisers believed the time was ripe for health insurance reform. A recent special senatorial election in Pennsylvania in which Democratic candidate Harris Wofford rode a call for universal health insurance to victory reinforced this view.

At the time, liberal advocates of universal national health insurance focused on two principle approaches: a single-payer plan, or "pay or play." Single-payer, the approach used in Canada and many other countries with universal national health insurance, was the most straightforward. The federal government would provide insurance coverage to all Americans financed through either a new payroll tax, as it now did with Medicare, or from general tax revenues. Provision of health care services would remain in private hands, but to avoid price inflation, the government would need to negotiate payments to physicians and hospitals, similar to what it now was doing with DRGs in Medicare. Some variants of single-payer plans proposed state governments or quasigovernmental regional agencies as the single health insurers in their geographic area.[31] Whatever the details, a single-payer approach would require a radical restructuring of the health care system, eliminate the private health insurance industry, and produce substantial increases in taxes and government regulation. In return, however, it would guarantee for the first time in history access of health care for all Americans and, through elimination of the administrative complexity and profits in the existing private health insurance system, reduce overall health costs.[32]

Pay or play involved a less-disruptive path to universal health coverage. It would require all employers either to pay for health insurance for their employees or pay a special tax to finance care for the uninsured. These taxes would support a new public program, replacing Medicaid to cover all those without employer-based insurance. Large businesses who already covered their employees and resented paying for the health coverage of the uninsured indirectly through their premiums found this approach attractive. In contrast to the single-payer plan, this approach left the existing system of employer-based care intact and, consequently, did not threaten the health insurance industry, nor did it change the coverage of the many Americans who already had health insurance through their employers. Not surprisingly, those businesses who did not provide health benefits opposed this approach, as did single-payer advocates who feared that taxes would not be high enough to fund adequate coverage for those in the public program and that it would facilitate employers now providing coverage to "dump" their employees into the new, probably underfunded, public program.[33]

As Clinton contemplated these two leading approaches to universal health insurance, he found strong reasons to avoid both. A single-payer approach, even if it eventually reduced national health expenditures in the economy, would involve a huge increase in federal expenditures, as national insurance costs were shifted from private industry to government, along with the additional costs of covering the uninsured. This did not seem feasible at a time when another Clinton priority was to reduce the massive federal budget deficit left over from the Reagan era. Instituting a single-payer plan also would require overcoming the political power of the health insurance industry that would fight ferociously to save itself. Moreover, the single-payer approach was at odds with Clinton's own ideological outlook as a New Democrat who rejected traditional liberal "big government" solutions to public problems in favor of new, innovative ones. Pay or play was more palatable to Clinton, but it involved alienating a substantial portion of the business community whose support he would need on other issues. Although its impact on the federal budget was much less than single-payer, it too would require increased federal spending at odds with the new administration's deficit-cutting agenda. As a New Democrat, Clinton sought an innovative path to universal coverage that would require minimal increases in government spending and regulation, build upon rather than replace the existing system of employer-based coverage, not threaten the health insurance industry, and win the support of the business community. He thought he had found such an approach in a market-based system called "managed competition."

Stanford University economist Alain Enthoven had been promoting the idea of managed competition for more than a decade. Like many policy advocates at the time, Enthoven looked to market-price competition among health insurers as the most efficient and effective way both to rein in health care costs and make insurance more affordable to more U.S. employers. He recognized, however, the limits of market solutions in health care, hence the need for *managed* competition. To prevent insurers from "cherry-picking" healthy subscribers and avoiding the sick, insurance had to be offered to large groups that spread insurance risk among a number of individuals of both potentially healthy and sick. Under his plan, large employers could continue to purchase insurance for their employees, but small and medium-sized employers would be organized into regional "health purchasing alliances" that would negotiate insurance packages with health insurers. Not only would these alliances prevent insurers from using experience rating to cherry-pick subscribers, they also would have the leverage to negotiate for low premiums. As members of these alliances, small employers who currently offered no insurance would be able to afford the smaller premiums. In fact, as in "pay or play," Enthoven advocated mandatory employer payroll contributions for health insurance.[34]

Under managed competition, health care costs would come down as health insurers competed for the business of large employers and health purchasing alliances. As an added incentive to encourage employers to buy the lowest-priced plans, Enthoven would cap the income tax deduction for employers to the cost of the lowest priced insurance plan in the region. This approach assumed an expansion of HMOs and managed care as a way of tamping down health care costs. Just as health insurance purchasers would negotiate aggressively for the lowest premiums, health insurers would have to negotiate lower prices with doctors, hospitals, and other health care providers as well as aggressively regulate treatment decisions to avoid overutilization and costly treatments and encourage preventive medicine if they were to be competitive.[35] Over time, health insurers would develop a variety of health insurance packages offering different levels of care based on market demand and differing consumer preferences. To ensure that these packages met the need for basic health services, however, regulations would be needed to prevent health insurers from underpricing competitors through denying coverage of expensive conditions or preventing access to legitimate treatments. Again, when it came to standards of care, the health care market had to be "managed" to reflect nonmarket values. Enthoven had great faith in the ability of price competition in the health insurance market, even when regulated to require minimum standards of care, to induce health insurance entrepreneurs to lower the cost of health services through the elimination of waste and inefficiency. Managed competition aimed to reverse the incentives that moral hazard, fee-for-service, and third-party payments created in the health insurance market.

At the time the Clinton administration had come into office, Enthoven had joined with HMO advocate Dr. Paul Ellwood to form the "Jackson Hole Group," a collection of health care reform advocates who met regularly at Ellwood's home in Jackson Hole, Wyoming. As they searched for a "middle way" between the existing health care system and liberal single-payer or pay-or-play health care reform, Clinton and his advisers gained inspiration from Jackson Hole to develop a non–big government, market-oriented approach to universal national health insurance. A Clinton health reform plan would utilize all the innovative ideas about the use of market incentives to reduce costs and encourage efficiency, something in line with the New Democrat vision, while keeping the need for new federal spending low; not threaten the health insurance industry but, instead, offer it new business opportunities; and require only minimal government regulation. Although the concept of managed competition seemed to offer all of these advantages, in practice, developing a comprehensive national plan that met these objectives while at the same time guaranteed health insurance to all Americans proved illusory.

THEN-FIRST LADY HILLARY CLINTON SPEAKS IN BALTIMORE IN FAVOR OF THE CLINTONS' PLAN TO ENACT UNIVERSAL HEALTH CARE INSURANCE. SINCE THE FAILURE OF THE CLINTONS' ATTEMPT IN THE MID-1990S, PROBLEMS IN THE HEALTH CARE SYSTEM HAVE WORSENED, MAKING A NEW APPROACH A CENTERPIECE OF SENATOR CLINTON'S 2008 PRESIDENTIAL BID.

The complete story of the failure of the Clinton health reform plan is beyond the scope of this chapter, but in brief, devising a plan to universalize health insurance and control health costs based on the ideas of managed competition turned out to be much more complicated than the group envisioned in Jackson Hole.[36] This is what the Clinton administration's health care task force under the leadership of First Lady Hillary Rodham Clinton and Clinton friend Ira Magaziner—a business consultant and, like Bill Clinton, a former Rhodes Scholar—was to discover. Designing a system of health care alliances throughout the country that "managed" the health insurance market to achieve crucial nonmarket values such as adequate care for all and nondiscrimination against those needing costly treatments proved to be quite complex. Despite echoing Jackson Hole rhetoric about minimal government regulation in managed competition, the Clinton health care bill eventually introduced in Congress ran to 1,342 pages.[37] Soon Republican opponents and editorial cartoonists across the nation were lampooning the Clinton plan as a bureaucratic boondoggle. A portion of the complexity and regulation in the Clinton plan derived from its attempt to ensure subscriber choice of at least three different insurance plan options, including at least one fee-for-service option that placed no constraints on choice of physicians.[38] Yet because the plan also encouraged enrollment in managed care plans, as a means of avoiding moral hazard, the plan's critics painted it as a threat to individual choice. Although the Clinton plan sought to prevent opposition from the health insurance industry by maintaining its central role in the system, many health insurers, particularly the smaller ones, objected to the prospect of increased regulation and soon joined in opposition to the plan. Much of the business community also objected to the mandates on their participation that were crucial if health care coverage were to be universal. By 1994, with much of the health insurance industry, the Republican Party, and business opposed and the Democratic Party divided over the Clinton plan, it died in Congress. The managed competition vision that market forces would control costs and allow expansion of insurance coverage, central to the Clinton plan, failed to account sufficiently for the inherent limitations of the free market in health care. Reliance on market forces, given their inherent limitations in health care, required heavy doses of government oversight if undesirable inequities and erosion of the quality of care were not to result.

Unmanaged Competition in Today's Medical-Industrial Complex

The defeat of the Clinton health reform plan did not mean the maintenance of the status quo in the health care system. In the absence of governmental reform of the system, the private sector proceeded with a top-down restructuring of the entire health insurance system.[39] Employers, seeking to escape higher premiums, imposed managed care plans as the sole option for their employees. Investor-owned, for-profit insurers responded in competing vigorously in offering managed care plans. To undercut rivals and maximize their profits, they moved aggressively to cut costs through treatment rationing, financial incentives to physicians in their networks to limit specialist referrals and tests, and capitation fees or negotiated fee-for-service rates. Capitation fees involved paying a physician a fixed sum for each subscriber taken on as a patient, with the physician assuming full responsibility for each capitated patient's care. All the approaches placed great pressure on physicians to limit care and obtain the insurer's permission before prescribing treatment. Employees also soon found that they had no choice among alternative health plans, the prevailing practice prior to the 1990s. Health insurance companies offered their lowest premiums to employers that gave them exclusive rights to enroll a given firm's employees.

Americans soon found they were forced into the health care plans their employers chose and compelled to receive their health coverage from physicians and hospitals in the insurer's network delivered under the terms the insurer negotiated with network providers. Ironically, all of the evils its critics had attributed to the Clinton plan soon came to characterize the health care system in spite of its defeat. Individuals found they no longer could choose their health insurance plan from a number of alternatives, nor did their plan allow them free choice of their health care providers. Physicians, who for years had resisted government health insurance for fear that it would interfere with the doctor-patient relationship, found this relation now governed by the regulations of private health insurance companies. Not only were these regulations intrusive, most physicians were compelled to satisfy different sets of regulations based upon the differing coverage of their patients. Because treatment rationing—limiting hospital stays, denial of certain treatments, refusal to approve diagnostic tests—became the main formula the private health insurance industry used to lower premiums, levels and quality of care soon began to erode. Health-insurer imposed limits on coverage of births—the "drive-by delivery" of babies—soon came to characterize the experience most Americans had of the health care system.

While patients and physicians may have found these developments disconcerting, profit-seeking investors found the health industry an attractive opportunity in the 1990s. The restructured and privatized health care system that evolved in the nineties had many features libertarians and other free market advocates ought to have admired. Investor-owned, profit-driven, and entrepreneurial health insurance companies now dominated the industry; the non-profit, community-rated insurance system of the 1950s had disappeared. These companies competed vigorously for the business of employers through offering discounts on premiums. As advocates of market competition in the insurance industry like Enthoven hoped, price competition in the insurance market led to price restraint in the medical care system as a whole, as insurance companies imposed "efficiencies" on medical care providers. More and more health care providers, themselves part of investor-owned private firms, sensitive to the bottom line, facilitated this process. In fact, health care costs as a percentage of GDP began to level off after 1995.[40]

Yet the very managed care techniques employed in the unregulated health care market to restrain costs proved massively unpopular with the American public and with health care professionals. Americans resented the intensive regulation and treatment rationing the insurance industry used in competing to offer low premiums. Physicians bridled at being required to obtain permission from insurance company bureaucrats before prescribing treatment. In many cases, patients suffered from insurance companies' denial of care. The belief that competing insurance companies could restrain health costs by squeezing efficiencies from the system proved mistaken. Very quickly, insurers learned that the best avenue to lower provider costs and more profits was simply denying care, but rationing treatment meant massive interference in the doctor-patient relationship and often denial of needed care. The political reaction was quick in coming as state legislatures and eventually even the Republican-controlled U.S. Congress began considering "patients' bills of rights" aimed at regulating the health insurance industry. To prevent such regulation, the private health insurance industry retreated. In 1999, United-Health Care, one of the country's largest national health insurance companies, announced it would no longer regulate physician treatment decisions, and the rest of the industry soon followed.[41] No longer able to employ the main tool of managed care to restrain prices, health care costs soon began to rise again. This does not mean that private insurers gave up on keeping their own costs down and their profits up. Rather than review physicians' decisions at time of treatment, insurers have relied more in recent years on rejecting claims, limiting payment to prescribed numbers of days in hospitals, and capping how much they will pay for particular treatments.[42]

The promises of market advocates of the past quarter decade that a more privatized, investor-owned, profit-driven, and competitive health sector would produce high-quality health care at a low cost and, as insurance became more affordable, reduce the number of Americans without insurance have not been fulfilled. For the last few years, health care costs have been rising faster than ever, outpacing both inflation and economic growth.[43] Health care expenditures rose to 15 percent of GDP in 2003. As health care costs once again soared at twice the rate of inflation by 2006, both insurers and employers shifted more and more costs to individual employees to cope with the rising costs.[44] Insurers have increased premiums, co-pays, and deductibles requiring patients to pay for a larger portion of their care. Higher insurance premiums have placed pressure on businesses, especially smaller ones, to eliminate health coverage or shift more of the share of premium costs to employees. Both developments have contributed to the steady increase in the number of uninsured Americans that reached forty-five million in 2003.[45] Yet this number understates the vulnerability of many Americans to be without insurance as about twice that number go without insurance at some time during the course of a year. Higher health costs have placed great pressure on Medicaid, forcing many state governments to reverse the trend of the 1990s in expanding coverage. Now many are tightening eligibility criteria and forcing recipients to shoulder higher co-pay costs.

The increase in the number of uninsured Americans has serious consequences for them, but also for all of society. Those without insurance, despite the supposed availability of emergency care, are sicker and more likely to die. Lacking preventive care, they usually are quite sick before they receive treatment at an emergency room. And when they are treated, the cost of treatment is much higher than it would have been had they received preventive or timely care. Some experts estimate that the overall costs associated with treating the uninsured are only slightly less than what it would cost to provide them with comprehensive insurance and cover all health costs.[46] Even though some uninsured people obtain care in emergency rooms, that care is uncertain and often too late to address serious problems. And the care they receive is expensive, since uninsured hospital patients usually are billed at much higher rates than the discounted ones that insurance companies negotiate.[47] As national hospital corporations absorb more previously nonprofit community hospitals across the country, access of the uninsured to emergency care has become more difficult. For-profit hospitals attentive to the bottom line are more likely to refuse or provide minimal treatment to the uninsured than the older nonprofits. They also tend to be quite aggressive in pursuing payment from those uninsured patients they care for—attaching wages and employing collection agencies. Such a system can be fatal to the uninsured, with about

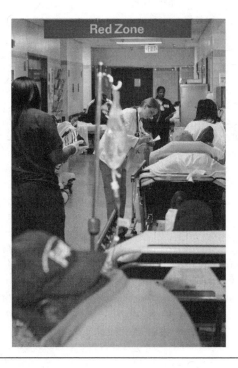

THE ONLY HEALTH CARE OPTIONS AVAILABLE TO AMERICA'S UNINSURED CITIZENS ARE TRIPS TO OVERCROWDED EMERGENCY ROOMS LIKE THIS ONE AT GRADY HOSPITAL IN ATLANTA, GEORGIA.

eighteen thousand uninsured patients dying each year because of lack of health insurance.[48] A more privatized, market-driven health care system has produced increasing numbers of the uninsured and impeded their access to care.

Not only have the trends of the last couple decades harmed those without insurance, those lucky enough to have coverage are not better off. All businesses have sought to shift more of the costs of health insurance premiums to their employees through higher co-pays of premiums and medical services. As their share of premium costs has risen, many lower-income employees have been forced to enroll in lower-cost plans that provide incomplete coverage, perhaps covering one's children but not oneself. To maintain their profits, insurance companies have become ever more adept at risk selection and experience rating so as to cherry-pick the more healthy subscribers and leave the less healthy vulnerable to more expensive premiums. Market competition among insurers has been central to this continuing trend away from broad insurance pools to the segmentation of risk.[49]

The mania to marketize health care eventually affected the country's popular and successful single-payer health insurance program for the elderly, Medicare. As noted earlier, insuring those over age 65, the least healthy and most costly segment of the population, is inherently risky for the insurer. The probability of needing to pay off on those insured is high, the reason why the market alone always failed to offer insurance to elderly citizens. Prior to Medicare, few of the elderly were insured because few private insurers were willing to take the risk. Since 1965, the government in the form of traditional fee-for-service Medicare has stepped in to insure this costly but vulnerable segment of the population. For government to do so successfully and in a program whose administrative overhead is below that of the private insurance industry conflicts with libertarian notions of the universal superiority of markets and private enterprise. In 1997, libertarian-minded members of Congress found a way to resolve this contradiction between their ideology and the realities of health insurance markets: they stuck to their ideology and opened up Medicare to competition from private insurers.

As a part of the Balanced Budget Act of 1997, the Republican majority in Congress created Medicare + Choice. Although a small percentage of Medicare beneficiaries had been enrolled in largely nonprofit HMOs as an alternative to the larger fee-for-service (FFS) program since the 1970s, the new Medicare + Choice program sought to encourage private insurers to offer a range of plans, including private fee-for-service plans, as an alternative to the government Medicare.[50] The new program was supposed to show how the wonders of market competition would lead these private insurers to cover seniors at lower than average cost and with a wider range of benefits than in traditional Medicare. Medicare would pay private companies a fee per enrollee (the capitation fee) equal to 95 percent of the average cost per enrollee in the traditional program. Initially, a number of insurers did entice a growing proportion of beneficiaries into their plans by offering the youngest and healthiest perks such as prescription drug coverage and lower co-pays and deductibles. This cherry-picking permitted companies to profit, despite the 95 percent capitation fee, because those they enrolled were less likely to incur health costs than the average Medicare beneficiary.[51] In the first few years, enrollment in Medicare + Choice programs rose to about 16 percent of the Medicare-eligible population.[52] Soon, however, enrollments began to drop as private companies discovered the limits of finding the young and healthy among seniors and applied more traditional managed care techniques, such as delaying care and restricting choice of physicians, to cut costs. Medicare beneficiaries deserted Medicare + Choice in droves.

So as not to allow reality to prove ideology wrong, the Republican Congress rode to the rescue of Medicare + Choice in 2003. A portion of the Medicare prescription drug bill enacted in that year changed the program's name to Medicare Advantage. Beyond this name change, clearly meant to assist private insurers in marketing their product to elderly consumers, the new program advantaged private insurers by now offering them subsidies to offer plans through capitation fees that were to be higher than average traditional Medicare costs. In effect, in the guise of using market competition to control costs, Medicare Advantage used Medicare taxes to subsidize the profits of the private health care industry. Currently, the per capita cost of enrollees in Medicare Advantage plans is 12 percent higher than in traditional Medicare and the program now contributes substantially to rising Medicare costs.[53] Now that an ample subsidy guarantees profits in the program, private insurers have aggressively marketed it, especially among low-income seniors, to attract enrollees. Recently, a number of state insurance commissioners have found health insurance agents working for some of the country's largest health insurers engaging in fraudulent practices to induce seniors to switch from traditional Medicare to their plans.[54] So far, the experience with trying to induce market competition into Medicare has been a colossal failure.

This blind adherence to market ideology pervades the entire prescription drug bill of which Medicare Advantage is a part. For years, the rising use of drug therapies has placed a huge burden on the pocketbooks of seniors because Medicare normally did not pay for prescription drugs, unless administered in a hospital. To correct this omission, the simplest and least costly approach would have been just to add a drug benefit to the traditional program. Instead, the bill enacted in 2003 relies solely on private insurance companies to offer prescription drug coverage through an enormously complex program requiring seniors to sort through hundreds of alternative plans. Aside from the inefficiency and anxiety that this program has created, the subsidies needed to induce private insurers to participate in the program increase its overall costs tremendously. At the same time, the program fails to adequately cover the costs of those who most rely on drug therapies. The legislation also prohibits Medicare, out of fear of "big government" interference in the market, from negotiating lower prices from the drug industry, a practice followed in most industrial countries. Because of the libertarian illusion, Americans will be paying more for less for years to come so that seniors might receive the medications they need.

Libertarian Health Reform: Consumer-Driven Health Care

The experience of the last two decades with privatization and pro-market approaches in the health care system ought to make one skeptical of the ability of the free market to improve health care. Not so for libertarians. Their ideological commitment to the free market as the universal cure for all social ills blinds them to experience with it in practice. So if recent market approaches such as competition in health insurance or expansion of for-profit health care have not worked, the problem must be that they did not rely enough on the market. Consumer-driven health care (CDHC), the latest libertarian nostrum for the health care system, aims to create the perfect free market in health care. CDHC would put health "consumers" in charge of choosing and paying for health care services just as they do when they purchase automobiles, dishwashers, or landscaping services. With consumers in charge of their own health care, a competitive market in both health services and health insurance would deliver them exactly what they need: high-quality health care at the lowest possible cost.

In a recent proposal from the libertarian Cato Institute, Michael F. Cannon and Michael D. Tanner identify two characteristics of this new, liberated health care market.[55] First, low barriers of market entry would create a wide pool of both health providers and health insurers competing vigorously for the health consumer's dollar. This competition would induce innovation in the kinds of treatments offered and promote efficiencies in their deliveries, driving down health costs. Naturally this would require freedom to experiment with ideas without the heavy hand of government regulation stifling innovation. Second, a successful health care market depends on consumer sovereignty—the complete freedom of consumers to choose their health care. CDHC means patients themselves—not their employer and not their health insurer—will choose their health care provider, the desired treatment from the options presented in the marketplace, and the type of health insurance product, if any, that best matches their individual situation. The choices of sovereign consumers will propagate through the market the precise signals to induce improvements in quality, lower prices, and stimulate technological innovation. As the Cato Institute study puts it, "individual choice actually promotes lower prices and higher quality . . . [consumers] will naturally choose the combination of health insurance and medical services that gives them the best mix of both. . . . The result is a market process that makes health care of ever-increasing quality available to an ever-increasing number of consumers."[56]

What practical measures are needed to bring about this ideal market in health services? First, health consumers need the cash to pay for the bulk of their health care directly rather than depend on insurance reimbursement. Libertarians view the third-party payment system and its accompanying moral hazard the main factor driving health care inflation and wasteful, unneeded, and low-quality care.[57] Instead of being dependent on health insurance reimbursement for their routine care, health consumers ought to have access to tax-favored *health savings accounts* (HSAs) from which they can pay medical bills. Deposits in an HSA would be in pretax dollars and their earnings accumulate tax free. With this money accumulating in their HSAs, consumers would shop carefully for the best care their money could buy. Cost-conscious consumers would see their HSA accumulations grow to cover future health costs or as part of their estate. (Most HSA proposals allow them to be available without penalty for any type of expenditure after age 65—to support retirement or to be left to heirs.)

Second, recognizing that HSAs alone might not be adequate if someone faced a catastrophic illness, CDHC advocates high deductible catastrophic insurance plans (HDCPs) as a supplement. Under these plans, subscribers cannot access their insurance until they have expended a large amount of money out of pocket (the deductible) in a given year. The advantage to health insurance consumers of high deductible insurance is its lower premiums. Since health insurers have a lower probability of reimbursing costs—many consumers may never expend all their deductible in a year, they can charge much less for the insurance. Typically, the higher the deductible the lower the premium will be. In the ideal libertarian system, consumers would have a choice between a wide range of HDCP options allowing them to pick the one best suited to their own calculation of risk. Some consumers might even choose to rely solely on their HSA and not purchase insurance at all.

In 2003, Congress included an HSA provision in the Medicare Prescription Drug Act.[58] The plan permits taxpayers to set up an HSA along the lines of the libertarian proposal. Contributions from both employers and employees are not taxed, nor are investment earnings in the account. Before age 65, an individual's withdrawals can be made for any approved medical expense tax free and after 65 for any purpose. To be eligible to establish an HSA, the taxpayer must enroll in an HDCP. The legislation assumes these will normally be offered as an option in an employee health benefit. Annual contributions to an HSA are limited to the size of the HDCP deductible, or $2,650 for individuals or $5,250 for families—limits that will increase with inflation. Eligible HDCPs under the legislation must have minimum annual deductibles of at least $1,000 for individuals or $2,000 for families and maximum deductibles of $5,100 for individuals or $10,200 for families. In fact, the plans limit out-of-pocket costs, including these deductibles and any other co-pays, to the maximum limits. All medical costs after the payment of these annual maximums are the full responsibility of the insurer. The purpose of these maximums is to protect participants in an HDCP from the risk of huge financial losses as the result of an expensive medical condition.

While libertarians Cannon and Tanner generally praise the 2003 legislation as a good start toward CDHC, they find fault with some of its elements.[59] First, they argue for a large increase in contribution limits. From a libertarian perspective, the key to consumer-driven health care is the HSA, not the HDCP. The magic of the marketplace for health services only kicks in as a result of health consumers spending their own money from their HSAs. Expenditures from an HDCP feature the same third-party payer drawbacks, including moral hazard, of traditional insurance. Consequently, real CDHC should encourage the accumulation of large sums in HSAs, so direct-consumer purchases of health services can be maximized. For this to happen, libertarians believe individuals should be allowed to invest from $10,000 to $17,000 annually in their HSAs.[60]

Second, Cannon and Tanner object to the requirement that investment in an HSA requires enrollment in an HDCP and the regulation of HDCPs, including the limits on the size of the deductible. In a free insurance market, consumers would be able to choose from the widest range of insurance products based on their own calculation of individual risk. From a libertarian point

Source: © 2007, Nick Anderson, Distributed by the *Washington Post* Writers Group. Reprinted with permission.

of view, this should include the choice to rely completely on one's HSA and not to purchase any insurance at all. They fear that regulation of deductible amounts would interfere with the ability of insurance companies to develop different insurance products with different deductibles targeted at different sorts of consumers. Choice among a variety of products catering to different tastes and different pocketbooks, libertarians point out, defines a truly free market. This feature is deemed essential if true price competition and its consequence—high-quality products at the lowest possible cost—are to be achieved.

The libertarian solution to the problems of the health care system relies on the blind faith in the virtues of the free market that characterizes the libertarian worldview. As we have seen, the nature of health care limits the efficacy of market solutions, but libertarians are blind to these realities. The idea of consumer-driven health care reflects the illusory nature of libertarianism. To begin, the idea of consumer-driven health care as a solution to problems in the health care system presupposes a faulty analysis of health care problems. Libertarians assume that the central problem with health care is overutilization of health services.[61] Due to the third-party payment system and moral hazard, health care costs skyrocket because consumers are opting for unneeded care. While moral hazard is a legitimate concern in health care, there are many other factors contributing to rising health care costs, including advances in technology, the labor-intensive nature of health care, and the administrative costs that a market-based system itself creates for the health care system.

The notion that smart shoppers spending their HSA dollars wisely will reduce overall health care costs ignores essential facts about health care expenditures. Even if CDHC makes millions of Americans wiser health care consumers, one should not expect a substantial reduction in health care expenditures. The fact is that most individuals do not spend that much on health care—a little over $2,000 per year for most people.[62] Reducing this amount will not have much impact on overall health care costs, because these costs are governed by the 80/20 rule—about 20 percent of the population accounts for 80 percent of the costs. Why is this the case? Most health care costs come from that relatively small proportion of Americans, mostly elderly, who are very sick. Their health care costs are high, not because they are not savvy consumers, but because they have conditions that are expensive to treat. HSAs may allow millions of relatively healthy Americans to shop for bargains, but this is unlikely to reduce the health care costs of the minority who need heart bypass surgery, kidney dialysis, or chemotherapy. Yet this minority comprises the bulk of national health care expenditures.

Consumer-driven health care also will exacerbate the risk segmentation—through cherry-picking and experience rating—that already plagues the health care market. HSAs with high deductible insurance are most attractive to the healthy and wealthy and least so to the sick and poor. Yet, as we have seen, any insurance system that fragments the insurance pool—separates those with little need for care from those who do—drives up insurance premiums and imposes more of the burden on the sick. In its purest libertarian version, individuals who anticipate the fewest health problems will select the HDCPs with the highest deductibles and the lowest premiums. This will impose higher premiums, since costs can no longer be shared with healthier people, on those with serious health problems. Inevitably, this will price insurance out of reach for many of the most vulnerable and likely increase the number of uninsured.[63] Moreover, individuals with expensive illnesses are unlikely to accumulate significant sums in their HSAs, since their health care costs will exhaust their contributions in a given year. Wealthy individuals with few health problems, however, especially if libertarian demands for high contribution limits are implemented, will find HSAs a convenient way to shelter much of their income from taxation and accumulate more wealth.

Finally, the whole idea of CDHC ignores the limits of health markets described earlier in this chapter. The HSA/HDCP approach cannot eliminate the basic asymmetry of information inherent in health care. Even if they are paying their health care costs with their own dollars, patients will depend on their health care providers to identify the best health care treatments. The image of sick patients facing life-threatening illnesses shopping around for the best deal on radiation treatments or an appendectomy is laughable. Buying health care is different from shopping for a car or a vacation. Consumers are more dependent on the judgment of those who provide the service being purchased and the professional standards that determine the best quality of care.

Quality health care cannot be provided equitably or effectively in a pure market system. Libertarian arguments about CDHC ignore this fundamental reality.

In sum, to return to our health care trilemma, consumer-driven health care offers a particularly undesirable trade-off among access, quality, and cost. Despite contrary libertarian claims, the practical impact of CDHC has to be less access to health care for people with lower incomes and an increase in the proportion of the uninsured. Most worrisome is the effect of this approach on the access of the sick—those most in need and more likely to be poor, whom higher premiums in traditional insurance, increased co-pays, and high deductibles will bar from access. Nor will CDHC produce high-quality care as it is premised on a mistaken expectation that the power of consumer choice will stimulate quality improvements. As we have seen, the asymmetry of information between provider and patient impedes such effects in health markets, requiring government regulations and professional standards to ensure quality. Finally, CDHC will not reduce health care costs. It places too much faith in savvy consumers driving down costs when the patients receiving the most expensive treatments, who are responsible for the bulk of health care costs, typically are not in a position to shop around for their care. If we were to adopt the libertarian formula, in a few years we would find the health care system to be as costly as it is today—probably more costly—and to provide access to quality care only for the "healthy and wealthy."

Nonlibertarian Alternatives to Better Health Care

There is no escape from the trilemma of health care. The libertarian illusion in health policy is their claim that the free market, in the guise of consumer-driven health care, offers an escape. Balancing the trade-offs among health care costs, access, and quality in a manner satisfactory to most of us requires prudent, sensible government regulation. Only when we begin thinking about health care more as a public good than a private market good will satisfactory trade-offs occur. We also must accept that a perfect resolution to the trilemma always remains out of reach. Like much else in public policy, outcomes involve compromises among competing goals—no one of which can be maximized except at the expense of another. In health care, this means setting priorities among our three goals. The reliance in the United States on market mechanisms has prioritized high-quality health care for some at the expense of universal access and high cost. As fewer and fewer Americans have access to high-quality care, the trilemma must be rebalanced to create a more satisfactory health care system. Rejecting the libertarian illusion and squarely facing policy trade-offs, including recognition of the need for governmental solutions, is the formula for a better health care system.

Central to better health care is a first priority on universal access. The most morally reprehensible aspect of our current health care system is how it rations access to medical care according to ability to pay. In the richest country in the world, those without insurance and those with inadequate coverage must not endure sickness and even death for financial reasons. Libertarian approaches to health care fail to acknowledge this moral problem and offer no adequate solution. Only a governmental guarantee of access to basic medical care along with governmental financing can provide this universal access.

The second priority should be quality. Over the past century medicine has developed the capacity to cure disease and prolong productive and enjoyable life. Providing sufficient resources and incentives to continue the invention of new procedures and technologies to improve health has to be part of any good health care system. Medical quality requires a steady supply of highly trained and well-compensated health care professionals. Like education, medical care is labor intensive and offers only limited capacity for productivity gains through the substitution of machines for labor, as in other industries. In fact, in medicine, the introduction of machines—as in new diagnostic devices— often leads to the need for more trained professionals to operate them and interpret their results. Higher-quality health care means, not only individual access to state-of-the-art treatments and skilled medical, professional, but also public health measures from quality environment to vaccinations that con-tribute to overall well-being. In many respects, public health measures and more widespread access are more important to measures of quality like higher life expectancy and low infant mortality than the latest technology.

Lower cost must be ranked as a third priority. Any good health care system needs to be attentive to costs, especially to the extent that they result from waste and inefficiency, but universal access and high-quality medical care can-not be bought cheap. Libertarians make a critical mistake when they focus on reducing health care costs through competition and barriers to "overutiliza-tion." A rich nation like the United States can afford to and should devote a large share of its resources to purchasing a valuable good like a healthier pop-ulation. More effective drugs, technology, and procedures, along with an aging population, are likely to lead to increasing health costs in the future, so we should be prepared to direct more societal resources to paying for them. The rising proportion of national income that will go to paying these higher costs should not be analyzed in isolation, but in relation to what is being pur-chased. To the extent that health care spending produces healthier people, it is a valuable investment.

This priority list effectively reverses that of the libertarians. Although, as I have said, they suggest free markets eliminate the need for trade-offs among cost, quality, and access, the real thrust of their prescriptions is to seek cost reduction first, quality second, and not worry too much about access. In order to make the trade-offs that I am suggesting, we would need to move to some form of government-regulated universal insurance. The precise form it would take would not matter so much as its commitment to these priority trade-offs. Two different approaches that make this commitment are a single-payer

"Medicare for all" long advocated by proponents of universal health insurance, and a more recently proposed "mandatory insurance" approach.

Mandatory insurance has gained attention since the state of Massachusetts recently adopted a variant of this approach for its citizens. The new law requires virtually all residents to obtain health insurance, just as it requires all drivers to purchase auto insurance. Most Massachusetts residents continue to receive coverage through their employers, while employers with over eleven employees are now mandated to offer a basic package of benefits or contribute $295 per employee to a fund subsidizing individual policies for the uninsured.[64] The state's poorest residents will receive free coverage from this fund, with contributions from state government. A key feature of the plan is the creation of a broad insurance pool including many younger, healthy people who are currently uninsured to help fund the overall system and keep premiums low. The gradual introduction of a system of fines for those who fail to purchase insurance are crucial to inducing the young and healthy into the system, but it remains to be seen if the fines are high enough and whether business will continue to back the program.[65] And despite the mandate rhetoric, no one expects the program to insure everyone in the long run.

While the Massachusetts model falls short of universal coverage, some advocates of mandatory coverage have proposed plans that do guarantee universal coverage. Leif Wellington Haase of the Century Foundation proposes a federal mandate that all American families purchase their own health insurance, with government subsidies to make it affordable. Each family will receive a subsidy sufficient to allow it, through a combination of its government grant and own resources, to purchase a "basic insurance plan."[66] Insurance companies will compete through developing insurance packages based on three levels of coverage that the federal government will devise and sponsor. Families will receive subsidies sufficient for the basic plan but would be able to purchase the more costly "Buick" and "Cadillac" plans from their own resources.[67] While insurance companies could develop a variety of insurance products to attract subscribers, including HMO and other managed care plans or fee-for-service plans, all must cover the benefits prescribed in each of the three federally sponsored plans. The federal government also will negotiate all premium levels with national and local health plans, thereby avoiding risk segmentation and cherry-picking of subscribers. With all Americans covered through this plan, employer-based coverage would no longer be needed and Medicare and Medicaid would be phased out.

Haase's approach to universal coverage has the political advantage that it carves out a role for the existing health care industry and thus offers the chance they would not oppose it. Unfortunately, in a manner similar to Clinton's ill-fated attempt to do the same with managed competition, the plan contains considerable bureaucratic complexity. Devising the appropriate subsidy to ensure that insurance is affordable for everyone, negotiating premiums, and developing the three levels of insurance packages will pose challenges to federal bureaucrats. The plan does promise universal access and support for quality improvements. Breaking the link between employment and insurance makes U.S. industry more competitive in the global economy, as employers, like those abroad, would no longer pay for health insurance. But one must be skeptical about insurance industry support for Haase's plan; as with the Clinton provision, the industry may bridle at the added regulation it requires.

A much more straightforward, simple approach to universal coverage would be a single-payer, Medicare-for-all approach.[68] Medicare already insures the most expensive portion of the population: the elderly. Extending coverage to all would widen the pool the program now "insures" to include healthier individuals who now pay, along with their employers, their health coverage through their employers. Although Medicare for all would increase federal expenditures substantially, the increase in society's total health care cost—even with extending coverage to the now uninsured—would be minimal. Without the administrative complexity of the current system, overall administrative costs would go down. Covering the current uninsured would be offset by the savings from their receiving preventive and timely care rather than costly emergency room treatment. As Michael D. Reagan points out, "universalizing Medicare would mean a switch in how health care is paid for, not an increase in how much it costs the nation."[69] The higher taxes that citizens would pay to fund a single-payer, universal insurance system would be less, in the long run, than what they would need to pay in private insurance premiums in the existing system. As it already does, Medicare could manage provider fees through DRGs without any substantial change in the way health care is currently provided. With all Americans now a part of the insurance pool, experiments in capitated managed care, as in the failed Medicare + Choice program, would be more successful because insurance plans could include younger, less risky subscribers. To ease the shock to the system that such a reform might produce, it could be phased in over time by gradually covering a greater range of ages, perhaps starting with children.

Critics of single-payer, universal insurance systems often decry the "rationing" of care that is supposed to characterize these systems. Horror stories about long waits for elective surgery for hip replacements are usually trotted out as decisive evidence of the undesirability of such systems. What this argument ignores is that all health care systems ration care. In the United States, care is rationed constantly by denying it to the uninsured and through the administrative regulations imposed by private insurers that limit access to care. Mandating limited time in the hospital; imposing high co-pays to discourage using medical services; and, most of all, not insuring a major portion of the population are our current means of rationing care. Rationing simply is more fair and efficient under universal care, done on the basis of the character of the health condition being treated rather than the patient's income, class, or race. Also, like all insurance, including private insurance in the United States today, a single-payer system would not pay for any and all medical interventions an individual might want. Cosmetic and other kinds of discretionary procedures probably would not be covered. But such a plan would meet the collective obligation we have to ensure that all have access to medical interventions needed to preserve life and the ability to function normally, to the extent that physical disability allows, in the world.

In sharp contrast to the libertarian consumer-directed health care plan, both mandatory insurance and single-payer plans face up to the realities of the health care trilemma and prioritize its components correctly. Any progress toward improving the United States' health care system requires discarding the failed notion that the free market alone will solve its problems. All of us, including libertarians—if they can set aside their ideological blinders—want a health care system that delivers much that a market can never deliver. We want a system that does not deny needed medical treatment to those without money in their pockets. When we are sick, we all want the most expert, state-of-the-art care possible. None of us want to face the prospect of bankruptcy on top of the misfortune of being seriously ill. Probably all of us would assent to directing a large share of national resources to pay for health care if the population as a whole could be made healthier as a result. None of these things that we want can be achieved in health care until we discard the libertarian illusion and tackle realistic ways to use government effectively for our collective good.

SUGGESTIONS FOR FURTHER READING

Cannon, Michael B., and Michael D. Tanner. *Healthy Competition: What's Holding Back Health Care and How to Free It.* Washington, D.C.: Cato Institute, 2005. The complete libertarian case for consumer-driven health care.

Morone, James A., and Lawrence R. Jacobs. *Healthy, Wealthy, and Fair: Health Care and the Good Society.* New York: Oxford University Press, 2005. A high-quality collection of articles by political scientists on various aspects of the health care system.

Reagan, Michael D. *The Accidental System: Health Care Policy in America.* Boulder, Colo.: Westview Press, 1999. Although now a bit dated, this book provides an excellent analysis of the policy issues confronting any attempt to reform the United States' health care system.

Relman, Arnold. *A Second Opinion: Rescuing America's Health Care.* New York: Public Affairs, 2007. A physician's analysis of the health care system, prescribing single-payer universal insurance as the only effective cure for what ails it.

Starr, Paul. *The Social Transformation of American Medicine.* New York: Basic Books, 1982. A now-classic study of the history of American medicine.

SELECTED WEB SITES

www.cato.org/healthcare/index.html. The Cato Institute's health policy site.

www.healthpolicywatch.org. A Century Foundation site on health policy.

www.nchc.org. The National Coalition on Health Care brings together business, labor, and medical professionals for bipartisan analysis of health issues.

NOTES

1. Michael D. Reagan, *The Accidental System: Health Care Policy in America* (Boulder, Colo.: Westview Press, 1999), 59.
2. Harold Wilensky, *Rich Democracies: Political Economy, Public Policy, and Performance* (Berkeley: University of California Press, 2002), 596.
3. Clarke Cochrane, et al., *American Public Policy: An Introduction*, 8th ed. (Belmont, Calif.: Thompson/Wadsworth, 2006), 253.
4. Anna Bernasek, "Health Care Problem? Check the American Psyche," *New York Times*, December 31, 2006, Bu-3.
5. Paul Krugman, "The Health Care Racket," *New York Times*, February 16, 2007, A19.
6. Cochrane, et al., *American Public Policy*, 254.
7. Bernasek, "Health Care Problem?"
8. Among the recent critical analyses of American health care are David Cutler, *Your Money or Your Life: Strong Medicine for America's Health Care System* (Oxford: Oxford University Press, 2004); and Donald L. Bartlett and James B. Steele, *Critical Condition: How Health Care in America Became Big Business—and Bad Medicine* (New York: Doubleday, 2004).
9. Cutler, *Your Money or Your Life*, xi.
10. For a discussion of Arrow's argument see Relman, "The Health of Nations," *The New Republic*, March 7, 2003, 23.
11. Julius B. Richmond and Rashi Fein, *The Health Care Mess* (Cambridge: Harvard University Press, 2005), 9.
12. Reagan, *The Accidental System*, 19.
13. Paul Starr, *The Social Transformation of American Medicine* (New York: Basic Books, 1982), 295.
14. Ibid.
15. Jacob Hacker, *The Divided Welfare State: The Battle over Private and Public Social Benefits in the United States* (Cambridge: Cambridge University Press, 2002), 203, 215–216.
16. Ibid., 214.
17. Ibid., 229.
18. Starr, *The Social Transformation of American Medicine*, 330.
19. Hacker, *The Divided Welfare State*, 225–237.
20. Ibid., 245.
21. Starr, *The Social Transformation of American Medicine*, 369.
22. Hacker, *The Divided Welfare State*, 247.
23. Ibid., 384.
24. Ibid., 320–327; for the coining of HMO, see 395.
25. Ibid., 415; Bartlett and Steele, *Critical Condition*, 88–89.
26. Arnold S. Relman, "Health-Care Financing: Profit and Commercialism," in *The Encyclopedia of Bioethics*, ed. Warren T. Reich (New York: Macmillan, 1995), 1064.
27. Bartlett and Steele, *Critical Condition*, 77.
28. Ibid., 72.
29. Richmond and Fein, *The Health Care Mess*, 81–82.
30. Theda Skocpol, *Boomerang: Health Care Reform and the Turn against Government* (New York: W. W. Norton, 1997), 25.

31. Ibid., 32.
32. Ibid.
33. Ibid., 34.
34. Ibid., 42.
35. Philip J. Fungiello, *Chronic Politics: Health Care Security from FDR to George W. Bush* (Lawrence: University Press of Kansas, 2005), 226–227.
36. See the following for accounts of the failure of the Clinton plan: Skocpol, *Boomerang;* Hacker, *The Divided Welfare State,* 260–269; and Fungiello, *Chronic Politics.*
37. Skocpol, *Boomerang,* 132.
38. Ibid., 196.
39. Arnold S. Relman, "The Market for Health Care: Where Is the Patient?" *Clinical Chemistry* (1997): 43, no. 12, 2226.
40. Richmond and Fein, *The Health Care Mess,* 60.
41. Fungiello, *Chronic Politics,* 281.
42. Paul Krugman, "The Health Care Racket," A19.
43. Leif Wellington Haase, *A New Deal for Health: How to Cover Everyone and Get Medical Costs under Control* (New York: Century Foundation Press, 2005), 1.
44. Milt Freudenheim, "Health Care Costs Rise Twice as Much as Inflation," *New York Times,* September 27, 2006, C1.
45. Ibid.
46. Richmond and Fein, *The Health Care Mess,* 233.
47. Bartlett and Steele, *Critical Condition,* 15.
48. Institute of Medicine, *Insuring America's Health: Principles and Recommendations* (Washington, D.C.: National Academics Press, 2004), 46.
49. Haase, *A New Deal for Health,* 23.
50. Arnold S. Relman, *A Second Opinion: Rescuing America's Health Care* (New York: Public Affairs, 2007), 83.
51. Ibid., 83–84.
52. Henry J. Kaiser Foundation, "Fact Sheet: Medicare Advantage, September 2005," www.kff.org/medicare/upload/Medicare-Advantage-April-2005-Fact-Sheet.pdf. Accessed July 7, 2007.
53. Peter R. Orszag, "The Medicare Advantage Program: Trends and Options," statement before the Subcommittee on Health, Committee on Ways and Means, U.S. House of Representatives, March 21, 2007.
54. Emre Peker, "Pushed into the Wrong Health Plan," *MarketWatch,* June 29, 2007.
55. Michael F. Cannon and Michael D. Tanner, *Healthy Competition: What's Holding Back Health Care and How to Free It* (Washington, D.C.: Cato Institute, 2005), 4.
56. Ibid., 5.
57. Ibid., 45–59.
58. This account of the 2003 HSA plan follows Beth Fuchs and Julia A. James, "Health Savings Accounts: The Fundamentals," National Health Policy Forum, April 11, 2005.
59. Cannon and Tanner, *Healthy Competition,* 68–73.
60. Ibid., 69.
61. Ibid., ix.

62. Fuchs and James, "Health Savings Accounts," 19.

63. Ibid., 28.

64. Reed Abelson, "Mandatory Coverage Is Easier Said Than Done," *New York Times,* June 11, 2007, H2.

65. Pam Belluck, "Universal Care Plan Faces Hurdles in Massachusetts," *New York Times,* July 1, 2007, N16.

66. Haase, *A New Deal for Health,* 5–7.

67. Ibid., 35.

68. Reagan, *The Accidental System,* 158–161.

69. Ibid., 159.

Chapter 6   Policies Regarding Birth and Death: Individual Autonomy versus Community Interest

Those under the spell of the libertarian illusion regarding the policies discussed in preceding chapters are typically Republican conservatives, people affiliated with the American political right. Deep tax cuts, deregulation, privatizing Social Security, and consumer-directed health care form the core of much of the Republican political agenda nowadays. All are based on libertarian assumptions about absolute property rights, the sanctity of voluntary contracts, and the magic of the free market. In this chapter, we turn to the left of the American political spectrum, where the libertarian illusion also has established itself and led to equally misguided policy thinking. While over the past three decades libertarians on the right have been enamored with unfettered market freedom, those on the left have sought complete independence in personal life choices. For these libertarians on the left, many of whom consider themselves Democratic liberals, the answer to the complexity of policy issues regarding abortion, recreational drug use, "victimless" crimes such as prostitution, sexual and other "lifestyle" preferences, euthanasia, and a whole range of bioethical issues is *individual choice*. In the same way that their ideological soul mates on the right celebrate the freedom of individuals to make voluntary exchanges in the marketplace without government regulation, libertarians on the left champion self-sufficient individuals' freedom to make personal life choices without the impediment of socially or governmentally imposed moral values. Both right and left libertarians base their policy prescriptions on the same conception of the human person—the unencumbered, autonomous, self-sufficient individual so at odds with the communitarian view of humanity's socially embedded nature. In this chapter, I will argue that these libertarian assumptions are as much of an impediment to achieving the common good through policies regarding personal life choices as they are those regarding the economic marketplace.

Some attribute the libertarian turn to the left to the 1960s counterculture.[1] Certainly, the hedonistic experimentation expressed in the era's slogan "sex, drugs, and rock and roll" promoted an ethic of radical individualism and self-expression. The blend of the counterculture with the civil rights movement imbued what otherwise might have been a superficial cultural trend with political significance. Many came to view the "right" to a countercultural lifestyle as analogous to the right of African Americans to civic equality; both were part of a new era of human liberation. Unlike the civil rights movement, however, which aimed at claiming rights for a disenfranchised group to participate as equal members of the political community, countercultural politics centered on freeing individuals from the constraints that community might seek to impose. The counterculture's mantra to "do your own thing" reflected a libertarian understanding of community in which every individual decided autonomously how to live. As a guide to policy, it sought to establish individual rights to choose every aspect of one's personal destiny. The demands for "rights" and "choice" became a core component of left-wing ideology in the post-1960s era.

Blaming the counterculture for the contemporary emphasis on personal rights, however, ignores the deep roots of this approach in U.S. culture and history. Over fifty years ago, political theorist Louis Hartz described how the liberal tradition, from which libertarianism is derived, has exerted an overwhelming influence over our culture and politics.[2] In no other society has the liberal governmental framework first envisioned in the theories of John Locke, with its emphasis on individualism, limited government, and individual rights, exerted so much influence. Locke's ideas hold a featured place in the Declaration of Independence and an echo in the fears of "majority tyranny" of those who wrote the Constitution. This liberal influence has included, as noted in chapter 1, a version of individualism placing the self-reliant individual, as championed in the works of Ralph Waldo Emerson and Henry David Thoreau, at odds with social conformity. An understanding of freedom as "pursuing your own good in your own way," as liberal theorist John Stuart Mill defined it, still resonates among U.S. individualists.[3] The libertarian assumption that personal conduct ought to be uniquely a matter of personal choice, as long as others are not harmed by the conduct, has always been as American as apple pie.

Not surprisingly, a bias toward individual autonomy has characterized U.S. law and, in the twentieth century, began to govern how the Supreme Court viewed personal rights. As we shall see in more detail, the development of a new legal understanding of personal privacy reflected a libertarian turn in jurisprudence. The Warren Court of the 1950s and 1960s, building on trends since the 1920s, made a jurisprudence of rights central to its legacy. Some, like the 1954 *Brown v. Board of Education* decision declaring segregated schools unconstitutional, promoted a more inclusive understanding of citizenship rights, but other decisions regarding rights of criminal defendants, free speech, and religious freedom focused on individual rights against the state. Eventually, in the 1965 *Griswold v. Connecticut* decision, the Court articulated for the first time a constitutional right to *privacy* that in subsequent decisions would be understood increasingly in libertarian terms. Like in the counterculture, the legal focus on rights tended to encourage many on the political left to think of politics as primarily a process of carving out areas of individual rights, usually through the courts, rather than building coalitions on behalf of the common good. Although not necessarily understood as libertarian, this political outlook resonated with the libertarian tradition in American political culture. In the nineteenth century, this tradition had emphasized the property rights so dear to today's right-wing libertarians, but it would encourage the new libertarian emphasis on personal autonomy as well. We will examine this evolution in more detail in the next section.

In this chapter, I will focus on that part of the new libertarianism of personal autonomy through an examination of some of the most controversial public policy issues of our time relating to both the beginning and end of human life. In the debate over abortion rights and the equally controversial debate over euthanasia, including "physician-assisted suicide," libertarian voices advocated policy solutions through the assignment of individual rights and ensuring individual choice. A largely libertarian solution has governed abortion policy since the 1973 Supreme Court decision *Roe v. Wade*. We will look at the limitations of this libertarian paradigm in resolving the political controversy over this morally significant issue. In regard to policies governing the "end of life," even though advocates of a constitutional "right to die" have sought a similar solution, thus far the Court has resisted a *Roe*-like rights guarantee. Consequently, policies regarding the termination of life have been more communitarian and less centered on merely granting a "right to die." Before looking at specific policy issues, we need to review some of the philosophical and legal reasoning, including the evolution of the jurisprudence of privacy, that undergird the libertarian stance toward these policies.

Individual Autonomy and Rights Absolutism

A number of years ago, when the People for the American Way asked young people to identify "what makes America special," most answered "rights and freedoms."[4] What they meant by "freedom" invariably reflected a libertarian understanding of the concept. America's freedom meant "individualism, and the fact that it is a democracy and you can do whatever you want," according to one young person, or "our freedom to do as we please when we please," according to another. These young people understood freedom in a radically individual way as their ability to choose for themselves how to live their lives and to do so free of any external constraint. In adopting this outlook, they tapped into the profound libertarian strain in American culture that provides an unconscious language for articulating the meaning of freedom. Legal scholar Mary Ann Glendon, in her well-known book *Rights Talk*, offers an anecdote that illustrates the almost automatic and unthinking connection people make between the United States and an individualistic understanding of freedom. She tells of a television interview with a representative of a veterans' group who loudly criticized a recent Supreme Court decision that had affirmed the right of individuals to burn the American flag as a form of political speech. When the interviewer pressed the opponent of this newly declared freedom to articulate what made the flag a cherished symbol that ought not to be desecrated in the name of political speech, he declared, with unconscious irony, that the flag "stands for the fact that this is a country where we have the right to do what we want."[5] Even his opposition to individuals exercising such an unbridled right in this particular instance could not diminish his commitment, in the abstract, to a libertarian understanding of freedom.

For both the young people in the survey and the befuddled flag defender, the automatic assumption is that freedom means autonomous individual choice of values and ends. As political philosopher Michael Sandel reminds us, this liberal (and libertarian) understanding is only one potential version of the complex concept of freedom.[6] Another, equally important within American culture, is based in "civic republican theory" that views freedom as the opportunity to share in self-government. Rather than as isolated individuals autonomously choosing by themselves what political ends to pursue, civic republican theory envisions people deliberating among themselves about the common good and the destiny of the community. Freedom, in this sense, is an ability to participate with others on behalf of common ends. The opponent of flag burning, for example, if thinking in civic republican terms, might have justified prohibiting flag burning because it symbolizes in a special way our democratic political community. To burn a flag as a means of political participation, then, is a symbolic attack on the very democracy that makes more meaningful forms of participation possible. While a complete sense of freedom demands both liberal and civic republican elements, the tendency in recent years has been to acknowledge only the liberal sense in looking to autonomous individual choice as the only means of resolving political conflict, especially in regards to controversial moral issues like those discussed in this chapter. In doing so, Americans have foregone exercising their freedom in the republican sense to deliberate about public policy issues.

By overlooking the civic republican understanding of freedom over the past few decades, Americans have sought to solve policy dilemmas on many issues simply by identifying those areas of life where individuals possess absolute rights to choose what to do. Individuals and groups demanding recognition of a right have come to dominate our politics. A host of rights—the right to bear arms, to smoke, to access pornography, to burn a flag as a political statement; and not to wear a seat belt, or inhale "secondhand" smoke, or wear a motorcycle helmet, to list only a few—has been the source of political controversy. In each of these areas, those claiming rights seek to carve out an area of life in which government and, often, other individuals are forbidden to intrude. This claim is often made in absolute terms that overrule or, as is sometimes put, "trump" any other public or social consideration that might be affected by a claim to rights. For example, those claiming a "right to bear arms" argue that this right overrides any consequences that gun possession could have on the community. Although gun rights advocates usually deny that widespread gun ownership encourages gun-related violence, even if it did, they would still claim that restricting gun ownership cannot be an option for addressing the problem. The slogan "guns don't kill, people do" implies this absolutist right to gun ownership—only punishing the person who uses a gun in a violent act is allowed, not regulating the availability of guns to law-abiding citizens. According to legal theorist Ronald Dworkin, "if someone has a right to do something, then it is wrong for government to deny it to him even though it would be in the general interest to do so."[7]

This absolutist understanding of personal rights and the "rights talk" of contemporary politics have evolved from nineteenth-century legal doctrines concerning the absolute right of private property.[8] Under the influence of the interpretation of Lockean political theory in Blackstone's *Commentaries*, the most widely read legal text of the period, legal scholars and courts in the United States viewed property rights as "absolute, individual, and exclusive."[9] Sir William Blackstone described property as "that sole and despotic dominion which one man claims and exercises over the external things of the world, in total exclusion of the right of any other individual in the universe."[10] At a time when small farmers dominated the U.S economy, this absolute protection of property represented a democratic guarantee of their security and independence. With industrialization, however, the absolute right to private property came to be an obstacle to regulation of corporations and the protection of workers. The federal courts, like contemporary libertarians, interpreted the right of property and the right of contract that derived from it in absolute terms that overruled any attempt by government to interfere with relations between employers and employees. Between the 1890s and the 1930s, the Supreme Court struck down nearly two hundred laws, both federal and state, that attempted to regulate prices, wages, working conditions, child labor, and labor union activities.[11]

The legal basis for most of these rulings lay in the Fourteenth Amendment to the Constitution. Enacted in the wake of the Civil War, this amendment was intended to guarantee civil liberties to the newly freed slaves. In time the Court came to apply the amendment's key phrase that no state may "deprive any person of life, liberty, or property without due process of law" not to protect the civil liberties of southern blacks, but to free corporations (legal "persons") from government regulation. In the most famous decision of its kind, *Lochner v. New York* (1905), the Court struck down a law limiting bakery employees' working hours to sixty hours per week. In this case, the Court saw the right to contract as a trump that overruled any effort by the state to improve working conditions for the bakers, arguing "interference with the rights of individuals, both employers and employees, to make contracts regarding labor upon such terms as they may think best."[12] As we saw in previous chapters, contemporary libertarians continue to hold this absolutist conception of property and contract rights, but after the 1930s and the New Deal, the Court ceased to adhere to such a rigid view and opened the door to wider government regulation.[13] Yet just as this libertarian vision of property rights absolutism waned, the Court began to apply the same rights-based jurisprudence of *Lochner* to certain personal rights in areas such as school prayer, free speech, rights of criminal defendants, and abortion. According to Glendon, "Much of the attention the Supreme Court once lavished on a broad concept of property . . . it now devotes to certain personal liberties that it has designated as 'fundamental.'"[14] Moreover, this shift has influenced the popular tendency toward "rights talk" in encouraging citizens to conceive of themselves primarily as possessors of individual rights that enable them to determine alone their life's purpose and goals.

The image of the "lone rights bearer" features prominently in how many Americans think about moral and life issues like abortion and euthanasia.[15] Much of the discourse about these issues and the way they are treated in U.S. law assumes an essentially libertarian conception of the human person as "a freely choosing unencumbered self."[16] To be "unencumbered" means that individuals choose the ends they pursue independent of any attachment to others. As pointed out in the first chapter, libertarians typically conceive of people as being self-owned. The ends chosen are considered equally good; "no person or way of life [is] intrinsically better."[17] When it comes to moral issues, self-ownership means individuals "determine for themselves what it means to lead a good and virtuous life."[18] In other words, only the autonomous individual can be the judge of the morality of his or her actions or the nature of the good. Government, in this view, has no business making judgments about what is good or moral because it has no grounds to do so. This particularly is the case when different groups or individuals disagree about the good in question; a minimal government response is demanded to "decide questions of justice and rights without affirming one conception of the good over others."[19] From a libertarian perspective, then, public policies touching on moral questions or differing conceptions of the good life ought to respect the rights of individuals to choose such things for themselves, and the government must remain neutral regarding competing ends and goals.

According to political philosopher Michael Sandel, this conception of the unencumbered self cannot make sense of moral obligations and social ties of real human beings.[20] In this libertarian moral universe, there is no room for those unchosen obligations we owe our families such as caring for a disabled child, supporting an ill spouse, or honoring the parents we did not choose, let alone broader solidarity with the communities that nurture us. Sandel criticizes liberal philosopher John Rawls, who embraces the conception of the unencumbered self, for his narrow vision of moral obligation. In Sandel's account, Rawls acknowledges two sorts of duties: those we owe other people as fellow human beings—not to harm them, to treat them fairly, and the like—and those based on agreements we consent to with other people. As unencumbered selves, "we must respect the dignity of all persons, but beyond this, we owe only what we agree to owe."[21] This constricted view of obligation does not account for solidarity with particular communities whose morally relevant histories may carry an obligation for us as, for example, a patriotic commitment to serve one's country. Can we make sense out of why soldiers dutifully serve multiple tours in an unpopular war in Iraq, one that many of the soldiers themselves regard as misbegotten and unjust, simply as fulfillment of a contractual obligation? Patriotic sacrifice and duty to country go beyond the language of contract. Beyond considerations of obligation, the vision of the unencumbered self denies the social character of the human person recognized at least since Aristotle's time as the defining feature of humanity. In sum, when we take into account the reality of social ties and solidarity, public policies based solely on an unencumbered individual's "right to choose" ignore how wider social concerns might bear on and potentially limit that choice.

As we have seen in the previous five chapters, this libertarian view regarding personal and moral issues is identical to the stance taken regarding economic and property issues. Individuals should have absolute ownership of any property they acquire without resorting to force or fraud, unencumbered with any obligation to any other individual or society at large. Taxation for the purposes beyond protecting property and contractual rights can never be legitimate because it employs an individual's property for something to which he has not agreed. Any attachments one has to others are based solely on voluntary contract and go no further than obligations to which contracting parties have mutually agreed. Beyond voluntarily contracted obligations, one only is obligated to respect the rights of others and not commit force or fraud. Government ought to be neutral regarding the goals or purposes of individual economic choices, including the goals of parties to contracts. If a worker contracts to take a hazardous job, for example, government has no right to interfere with that choice. As with moral judgments, economic choices in a libertarian world are best left for individuals to make on their own. In light of this consistency between the worlds of unencumbered moral and economic selves, the manner in which legal jurisprudence adapted ideas of absolute property rights for defining absolute personal rights comes into focus. The libertarian vision of rights-bearing, unencumbered, self-sufficient individuals holds consistently across both moral and economic realms.

The emergence of a constitutional right to privacy in American law illustrates the connection between nineteenth-century understandings of absolute property rights and contemporary conceptions of absolute personal rights.[22] The first mention of a "right to privacy" in American jurisprudence came in an 1890 *Harvard Law Review* article by Samuel D. Warren and his law partner (and future Supreme Court justice), Louis D. Brandeis. The concern of the article was gossip: should individuals have any legal protection against their private lives being exposed in the press? This may seem a quaint concern in light of today's world of paparazzi and the widely reported goings on of starlets and pop stars, but Warren and Brandeis wanted to find within the common law some justification for someone to sue to protect privacy. They found their principle in cases, based on property rights, that prevented publication of individuals' private letters, lecture notes, drawings, and the like. Pulling privacy "from the hat of property," Warren and Brandeis discerned the "inviolate personality" of the author or artist in these cases being protected, not the physical objects themselves.[23] They extrapolated from this a person's "right to be let alone" when it came to public exposure of the elements of one's private life. Over the next few decades, lawyers and judges would assert this "right of privacy," as a common law principle, in a variety of cases protecting individuals from intrusion into their personal lives in areas such as public disclosure of personal information and commercial appropriation of name and image.[24] As yet, however, this understanding of privacy was narrow, encompassing only intrusion into private areas of life, not any individual action, and it was not asserted as a constitutional right.

It took *Griswold v. Connecticut* in 1965 to raise the right of privacy to a matter of constitutional principle, yet in doing so the Supreme Court retained much of Warren and Brandeis's understanding of privacy as a right against unwarranted intrusion into personal affairs. The case involved an antique and unenforced Connecticut law prohibiting the use of contraceptives. The Court's majority found the law to violate the "intimate relation of husband and wife" and a "right of marital privacy" implicit in the guarantee of liberty in the Fourteenth Amendment. Like the common law understanding of privacy, the Court's concern was more with the law's intrusion into a personal relationship between married couples that ought to be free of governmental scrutiny than a right to take a particular action. While this case clearly articulated a "right of privacy" as a constitutional right, the decision did not necessarily envision it as an individual right. Rather than affirm any personal choice a person might make regarding contraception, the decision advanced a substantive moral judgment about the value of the social institution of marriage that would be harmed if government intruded.[25] In fact, legal scholar Glendon believes that the right to privacy, left as it was in *Griswold,* would have remained a feature of family and marital law rather than an individual right.[26]

In 1972, the Court took the fateful step of expanding the right to privacy into an individual constitutional right. This time the case also involved contraception, but it concerned a Massachusetts law prohibiting the sale of contraceptives to unmarried individuals. In *Eisenstadt v. Baird* the Court no longer confined the right to privacy to the marital relation but identified it as an individual right. According to the majority, "if the right of privacy means anything it is the right of the individual married or single to be free from unwarranted governmental intrusion into matters so fundamentally affecting a person as the decision to bear or beget a child."[27] Nothing could be clearer—individuals now had certain rights to privacy that the Constitution protected. And, as the quote indicates, the right now involved not just intrusion into an area of personal privacy, like a marital bedroom, but into an individual choice to purchase a contraceptive. This new description of a right to privacy fit perfectly the libertarian view of absolute individual liberty to pursue one's preferences as one wished.

The Beginning of Life: A Right to Choose Abortion?

The Roe v. Wade Decision

In the 1973 case *Roe v. Wade,* the Supreme Court overturned an 1854 Texas law, then still in effect, that prohibited abortion. In doing so, the Court adopted the libertarian paradigm that the government should not impose a particular moral judgment regarding the act of aborting a fetus, as least in the early stages of pregnancy, but left that judgment to the choice of the individual woman. Drawing on the new right to privacy, the Court said this constitutional right applied to abortion and gave the individual woman an absolute right not to be interfered with if she chose to terminate her pregnancy. Leaving such a morally charged issue to individuals to decide for themselves, the Court argued, was the best way to resolve the problem in a pluralistic society lacking a clear consensus on whether or not abortion was morally permissible. In the years since, the country's experience with politics around the abortion issue has clearly shown the limits of a libertarian approach to policies regarding moral questions. Regulating abortion merely through the assignment of an absolute individual right to choose has not produced an abortion policy that satisfies either those who oppose a woman's access to abortion or those who favor it. Rather than diffusing the politics surrounding the issue, which seemed to be the Court's expectation in *Roe,* abortion has turned into one of the most politically divisive issues of our time. At the same time, this approach to abortion politics has impeded rather than facilitated constructive deliberation about what to do about abortion, as well as maternal and child care issues in general. And, most tellingly, the *Roe* decision has failed to offer many women the actual freedom to choose, with dignity, their reproductive future.

Roe v. Wade concerned a Texas woman, identified as Jane Roe in court documents, whom Texas law had prevented from obtaining an abortion. The Texas law resembled many such laws enacted in the latter half of the nineteenth century that prohibited abortion except when performed to save the life of the mother.[28] Before that time, most states either had no laws regarding abortion or proscribed the procedure only after "quickening"—the time of the fetus's first movement in the womb. By 1973, only about half the states retained restrictive abortion laws comparable to the Texas law. Most of the other states had liberalized their statutes to allow abortions when pregnancy risked the physical or mental health of the mother, when the child was likely to be born with grave mental or physical defects, and in cases of rape or incest. Four states at the time—Hawaii, New York, Washington, and Alaska—had enacted laws that allowed unrestricted abortion in the first trimester of pregnancy, the standard the Court would articulate in *Roe.* In sum, the legal status of abortion in 1973 was very much in flux, as states deliberated about the complex moral issues that the procedure raised.

In intervening in the abortion issue, the Supreme Court nationalized it, and in imposing a uniform federal policy effectively halted state legislative deliberation on the core question of the permissibility of abortion. States would be prevented from interfering with a woman's decision to terminate her pregnancy in the first trimester, while retaining the ability to impose restrictions in the interests of maternal health starting in the second trimester, and to proscribe abortion based on the state's interest in protecting fetal life after "viability"—the point at which a fetus could survive outside the womb.[29] The Court based its decision on a substantive right to privacy regarding matters of reproduction and sexual intimacy implicit in the Fourteenth Amendment's due process clause.

In its decision, the Court claimed it was not providing an absolute right to abortion, per some of the amicus briefs' arguments, but one limited by the various rules defining the extent of the right within the trimester scheme. But a woman's right to choose could not be limited within the first trimester and, after that, the restriction in the second trimester related to state regulation of the safety of the procedure, not whether an abortion could be permitted. Only after viability did there seem to be some room for legislative intervention to regulate abortion, but that could be limited in the interests of protecting the mother's health.[30] Certainly, after *Roe,* any legislature seeking to regulate abortion had to do so without placing, as Justice Sandra Day O'Connor would eventually put it, "an undue burden" on the core right to choose. This clearly meant there was, in the abstract at least, an absolute right with which a legislature could not interfere, although a tug of war defining the precise line a legislature could not cross in regulating abortion came to dominate abortion politics in the coming decades.

In making its decision, along with determining a pregnant woman's rights, the Court had to address the fact that a decision to terminate a pregnancy would result in the destruction of a fetus. Should the fetus also be regarded as a "person" under the Fourteenth Amendment and thus invested with guaranteed rights? And, if so, how should these fetal rights be weighed against the privacy rights of the mother? In defending the Texas statute, the state's lawyers argued that life begins at conception and that the fetus is a person whose life the state is compelled to protect from and after conception. The Court acknowledged a state interest in the potential life of the fetus after viability, but prior to that point it refused to recognize the unborn fetus as a person with rights under the Fourteenth Amendment. To recognize the fetus as a person after conception would require accepting the Texas law's view that life began at conception, but in pointing to the absence of consensus among doctors, philosophers, and theologians regarding when life began, the Court held it "need not resolve the difficult question." Instead, it opted to remain "neutral" on the question of when life began and simply ruled that the view in the Texas law did not outweigh the privacy rights of the pregnant woman. In effect, the Court's presumed neutrality gave to the individual woman the right to decide, prior to viability, whether her fetus were alive and how that judgment might bear on whether to terminate a pregnancy. In sum, the decision adopted the essentially libertarian paradigm that government and law must remain neutral regarding contentious moral, philosophical, and religious issues and only the autonomous individual—the "lone rights bearer"—could decide such questions.

Despite *Roe*'s claim to neutrality regarding when life begins, in permitting abortion the Court did presuppose an implicit position on the issue. Certainly, those who held the belief that an embryo or fetus was a human life from conception saw permitting abortion as anything but neutral—it permitted killing a fetus, which from their point of view was a morally abhorrent act. The claim to remain neutral and leave the decision to the individual as a constitutional right was no different in practice than affirming the view that, prior to viability, the fetus was something less than a human life; otherwise, how could women be permitted to choose abortion? Neutrality meant, in reality, taking a stand on the very issue the Court claimed to avoid. Despite its claim to sidestep the issue, the Court had to assume this moral difference prior to viability; otherwise, it could not justify why the state's interest in the life of the fetus begins then and not before. As philosopher Michael Sandel points out, "The case for respecting a woman's right to decide for herself whether to have an abortion depends on showing that there is a relevant moral difference between aborting a fetus at a relatively early stage of development and killing a child."[31] In *Roe*, the Court claimed it was only preventing Texas law from imposing a particular answer on the morally controversial issue of when life began, but it decided the question itself that life began, at least as a political and constitutional matter, at viability. What the decision failed to do was offer any compelling moral, political, or philosophical argument why its judgment regarding when life began was superior to that of Texas. As one constitutional scholar put it, "Why wasn't Texas free—free as a constitutional matter, free under the Fourteenth amendment—to proceed on the basis of the assumption that a pre-viable unborn child is no less a subject of justice than a post-viable unborn child or a born child?"[32] The *Roe* decision seems to reflect the libertarian illusion that society can resolve moral controversy simply by leaving such issues to individual choice. The political storm that *Roe* ignited showed that leaving moral choices to individuals will only fuel conflict when some regard the choices made as morally unacceptable.

Abortion Politics after *Roe*

In removing abortion policy from the state legislative arena and nationalizing the issue as a matter of constitutional right, the *Roe v. Wade* decision intensified, rather than diminished, political controversy over abortion rights. Soon the public debate became focused around two dichotomized views: pro-choice and pro-life. Adopting the "rights talk" frame of contemporary

THE "RIGHTS TALK" POLITICS OF ABORTION, SINCE *ROE V. WADE*, ENCOURAGES PRO-CHOICE AND PRO-LIFE ACTIVISTS TO TAKE ABSOLUTE POSITIONS AND PREVENTS COMPROMISE.

politics, two incommensurable and absolute rights—a woman's right to choose and a fetus's right to life—were pitted against each other. Rhetorically at least, the bodies of pregnant women became battlegrounds within which warring factions contended over which absolute right would trump the other. Both sides seemed to lose sight of the possibility that within those bodies there might be a common interest that could lead to compromise. The libertarian assumptions, implicit in the rights rhetoric of both sides, that only an assignment of rights could resolve the matter, have stifled any policy deliberation that might help find where the common good rests with respect to the abortion issue. The rigidity with which the conflict has raged has politicized the U.S. judiciary, as both sides intervene to obtain judicial appointees sympathetic to their position, and deformed our electoral politics, as the parties have divided on the issue and activists on both sides make abortion stances a litmus test for nominations.[33] The abortion controversy has been central to the increasingly polarized politics of the contemporary era. Trying to resolve the moral complexities in abortion policy through leaving it a matter of choice and constitutional right have not encouraged the productive political deliberation needed for good policymaking.

Nor has this approach to abortion policy provided the meaningful choice and reproductive freedom advocates of a woman's right to choose expected from *Roe v. Wade*. In libertarian fashion, *Roe* offered women only the *negative* freedom from government interference in choosing whether to have an abortion; it provided neither the capacity to exercise that freedom, the resources to assist them with the decision, nor support for the decision's consequences—whether the impact of an abortion on a woman, her friends and family, or the burdens of parenthood. Soon the negative character of the freedom became clear as abortion opponents, once they realized *Roe* would not be easily repealed, focused their attention on restricting access to the procedure.[34] A struggle over defining how the abortion right might be exercised came to dominate abortion politics from the late 1970s to today. The approach of opponents was to enact a restriction on abortion access at a state or national level, defend the inevitable constitutional challenge in court, and require the Supreme Court to determine the constitutionality of the restriction. For the past three decades, the Court has had to revisit the issue of abortion rights in case after case. Over time, these cases have created a more restrictive environment that with other factors have reduced access to abortion across the country.

Initially the focus was on denying public funding for abortions and, reflecting an understanding of the right to choose as a private, negative freedom, the Court upheld denial of any federal or state funds to pay for abortions. As a result, while a few states continue to provide some funding of abortions, most women seeking an abortion must pay for it privately.[35] By the early 1990s, the Court agreed that a variety of state regulations on abortion access, such as a twenty-four-hour waiting period, state-mandated counseling, and parental consent for a minor seeking an abortion, as not creating an "undue burden" on the right to choose an abortion. Today, while there are substantial variations across the country, state legislatures have imposed a wide variety of statutory regulations on abortion that, along with funding restrictions, impede the ability of many women, particularly poor women, to obtain an abortion, although all pass constitutional muster as not violating the "right" to one.[36] In addition to these legal developments, a woman seeking an abortion today will find many practical obstacles, including a declining number of abortion facilities—many women need to travel hundreds of miles to reach one, fewer doctors trained in abortion procedures or willing to perform them, and the agony of having to run a gauntlet of antiabortion protestors outside abortion clinics.[37] As with libertarian approaches to public policy in general, the negative freedom approach to abortion gives women a right to choose but provides no guarantee that the resources needed to take advantage of the right will be available. As the title of a recent book says, in America today, abortion is "safe, legal, and unavailable" for many women.[38]

The rights talk that dominates our national discussion of abortion policy overwhelms any meaningful discussion of the socioeconomic realities that lead women to seek an abortion or the formulation of constructive public policies that could reduce the number of unwanted pregnancies. Although pro-life and pro-choice advocates argue about the legal right to an abortion, comparative studies show that whether or not abortion is legal in a country is unrelated to the actual abortion rate.[39] Poorer, developing countries where abortion tends to be illegal have much higher abortion rates than developed, industrialized countries where the procedure is legal but women have better access to birth control. Arguments over the legal right to an abortion also have little to do with how women view their situation. Few women regard the agonizing decision to seek an abortion in terms of a right to choose; for most it is a tragic necessity when no other meaningful option seems available. Studies show that nearly half of all pregnancies are unintended and of those about half end in abortion. Usually lack of access to effective contraception was the reason for the unintended pregnancy. The reasons most women give for seeking an abortion are overwhelmingly economic; chief among them are concern about having the financial resources to support the child or the impact on work responsibilities and the need to care for other dependents.[40]

Yet for all the uproar abortion politics has created, very little attention is paid to practical policy efforts that would address the reasons abortions occur. Given the relationship between access to contraception and abortion, devoting resources to reproductive health education and availability of contraception, including the health insurance needed to pay for them, would more effectively prevent abortions than legal battles over abortion. Increased investments in child care, maternal health, and family support, as well as more generous maternity leave policies, would reduce the financial anxieties that lead women to choose abortions. In recent years, as we have seen in the previous chapters, the libertarian campaign to shrink government has reduced spending on such programs, and libertarian fiscal and regulatory policies have increased economic pressures on most Americans while increasing poverty and economic inequality. These factors may explain why, as overall abortion rates have declined in the past decade (by about 11 percent between 1994 and 2000), abortion rates for women with incomes less than 200 percent of the poverty rate have increased by 25 percent.[41] Besides easing the financial burdens of parenthood, particularly for low-income women, as an option to abortion, making adoption a realistic alternative requires investment of community resources in caring for a woman and her family through pregnancy and supporting adoption services. When it comes to policies that address the overall context and socioeconomic factors that impact abortion, neither the libertarian outlook on government programs nor its individual rights orientation to matters of personal morality have much to offer.

Since *Roe*, the federal judiciary has placed itself as the ultimate policy decision maker on the abortion issue, yet court adjudication is deficient as an arena for building public agreement around such a complex issue. Judicial policymaking involves an adversarial process in which contending parties attempt to convince judges to accept one side of an issue rather than another. This process encourages both sides to differentiate their arguments as sharply as possible from those on the other side and excludes any mutual deliberation to find common ground. In the case of abortion, as we have seen, this has meant defenders of the right to abortion fighting to protect the broadest possible interpretation while the antiabortion side has tried to chip away at the right. The adversarial judicial process reinforces a polarized abortion discourse that pits a woman's absolute right to choose and a fetus's absolute right to life into an unequivocal choice. But this rights dichotomy does not reflect the nuanced, ambivalent, and ambiguous way most Americans think of the issue.

Despite the ups and downs of abortion politics over the past thirty years, public opinion on abortion has remained remarkably stable and provides little support for how activists on either side frame the issue. Since the 1970s, the percentage of Americans adopting a pro-choice position—that abortion should be legal under any circumstances—has remained between 20 and 25 percent, while those who think it should be illegal under all circumstances has attracted only a slightly smaller percentage.[42] When respondents are specifically asked to choose between the pro-choice and pro-life labels rather than characterize the issue's legality, Americans divide evenly, with a little over 45 percent on each side. Polls have consistently found that Americans strongly supportive of a decision to abort in the cases of threats to the life of the mother, fetal deformity, and pregnancies resulting from rape and incest, with over 80 percent supporting the decision in these cases.[43] When it comes to matters that respondents see as more within the discretion of pregnant women, such as unwillingness to marry, concern about having too many children, or financial pressures, support drops dramatically, although from 40 to 50 percent of Americans have consistently supported the choice to abort even in these cases. The latter suggests, given the fact that the reasons that inspire less public support are precisely those more likely to lead to abortions (particularly concerns about financial pressures), pro-choice advocates might be correct in seeking a constitutional right to protect women from a potential "tyrannical majority." But, despite less willingness to see factors like financial pressures as justifying an abortion, most Americans remain unwilling to have government intervene heavy-handedly in the decision to have an abortion. Respective of their own attitudes, nearly 70 percent of respondents are willing to leave the choice to a woman and her doctor. This is true even though over half of Americans regard abortion as immoral. Large majorities support the kinds of abortion regulations that states have enacted in recent years, such as waiting periods and parental notification, but a 2003 Gallup Poll found that 58 percent of Americans opposed an outright constitutional ban on abortion, even if it included an exception for saving the mother's life. What emerges from this and other polling data is a picture of the American public that is divided on the abortion issue but, consistent with public opinion on many issues, is neither ideological nor consistent in its views. The public seems to regard abortion as wrong in the abstract, but justified depending on the reasons; it approves of some government regulation, but does not want government to be too intrusive or meddlesome. If abortion policy were to be democratically responsive, reflective of these ambivalent public views, it would need to be nuanced and steeped in compromise of moral principle.

Turning the issue into a matter of constitutional rights has left politicians free from actually deliberating with one another about crafting public policy that reflected the complicated views of the American people. With the judiciary in control of abortion policymaking, elected politicians have used the issue for symbolic purposes—carving out extreme and absolutist positions on the issue to gain the support of party activists without the need to formulate practical solutions that might gain wider public support. At election time, politicians adopt either pro-choice or pro-life labels as a means of gaining support in low turnout primary elections where issue activists' votes matter and in raising money from those ideologically devoted to the issue. In doing so, however, they know that they will not face tough questions about the nitty-gritty of how abortion should be regulated—for example, who ought to be penalized and how if it were prohibited—nor address the specific needs facing pregnant women and their families contemplating an abortion. Nor do they need to fear being held accountable for how abortion policy affects constituents and society at large, such as its impact on women or on the unborn, because the judicial arena has predominated in controlling the issue and can be blamed for any negative outcomes. In fact, since abortion politics has been largely symbolic politics for politicians for so long, the tendency has been to legislate irresponsibly on the problem, more for the purpose of symbolic position taking, rather than to seek realistic solutions to this complicated issue. The Partial-Birth Abortion Ban Act, enacted in 2003, illustrates the irresponsibility of such symbolic politics.

The Conflict over Partial-Birth Abortion

In the mid-1990s, the pro-life movement targeted a specific abortion procedure as a means of rallying its supporters and making a largely symbolic statement against abortion. The procedure, labeled "partial-birth abortion" (technically *intact* dilation and extraction [D&E]), is a particularly gruesome one involving crushing a fetus's brain as it is removed from the birth canal.[44] The procedure, like its more often performed variant *simple* D&E, involving dismemberment of the fetus in the womb prior to extraction, is performed rarely and only in cases when a well-advanced pregnancy goes disastrously wrong. Physicians who perform the procedure argue that in those rare cases when necessary, intact D&E sometimes is less likely to risk injury to the mother than its variant. In combating the procedure, the antiabortion activists thought they could raise awareness of the seeming brutality of the procedure and, since it involved removal of a well-developed fetus that was killed in the process, they sought to highlight a comparison to infanticide. In 1996, the Republican Congress passed legislation outlawing the procedure, only to have it vetoed by President Bill Clinton. After the 2000 election, the legislation was passed again, this time signed by President George W. Bush. In the spring of 2007, in a narrow 5–4 decision in *Gonzalez v. Carhart*, the Supreme Court's conservative majority, now with Bush appointees Chief Justice John Roberts and Justice Samuel Alito in the majority, found the Partial-Birth Abortion Ban Act to be constitutional.

Although the pro-life movement celebrated passage of the legislation as a great victory, it is important to note that the law prevented no abortions. All it does is to require surgeons to use only the equally gruesome regular D&E procedure in late-term abortions rather than have the option to use the sometimes safer intact D&E. Critics of the law saw it as an outrageous interference in a physician's discretion and professional judgment as to which method was medically required in a particular case. The legislation seemed to bring the government into the operating theatre to second-guess physician judgment in a potentially dangerous operation. From a constitutional standpoint, the *Gonzalez* decision broke new ground in finding the law constitutional, although it provided no exception for saving the life of the mother—the first time the Court had not done so in the history of abortion jurisprudence. The legislation claimed, and the Court agreed, that such an exception was unnecessary in this case because the D&E option involving uterine fetal dismemberment remained—although many specialists in obstetrics had testified that this D&E procedure often posed severe risks for death and injury from bleeding and punctures to the uterus.

The now conservative majority on the Supreme Court has not yet over-turned a woman's right to choose, but it is willing to countenance substantial interference into the complexities of medical decision making in carrying out the choice. Independent of the abortion controversy, all Americans have to wonder whether other sorts of surgical procedures might become subject to legislative prohibition now that Congress had established the precedent of doing so in this case. Because the libertarian paradigm of abortion policy-making foreclosed legislative deliberation on the substance of the issue, abor-tion opponents had embarked on a thirty-year campaign of attrition through legislative efforts to limit the right. With the Partial-Birth Abortion Ban Act, these efforts have culminated in the alarming spectacle of Congress prescrib-ing appropriate medical procedures. Even nonlibertarians have to regard this step as potentially threatening to the liberties of physicians and their patients to make medically appropriate decisions. Instead of protecting liberty, the lib-ertarian rights paradigm and reliance on judicial policymaking has produced a substantial threat to freedom. These developments seem to underscore James Madison's famous observation that rights are mere "parchment barriers" absent majority political support for rights and the capacity of a democratic majority to protect them.

A Communitarian Approach to the Abortion Controversy

The United States needs an abortion politics where sides do not yell at one another about whose rights trump whose or think a "morally neutral consen-sus" can be found on the issue, but one where all hammer out the practical measures required to address the existence of unwanted pregnancies. On the pro-life side that would mean moving beyond simply a vague demand that abortion be prohibited to detailing how such a ban would be enforced, who would be sanctioned when abortions occurred, and what those sanctions would be. Those who believe that life begins at conception would need to convince a democratic majority of what concrete legal steps follow from such a belief. Would killing an embryo or early-term fetus be equivalent to murder, or would distinctions be possible allowing such an action to be something less? If life begins at conception, does that mean there could be no exceptions within an abortion ban, or would exceptions for rape, incest, or dangers to a mother's life and health be allowed? And how would those exceptions be rec-onciled with the taking of a human life as the fetus was destroyed in those cases? While many of these questions now receive attention in philosophical and legal journals, elected politicians rarely have to address them when dis-cussing the issue today, but these questions would come to the fore were abor-tion opponents given the opportunity to deliberate about a comprehensive abortion policy. At the same time, abortion opponents would need, in the context of the abortion debate, to address the broader concerns of women fac-ing unwanted pregnancies and what should be done if abortion were not an option. How issues of reproductive health, access to contraception, child care, family-leave policies, maternal support during pregnancy, and policies regarding adoption and foster care bear on the abortion issue would have to be integral to the discussion.

Likewise for those favoring the permissibility of abortion, the debate would need to move beyond simply defending the right to choose. As for the pro-life side, more attention would have to be given to the broader context surrounding those facing the agonizing choice to seek an abortion. If attention turned from the right at stake to the broader community responsibility to those faced with unwanted pregnancies, social supports could be demanded to assist women who believe they need to make a choice to abort. Also, defenders of the need for recourse to abortion in some cases would need to convince a democratic majority what community goods, as well as individual ones, were threatened if such an option were denied. Defending abortion would demand facing the moral issues surrounding abortion as a matter for communal judgment, not merely one of individual choice. Rather than a pro-choice position that sidesteps the moral controversy abortion entails, those who believe abortion is permissible need to make a public, substantive, and moral case why an embryo or fetus should be regarded differently than a fully developed human being. Such an argument might be based on how, as Philip Selznick suggests, "biological changes between conception and birth are accompanied by progressive transformations of meaning, attachment, and obligation."[45] Public deliberation would never reconcile completely opposing moral, religious, and philosophical views on the issue, but it could allow majority compromise on what these transformations in meaning, attachment, and obligation bear on the legal status of the fetus and when abortion might be permissible. This approach would allow an abortion policy that both acknowledges the sanctity of developing human life and the dignity of a pregnant woman grounded in community values.

To Americans familiar with our abortion politics, developing abortion politics outside the language of competing rights and through democratic deliberation based in community values as just described might seem absurd. How could anyone resolve the competing moral, religious, and philosophical views regarding the matter through legislative deliberation, independent of judicial fiat? Yet this has been the approach of most other industrial democracies, and many have been more successful than the United States in both asserting respect for the potential life of the unborn fetus while also offering women faced with an unwanted pregnancy a dignified way of considering options, including access to abortion.

As in many matters of social policy, the French seem to have developed one toward abortion that is humane, supportive, and respectful of human life. Initially enacted in 1975, during a period of extreme controversy over the issue, the French legislation reached "a humane, democratic, compromise."[46] The statute's opening clause "guarantees the respect of every human being from the commencement of life . . . [with] no derogation from this principle except in cases of necessity."[47] This clearly places the abortion decision in the realm of "necessity" rather than choice, reflecting more accurately the reality involved and signaling symbolically that abortion is an exceptional event. At the same time, the law emphasizes the state's responsibility toward women and children, citing "education towards responsibility, the acceptance of the child in society, and family-oriented policy are national obligations."[48] In France, a woman facing an unwanted pregnancy is not considered responsible alone in the situation, but can count on broad governmental support. The law forbids abortion as a means of birth control, but in the same clause cites the government's obligation to provide birth control and family planning education. It then authorizes abortion in the first twelve weeks of pregnancy in cases of "distress," left undefined; the woman and her doctor determine whether such distress exists. Again, rhetorically, abortion is characterized as a serious matter and not given absolute sanction, but a woman and her physician have discretion in making the ultimate decision. Prior to obtaining an abortion, a woman must undergo a waiting period (although a doctor may waive this requirement if deemed necessary), receive a brochure describing the abortion law, be informed of all medical risks in the procedure, and accept counseling from a social worker regarding alternatives—including description of the generous French system of social benefits for pregnant women and for child care. After the first twelve weeks of pregnancy, abortion is possible for "therapeutic" reasons, as certified by two physicians, such as danger to the health of the mother or fetal deformity.

In contrast to the U.S. libertarian approach, the French law is communitarian in placing the decision within the context of the connections between a woman and the community. It emphasizes not the rights involved but the communal interest in both the sanctity of life and the welfare of the woman. This law forces no woman to carry a child to term—the "distress" criterion and other requirements are low hurdles for any woman seeking an abortion— but it does not simply say an abortion can be obtained on demand. The law allows encouraging a woman to have a child but underlines the government's obligation to assist families and children, backed up with generous benefits. While the French statute would satisfy neither the pro-life view (abortion is permitted) nor the pro-choice view (conditions are placed on receiving abortions), it does acknowledge both the concern to emphasize the sanctity of life yet not obstruct a woman's ability to determine the outcome of her pregnancy. Since the law was enacted, abortion controversy has diminished in France and has rarely been a salient issue in French politics. Although most Americans, given our experience since *Roe v. Wade,* believe the moral controversies surrounding abortion can only be addressed through the libertarian paradigm of rights and personal autonomy, the French example shows that there is a communitarian alternative. It both respects human dignity, with considerable freedom from governmental intrusion concerning such a personal and difficult decision, and provides important community support to those facing the decision.

The End of Life: A Right to Choose Death?

Like the debate over abortion, the policy debate about physician-assisted suicide—whether terminally ill or severely disabled individuals ought to be able to seek the help of doctors to end their lives—raises profound moral and philosophical issues. And like the abortion issue, there is great disagreement over whether such a procedure is permissible. Views on the issue range from those who believe in the absolute autonomy of the individual to choose death to those who believe only the God who gives life can take it.[49] While many Americans hold one or another of these extreme positions, most probably find themselves somewhere in between and, much like on the abortion issue, are torn by the competing moral claims. Everyone can easily understand the anguish of a person facing a life of extreme pain, suffering, or severe limitations who would see death as a release from misery. As recently as forty years ago, few people were likely to face this situation—a serious accident or illness would bring a fairly quick death—but advances in medicine, such as organ transplants, heart-lung machines, and advance drug therapies can now keep people alive but not always guarantee a good quality of life.[50] In recent years public policy has had to address the desire many people have to seek the help of a physician to quietly end lives they find unbearable. And these policies have needed to address the issue of how to treat a physician who might agree to assist in such a case. Given the strength of libertarianism and individualism in our culture, for many Americans the best policy solution in these cases is to grant individuals a "right to die" so that they can make the individual choice of seeking the help of a physician to end their life. While, as in the case of abortion, such a policy solution might seem appealing, it faces similar limitations.

To understand this debate, we need to review briefly traditional law and policy regarding suicide, euthanasia, and a variety of "end-of-life" issues raised by advances in medical knowledge. The dominant Western religious traditions and many philosophical ones condemn suicide as immoral, although some Western philosophers, such as David Hume, considered it an appropriate, rational choice for those who no longer saw value in living. Not surprisingly, in view of these dominant philosophies, suicide traditionally was considered illegal in Western societies until the twentieth century—with legal penalties for those who survived suicide attempts. Nowadays, in most American states, suicide has been decriminalized, although still condemned, and treated more as a matter of mental health policy.[51]

While willfully killing oneself has been considered illegal, legal tradition never imposed an obligation on an individual to accept medical treatment even if that refusal would result in death. Common law asserted a person's control over his body against unwanted action, whether it was a punch in the face or a medical syringe. This notion speaks not of a right to die but of people's ability to control the medical interventions to which they are subjected.[52] In fact, legal principal requires that individuals' consent to the care they receive—the reason we all have to fill out consent forms so often in doctors' offices. The key idea here is *informed consent,* the ability of someone to rationally decide on medical treatment. In practice, the idea of informed consent allows, for example, people with cancer to weigh for themselves, presumably with their physician's advice, whether chemotherapy's probability of saving their life is worth its pain and discomfort or whether they would prefer to let the disease take its course. Most ethicists distinguish such a decision as distinct from suicide because the cause of death, in this instance, is the underlying disease, not the refusal of treatment.

Such decisions to refuse or forego additional treatment of an illness leading to death usually are accompanied by efforts to ease the pain and suffering accompanying that death. This process can be seen as a form of *passive euthanasia.*[53] The term *euthanasia* derives from the Greek for "good death," connoting a process of peaceful, pain-free "death with dignity." Euthanasia has most often been associated with the active form, in which someone willfully acts to help a person die. For critics, euthanasia is a form of murder, even if the person being killed consents. The Nazi use of involuntary euthanasia to kill a variety of groups they deemed undesirable, such as the mentally and physically disabled, as well as the other Nazi atrocities of the Holocaust forever associated the term with unspeakable evil. While many see a large moral difference between voluntary and involuntary euthanasia, the Nazi example remains an important reminder of the moral gravity associated with any public policy addressing the care of the terminally ill, decisions regarding how they are treated and the danger of its misuse for evil ends.

Yet the issues of care at the end of life and how public policy should address it are inevitable. For millions, death is not a sudden or immediate event but rather a process ranging from days to years during which a patient, though terminally ill, remains alive. During this period numerous difficult decisions are involved regarding the forms of palliative care to be provided and whether to seek medical intervention to further prolong life. For many, the best solution in these cases is hospice care aimed at assisting in a "good death" through treating pain and easing discomfort and suffering, but avoiding interventions that prolong life without improving the quality of life. Fortunately, specialists in end-of-life care are continually developing better medication and procedures to increase the comfort of those in the process of dying.

In offering comfort to the dying, however, the line between simply allowing death to occur, what might be termed passive euthanasia, and actively producing death is often blurry. For example, morphine is commonly used to ease the pain and discomfort of the dying, but usually steadily increasing dosages of morphine are needed to be effective. This means that at some point the level needed to control pain will produce death. Ethicists tend to regard death brought about in this matter as permissible based on the principle of "double effect." The act of administering the drug is intended to relieve pain, not induce death, although the act in question has the double effect of producing both ends. Professional medical standards approve of such practice and have been found acceptable by hospital review boards, courts, and usually families.[54]

For the vast majority of those facing death, the most important public policy issues involve access to hospice care rather than abstract issues like the "right to die." This means requirement that such care be covered under private insurance and that those without coverage receive public assistance. Given the blurry line between palliative care and bringing about death, policies regulating end-of-life care need to focus on the professional competence of caregivers, adherence to professional standards, and the participation of family members in care decisions. A libertarian approach to dying that focuses solely on the individual rights at stake cannot encompass the reality people face in such a situation. Rather than being a self-sufficient decision maker at death, one is dependent on the compassionate care of families, caregivers, and access to community support. A communitarian vision recognizes individual dependency and concerns itself with providing communal support and recognizes the obligation of communities and governments to make "death with dignity" possible. Rights talk has little relevance to the important issues people deal with when a loved one nears death.

Rights of the Dying: The *Cruzan* Case and Living Wills

Public controversy regarding the "right to die" has arisen more often in terminating life support in the form of a respirator or a feeding tube when there is no longer the prospect of curing an underlying condition. In cases involving individuals who may be competent to decide for themselves, life support can be terminated based upon the broader right of informed consent. The difficulty arises when the person on life support is not competent, either because they are disabled or comatose. Medicine now defines death as a flat electroencephalogram (EEG), but people in comas continue to exhibit some brain activity even if there is no prospect of their returning to consciousness. Persons in a persistent vegetative state may survive for years with only a feeding tube providing water and nutrients yet be totally unaware of their existence and never regain consciousness. But given medical uncertainties (there are cases when people emerge from comas after many years), a judgment needs to be made whether the prospects for revival merit continuing life support and who is going to decide—the state, medical providers, or family members. A combination of state statutes and court decisions has recognized close family members, who are aware of the patient's likely wishes regarding care, as surrogates who can make decisions for a legally incompetent person in these cases. Most state laws shield physicians who terminate treatment from liability if done according to the patient's wishes expressed through surrogates.[55]

To prevent uncertainty regarding a comatose patient's wishes, all fifty states have passed "living will" statutes allowing individuals to give advanced directives defining how they would want to be treated under given circumstances and specifying a surrogate to decide if they are incompetent. In the case of a living will, decisions to terminate care need not involve the courts. Unfortunately, few Americans have living wills, and in their absence issues may be raised about whether a close family member actually expresses the wishes of the comatose individual. This was the issue in 1988 in Missouri in the case of Nancy Beth Cruzan.

In 1983, Cruzan was involved in an automobile accident that left her in a persistent vegetative state. Although she was able to breath on her own, a feeding tube kept her alive as she lay in a constant fetal position. After five years, her parents, certain Cruzan would never revive and convinced she would not wish to continue as she was, went to local probate court seeking permission to remove the feeding tube. The probate judge agreed, but the state attorney general appealed the decision to the Missouri Supreme Court, which reversed the probate court, citing the state's interest in preserving life and the absence of "clear and convincing evidence" that Cruzan's parents knew her wishes.[56] The Cruzans appealed the decision to the U.S. Supreme Court, confronting the Court for the first time with the question whether the Constitution guaranteed a "right to die." Writing for the majority in *Cruzan by Cruzan v. Director, Missouri Department of Health,* Chief Justice William Rehnquist acknowledged a competent individual's constitutional right to die through the refusal of medical treatment as a matter of due process under the Fourteenth Amendment, but he upheld Missouri's power to determine what evidence needs to be presented for an incompetent person's wishes. In the decision, Rehnquist found that the individual's interest needed to be balanced by the state's concern for the value of human life. In effect, he supported Missouri's claim that the Cruzan parents had the burden of proof that they expressed their daughter's wishes. The ultimate impact of the decision was to decline to nationalize the issue of the "right to die," as had occurred with abortion in *Roe,* and leave to the states the complex issues surrounding death and dying. After the Supreme Court decision, the Cruzans returned to probate court with new evidence of their daughter's wishes based on further comments from friends and family. The judge, based on this evidence, again allowed removing the feeding tube, and the Missouri attorney general did not appeal, having made his legal point. (Missouri public opinion had already turned decisively in favor of the Cruzans.) In December 1990 Nancy Cruzan died, two hours after her feeding tube was removed.

The legal and policy framework after *Cruzan* in the United States governing the withdrawal of life support bore little resemblance to the libertarian paradigm of absolute rights as trumps. The Supreme Court had affirmed the traditional doctrine of informed consent over medical interventions, but left it up to state legislatures and courts to determine how the wishes of an

incompetent individual were to be ascertained in light of a state interest in preserving life. In practice, given most state law on the matter, this meant nearly
complete autonomy of patients, their caregivers, and family members in decisions surrounding withdrawal of care if a "living will" is in force and, in most
cases, a near autonomy in most cases when state law acknowledges close rela-
tives as appropriate surrogates to decide the fates of their loved ones. Unlike
Missouri and a handful of other states, most state laws do not place a high burden of proof on family surrogates in the decision to withdraw life support.[57]
The overall situation reflects a more communitarian understanding of the
termination of an individual life that acknowledges the dying person's ties to
family and the legitimate obligations of both professional caregivers and
government.

This framework was upheld in the tragic and emotional case of Terri
Schiavo in 2005, who had survived in a persistent vegetative state since 1990.[58]
The difficulty in this case arose because of a family conflict over what her wishes
would have been regarding withdrawal of the feeding tube that kept her alive.
Because she had no living will, her husband and guardian, who claimed Schiavo would rather die than live in this state, had to petition the local Florida
court for permission to remove her feeding tube in 1998. Her parents, who
believed Schiavo would not have wished the tube removed, appealed when the
local judge granted the husband's petition. After seven years of litigation and
the unprecedented intervention by the Republican-led Congress to require a
final federal court review of the case in March 2005, the Supreme Court, consistent with its stance in *Cruzan,* refused to intervene and the local court order
prevailed. In seeking federal intervention in the case, the parents framed the
issue in terms of a constitutional "right to life" but, as in its refusal to decide
Cruzan on the basis of a "right to die," the Court left responsibility for weigh-
ing state interest in the value of preserving life to state law and the state court.
The preferred judicial framework was not to choose between competing rights
claims but to allow review of who represented Schiavo's wishes to proceed
according to state law and in the state court system.

Physician-Assisted Suicide

None of the end-of-life situations described thus far raises the issue of a right
to die as starkly as the practice of physician-assisted suicide. Advocates of the
practice claim that individuals suffering from debilitating illness should have
the right to choose death rather than continue a life they regard as miserable
and without hope. Usually these are people, unlike those receiving hospice
care at the end of life, who suffer from conditions such as Alzheimer's or Lou
Gehrig's disease, which may allow them to live for a long period of time, but
with a steady decline in the quality of life and without any possibility of a cure.
In these cases, according to right-to-die advocates, physicians ought to be
able, without any legal sanction, to prescribe a painless means of ending life,

usually a drug. Unlike the examples of passive euthanasia discussed earlier, physician-assisted suicide involves active euthanasia, because the administered drug is given for the sole purpose of causing death. Since the 1980s, the most publicly visible advocate of this position has been Dr. Jack Kevorkian, nick-named Dr. Death, who claims to have conducted over 130 such "mercy killings."[59] While most observers acknowledge that instances of some physi-cians administering or making available to their patients lethal doses of drugs to end a life they no longer wish to continue may not be uncommon, Kevorkian's advocacy of the right to die has led him to publicize his actions. In 1999, after the broadcast of a tape on *60 Minutes* showing him adminis-tering a lethal drug to a man suffering from Lou Gehrig's disease, Kevorkian was tried and convicted of second-degree manslaughter and sent to prison. (He was released on parole in 2007.) Public policy regarding physician-assisted suicide, however, has involved not the flamboyant Kevorkian but cases involving physicians who sought quietly to end lives their patients considered unbearable.

DR. JACK KEVORKIAN, SHOWN HERE UPON HIS RELEASE IN 2007 FROM AN EIGHT-YEAR PRISON SENTENCE, CLAIMED TO HAVE ASSISTED 130 TERMINALLY ILL PATIENTS IN COMMITTING SUICIDE.

In 1997, the U.S. Supreme Court decided two cases, *Washington v. Glucksberg* and *Vaceo v. Quill,* that both addressed directly the issue of a right to physician-assisted suicide.[60] The first case involved a challenge by a group of physicians and terminally ill patients to a Washington statute prohibiting physician-assisted suicide. They claimed the statute violated a constitutional "right of privacy" under the due process clause of the Fourteenth Amendment to physician-assisted suicide. The *Quill* case emerged from New York doctor Timothy Quill's public revelation that he had helped one patient commit suicide. Facing indictment, Quill, along with several other physicians, challenged the constitutionality of New York's ban on assisted suicide on equal protection grounds. Their suit argued that since the state permitted the terminally ill to stop life support, equal protection required it to allow persons to seek assistance in ending their lives. In a unanimous decision, the Court rejected the right to assisted suicide claim of the Washington case, arguing that to do so would "reverse centuries of legal doctrine and practice and strike down the considered policy choice of almost every State."[61] It opted to leave to the states the power to "how best to protect dignity and independence at the end of life," including whether to sanction physician-assisted suicide.[62] In the *Quill* case, the equal protection claim was rejected on the ground that the act of refusing medical treatment, long acknowledged in the law, differed from that of committing suicide. Like the *Cruzan* case, the Supreme Court majority refused to take charge and constitutionalize policies regarding end-of-life care, but deferred to state legislatures and local communities as better equipped to make the difficult moral choices involved. As these cases had moved through the federal courts, however, they had produced considerable scholarly and legal commentary of whether there should be a "right to die."

The strongest statement of the libertarian position on a constitutional right to die came in "the philosophers' brief," a friend-of-the-court brief filed by six moral philosophers, including libertarian Robert Nozick, distinguished liberal theorist John Rawls, and legal scholar Ronald Dworkin (noted for his advocacy of a rights-based approach to social policy).[63] At the core of their argument were the twin libertarian principles of absolute personal autonomy in the making of life choices and the neutrality of government toward morality. According to the philosophers, the right to physician-assisted suicide derived from an individual's "more general right to make 'intimate and personal choices' for himself."[64] In support they cited the broad assertion of personal autonomy in the 1992 *Casey* decision that had affirmed the right to an abortion derived from "the right to define one's own concept of existence, of meaning, of the universe, and of the mystery of human life."[65] This rhetoric envisions the person considering ending his life as the lone, unencumbered individual of the libertarian worldview; obligations that tradition, community preferences, family ties, or religious commitment might play in his decision are completely a matter of free choice. Most important, any governmental obligations are considered illegitimate. Because "different people, of different religious and ethical beliefs, embrace very different convictions about which way of dying confirms and which contradicts the value of their lives," then government must remain neutral and permit individuals to seek or not seek assistance to die according to their individual wishes. In libertarian fashion, this argument addresses the absence of moral consensus by deferring to individual choice. As Michael Sandel would point out, the argument ignores the *de facto* bias of assigning a right to physician-assisted suicide. It would affirm the moral position of those who consider assisted suicide permissible and reject the view of those who see it as an immoral act either for themselves or for others. The illusion of government neutrality regarding the morality of suicide prevails here as it does in the case of abortion.

The philosophers believe the right to seek physician-assisted suicide trumps both traditional condemnations of suicide and any opposition from state legislative majorities. They do acknowledge, however, that states will have to devise regulations to make sure that the right is not abused and lead to involuntary suicide or that incompetent individuals exercise the right. In fact, much of their brief seeks to refute the arguments U.S. Solicitor General Walter E. Dellinger had made against physician-assisted suicide based upon the difficulties states would face ensuring that the right be confined to those making a competent, rational choice and not lead to abuse.[66] For the philosophers, implementation challenges should not deter individuals who are "competent, rational, informed, stable, and uncoerced" from seeking physician-assisted suicide. The person who should have this right, in the philosophers' account, conforms to the libertarian vision of the self-sufficient individual in control of his life choices. But a communitarian is likely to question whether anyone suffering from a debilitating illness so severe that they would consider ending their life to be "competent, rational, informed, stable, and uncoerced." In fact, the philosophers' own description of someone for whom the right to die would be appropriate—"intubated, helpless, and often sedated near oblivion"—is hardly a person who fits their own definition of competence. As libertarians do so often, the philosophers avoid the reality of human dependency and the limits to one's capacity, particularly in circumstances of physical pain and illness, and focus instead on the abstract self-sufficient choice makers envisioned in libertarian ideology. Even if one might acknowledge a right to assisted suicide to the "competent, rational, informed, stable, and uncoerced," I find it doubtful that many of us suffering from a debilitating, painful disease would meet the standard required to exercise it.

For some critics of a right to physician-assisted suicide grounded in libertarian notions of personal autonomy and government neutrality, the right once granted to the terminally ill could not be confined to them alone. If a right to assisted suicide is based on an absolute "right to define one's own concept of existence, of meaning, of the universe, and of the mystery of human life," then anyone in contemplating their existence and who concludes it not worth continuing should have the right to commit suicide.

Legal scholar Stephen L. Carter points out that "constitutional rights arise by virtue of citizenship, not circumstance . . . each of us . . . possesses an identical set of rights . . . if there is indeed a constitutional right to suicide, assisted or not, it must attach to all citizens."[67] In fact, many legal scholars expected that, had the Supreme Court affirmed a constitutional right to physician-assisted suicide, it would have faced years of litigation from persons seeking to expand the right. The slippery slope from the right to physician-assisted suicide to a general right to suicide seemed, to many, a steep and slippery one indeed.[68]

In contrast to the philosophers' brief, some scholars found strong reasons why states were justified in prohibiting physician-assisted suicide. Cass R. Sunstein, writing in the *Yale Law Journal*, succinctly described five reasons justifying state prohibitions on assisted suicide.[69] First, he began with the observation that "People who are in intense pain or emotional distress, and who face a bleak future, may well be unlikely to think clearly."[70] Distorted judgment might lead them to seek the simple solution of suicide rather than alternative ways of coping. If physician-assisted suicide were available they might not seek help from professionals and family members in trying to resolve their fears and distress. Second, a ban on assisted suicide protects a vulnerable patient from psychological pressures, such as concern for the emotional and financial costs their condition imposes on family members that might cause them to seek assisted suicide. Family members themselves might exert subtle, even unconscious, pressures toward suicide, if it were an option, to remove the burden of a dying relative. Rather than increase an individual's autonomy, given these realities, a "right to die" might reduce one's ability to refuse to die. As Sunstein puts it, "the social meaning of a refusal to terminate one's life would be very different from what it now is."[71] Third, a right to physician-assisted suicide would make patients vulnerable to pressure from physicians who, as authority figures, might consciously or unconsciously encourage suicide. The costs in time and money to care for "hopeless" cases might lead to pressures—particularly in the case of the poor, uneducated, and disadvantaged—to accept a lethal injection. Sunstein cites evidence from the Netherlands, the only nation where physician-assisted suicide is legal, of such pressure. Fourth, again drawing on the Netherlands experience, Sunstein warns of slippage from voluntary to involuntary suicide. Safeguards to ensure that those receiving an "assisted" death have competently and freely chosen the option are not foolproof. Health care providers, based on their own judgment of whose life is worth living, may report a choice to die when the patient's preference is not clear. Finally, Sunstein cites the expressive value of a ban as a way of the state affirming social attitudes about the sanctity of life. Such an affirmation establishes "an entrenched norm in favor of the preservation of life" that has salutary social effects ranging from discouraging suicide generally to preserving the role of the physician as life preserver rather than life taker.[72]

In its 1997 decisions, the Supreme Court rejected the libertarian positions expressed in the philosophers' brief and, citing many of Sunstein's concerns, left the matter of physician-assisted suicide to the states. The sentiment of the Court majority, as expressed in a concurring opinion by Justice David Souter, was not to preempt state-level deliberation and experimentation with physician-assisted suicide.[73] The overwhelming choice in the states is to keep the prohibition on physician-assisted suicide. Statutes prohibiting it are in place in forty-six states with three—Nevada, Utah, and Wyoming—with no laws on the matter.[74] Only one state, Oregon, permits physician-assisted suicide. In 1997, after similar referenda failed to pass in California and Washington, Oregonians approved a measure legalizing physician-assisted suicide by a narrow 51 percent margin.[75] The Death with Dignity Act established strict guidelines regulating physician-assisted suicide to be administered by the Oregon Department of Health. Between 1997 and 2006, only 292 people availed themselves of the option, a miniscule percentage of those who died in Oregon over that period. While the Oregon law allows physician-assisted suicide, it does so not as a constitutional right but through a simple statute. This means Oregon citizens have access to physician-assisted suicide only as long as a majority of them continue to support the practice. In 2006, the Supreme Court refused to interfere with physician-assisted suicide in Oregon when, in *Gonzales v. Oregon,* it refused to approve the Bush administration's attempt to prevent Oregon physicians from prescribing lethal doses of drugs under the Federal Controlled Substances Act. For now, physician-assisted suicide remains an issue for citizens to decide at the state level.

In contrast to the abortion issue, where *Roe v. Wade* nationalized and constitutionalized the issue, end-of-life care in the United States remains a matter regulated at the state and local level. In this regulation, states have opted to provide considerable discretion to individuals, their families, and medical professionals over the complex and difficult decisions about the end of life. To a certain extent, the dominant experience of Americans with end-of-life issues reflects a principle identified in the social teachings of the Roman Catholic Church as *subsidiarity*.[76] According to this principle, human dignity is best respected if human needs are satisfied, locally, through the participation of families and community institutions, rather than through regulations of a distant state. This approach does not deny the importance of state regulation when appropriate, but the common good as well as that of individuals can best be achieved if those closest to and most familiar with an issue are involved. If any issues require subsidiarity, the intimate, emotional, and complex decisions often needed at the end of life certainly do. Despite sensational cases, such as that of Terri Schiavo, U.S. public policies regarding the end of life do seem to offer most people the ability to make decisions regarding termination of life support and hospice care to ease pain and suffering as death occurs without heavy-handed government regulation. Subsidiarity also implies a communitarian approach to such issues that does not treat individuals as lone rights bearers but understands people to be embedded in their families and communities whose participation in their situation is required. Such a view of the complexity of end-of-life policy seems to offer much more than the libertarian one.

Despite the implicit recognition of subsidiarity in the overall policy framework regarding end-of-life care, one should not paint too rosy a picture of the experience of most of those who face the heart-wrenching decisions regarding medical treatment at life's end. Even with advanced directives and the right to terminate care, the end of life for many involves intrusive medical intervention and, in retrospect, pointless treatment.[77] The difficulty for both physicians and patients seems to be uncertainty about determining the hazy line between the use of technology to preserve life while maintaining a reasonable quality of life and simply excessive treatment. According to medical ethicist Daniel Callahan, physicians find that with modern technology both the moral and technical challenges regarding terminating care are more difficult.[78] One cannot be sure that an intervention will be helpful, in a particular case, until after it has been tried. Patients themselves seeking to cling to life are eager many times to seek the one additional treatment that might make a difference.[79] Deciding when a condition is truly terminal or when a given treatment is futile have become increasingly ambiguous. This is a reality for which there is no satisfactory policy solution. Certainly, providing a "right to die" does nothing to help people navigate the complexities of end-of-life care. And, as Sunstein points out, the existence of such a right, particularly one for physician-assisted suicide, might introduce as bias toward life termination into the complex, uncertain deliberations of patients, their physicians, and families in making these decisions. For many of us, a bias on behalf of life in these situations is to be preferred, even if life is sometimes needlessly prolonged.

Stephen L. Carter poses a key question at the heart of a debate between a libertarian or communitarian approach to end-of-life policy: "Do our mortal lives belong to us alone or do they belong to the communities or families in which we are embedded?"[80] A libertarian answer to this question may respect an idea of individual autonomy, but it offers individuals nothing more than a "right to die." A communitarian response emphasizes obligations more than rights: to the extent that our lives are embedded in our communities, we are obliged to adhere to community judgments and traditions regarding how we end our lives. But our families and communities are obligated to support us as well. This means a communitarian approach demands maximum opportunity for participation of family or others dear to us in all decisions regarding our fate and a chance to offer advice and emotional support. It also demands access to institutional resources needed to ensure a death as pain-free and comfortable as possible, including adequate medical and hospice care. Overemphasis on a right to die does nothing to make available what most people need when facing death—compassionate palliative care. Recognition of ourselves as embedded beings offers a better chance that governments will enact public policies providing the resources that most of us will need at the end of life.

Conclusion

The libertarian illusion that empowering lone, rights-bearing individuals with a right to choose an abortion or a right to die can solve agonizing and morally significant issues regarding both the beginning and end of life fails in much the same way it fails to solve the policy dilemmas discussed in earlier chapters. On all these issues, libertarians claim giving individuals "ownership" of the problem frees them to control their destiny without the constraint of societal pressures or obligations. How to meet the need for financial security in old age? The libertarian response is to empower individuals to save in tax-free private retirement accounts. This empowerment, as we saw in chapter 4, also means the individual bears alone the risks and burdens involved in ensuring retirement security rather than the responsibility for security being shared collectively among all. A right to an abortion or a right to die can be thought of in much the same way. The recipient gains individual ownership over these difficult decisions yet, although empowered as an individual, these rights are silent regarding the solidarity the broader community owes those facing these choices. Offering merely a right also ignores the reciprocal obligations individuals owe society at large and the reality of individual dependency on others when dealing with momentous life-and-death decisions.

Rather than leave individuals alone to face decisions about either abortion or death, a communitarian approach emphasizes the collective stake in terms of both interest in the outcome and obligation toward the individuals involved. Society cannot avoid the moral issues involved simply by leaving them to individual choice. As the history of conflict over abortion rights demonstrates, those who oppose the morality of what individuals might choose will not remain silent in the face of what they regard as a moral outrage. Pro-life advocates point out, correctly, that in allowing individuals to choose either an abortion or active euthanasia, society through its government is taking a moral position that such actions are permissible. From a democratic perspective, deciding morally significant issues demands open, public deliberation in the legislative arena, not in the judicial system. A battle of contending rights within adversarial court proceedings is ill suited to produce resolution to moral conflict. Instead of just leaving the decision to the individual, democratic deliberation must occur to define the moral status attached to terminating a pregnancy or seeking assistance to die. All of us have a stake in how society views the sanctity of life, and this interest requires collective deliberation and the exercise of collective power over the matter.

Society also has important obligations toward both women facing unwanted pregnancies and those facing terminal illness. A libertarian rights approach does nothing to ensure that the support and resources to both will be available and tends to separate such issues from the problem with its focus on merely a right to choose. Of course, many advocates for choice in these areas are in the forefront of demanding better reproductive education, maternal support, and child care in the case of abortion rights, or better palliative care and more hospice funding in the case of a "right to die." Yet the debate over a right to choose in these areas tends to be conducted separately from advocacy for better societal support. If policy deliberation regarding access to abortion or to terminating life occurs in the legislative arena, then the connection between how these will be regulated and the broader needs of pregnant women and the dying become immediately relevant. Those who wish to constrain abortion access, for example, can be challenged to support public expenditures on measures to prevent unwanted pregnancy, obtain better child care support, or facilitate alternatives like adoption. For many years advocates on both the pro-choice and pro-life sides of the conflict have sought common ground on these issues, yet finding it becomes impossible when the contending groups are locked in an absolutist battle over rights. Democratic deliberation over the pragmatic issues involved in regulating abortion would facilitate finding the common ground on societal supports as a part of resolving the larger issue.

The communitarian approach advocated here, of course, requires faith in democracy. One of the principle reasons the libertarian solution of rights and individual choice seems attractive is that it offers protection from "majority tyranny." Since the American founding, a preoccupation with a tyrannical majority has been a prime factor in seeking a regime of individual rights that could trump majority preferences that would be unjust to the minority or to dissenting individuals. In the early days of the republic, the preoccupation was with, as James Madison wrote in *Federalist* No. 10, a majority faction expropriating the propertied. In the *Lochner* era, the concern was with a majority favorable to the interests of workers overwhelming the property rights of owners of capital. Both these fears proved unfounded. In the early republic, the small, freehold farmers who made up the majority were as anxious to support the acquisition and protection of property as the rich merchants and plantation owners who initially feared them. And after the New Deal, an economic structure evolved that recognized the common interests of both capital and labor, although libertarian measures in recent years have undermined this consensus, largely through a *Lochner* mindset.

This experience suggests that the fears of "majority tyranny" producing injustice and abuse of either women facing unwanted pregnancies or the terminally ill are unwarranted. Certainly, public opinion polls offer little support of a tyrannical majority on either issue. In both areas, opinion seems strongly opposed to heavy-handed government control and prefers leaving decisions in both areas, primarily individuals, families, and medical professionals. If *Roe* were overturned, the national imposition of overly restrictive antiabortion laws seems unlikely.[81] More likely would be a renewal of the process of state statute liberalization underway in the late 1960s, leading potentially to policies in most states more akin to what prevails in France today than had been the norm in Texas in 1970. Of course, there would be substantial inter-state variation in abortion law—with access more restricted in more conservative states, but access, as a pragmatic matter, is currently quite limited in those areas and likely would be no more limited in the absence of *Roe*. Yet even legislators in conservative states might find little support among their constituents for draconian antiabortion laws. In March 2006, pro-life legislators in conservative South Dakota, seeking the basis for a legal challenge to *Roe*, passed such a law. To their surprise and to many observers nationwide, a referendum repealed the law by a large majority the following November. Likewise, experience has demonstrated little to fear from "majority tyranny" imposing itself on those facing difficult decisions regarding the termination of life. The public revulsion against congressional leaders' attempts to insert themselves into the Terri Schiavo case proved the moderation of the majority of ordinary Americans on the issue. Moving these issues out of the libertarian realm of absolute rights into the arena of democratic deliberation and control should not raise fears of a tyrannical majority enacting unjust laws. We need to embrace a democratic faith in the wisdom of the American people through their representatives to craft laws that are just to individuals while expressive of society's deepest moral commitments.

Finally, the most profound libertarian illusion is that assigning absolute rights and providing individual choice can provide the individual control and mastery over life. Medical ethicist Daniel Callahan, writing about the right to die, identifies as a dual illusion regarding this ambition to mastery: "the naïve belief that the watchful self . . . can master the body by means of carefully controlled medical technology . . . [and] . . . that we can know ourselves and our own wishes well enough to manage ourselves."[82] The libertarian frame within which policies regarding both the beginning and end of life are discussed implicitly assume this mastery, but we should be skeptical, as Callahan warns, that the right to choose can provide it. In years to come, the issue undoubtedly will be raised regarding a host of new policy dilemmas. Now that medical technology offers the coming prospect for parents to manipulate the genes of their children, there will be those seeking to choose "biological enhancements" such as improved athletic ability, good looks, musical talent, or intelligence.[83] When technology allows systematic genetic engineering there are sure to be those who demand a constitutional right to choose the genetic makeup of their children, but there are good reasons to resist this libertarian solution. Surely, as with abortion and the termination of life, society as a whole has a tremendous stake in what choices individuals make. Already, in countries like India and China, parents' gender preferences for boys lead to the abortion of female fetuses, resulting in projections of a future social crisis. Given our experience with policies regarding birth and death, we must not allow the illusion of mastery to lead to a libertarian approach to genetic engineering policy framed solely as a debate over individual rights. Only through facing the moral issues and social dimensions of policies regarding birth, death, or the brave new world of genetic manipulation can we hope to find the common good.

SUGGESTIONS FOR FURTHER READING

Callahan, Daniel. *The Troubled Dream of Life: In Search of a Peaceful Death.* Washington, D.C.: Georgetown University Press, 2000. Profound wisdom about the reality of death and dying and the limits to our attempts at mastery.

Dworkin, Ronald. *Life's Dominion: An Argument about Abortion, Euthanasia, and Individual Freedom.* New York: Alfred A. Knopf, 1993. A strong case for a libertarian approach to these issues made by one of the country's leading legal philosophers.

Glendon, Mary Ann. *Rights Talk.* New York: Free Press, 1991. A systematic analysis of how our focus on rights impedes Americans from finding the common ground.

Rose, Melody. *Safe, Legal, and Unavailable: Abortion Politics in the United States.* Washington, D.C.: CQ Press, 2007. A comprehensive analysis of all aspects of abortion policy.

Urofsky, Melvin. *Lethal Judgments: Assisted Suicide and American Law.* Lawrence: University Press of Kansas, 2000. A well-written review of the cases that have defined the United States' jurisprudence regarding the right to die.

SELECTED WEB SITES

www.cbctrust.com/history_law_religion.php. A site favoring abortion rights, but with links to various views and, especially, the experience around the world.

www.euthanasia.com/. Information site with links to a wide range of views on euthanasia despite a clear bias against the practice.

www.findlaw.com/casecode/supreme.html. An easy-to-use, comprehensive legal site providing access to all the Supreme Court cases discussed in this chapter, plus many more.

NOTES

1. This is the thesis of Brink Lindsey's *The Age of Abundance: How Prosperity Transformed America's Politics and Culture* (New York: HarperCollins, 2007).
2. Louis Hartz, *The Liberal Tradition in America* (New York: Harcourt, Brace, Jovanovich, 1955).
3. Mill quoted in Stephen Holmes, *Passions and Constraint* (Chicago: University of Chicago Press, 1995), 182.
4. Mary Ann Glendon, *Rights Talk* (New York: Free Press, 1991), 9.
5. Ibid., 8.
6. Michael J. Sandel, *Democracy's Discontent: America in Search of a Public Philosophy* (Cambridge: Harvard University Press, 1996), 4–5.
7. Ronald Dworkin, *Taking Rights Seriously* (Harvard University Press, 1977), 269.

8. Glendon, *Rights Talk,* 22–23.
9. Ibid., 23.
10. Ibid.
11. Sandel, *Democracy's Discontent,* 40–41.
12. Quoted in ibid., 41.
13. Libertarians, however, would like to return to the *Lochner* era; see Randy Barnett, *Restoring the Lost Constitution* (Princeton: Princeton University Press, 2004).
14. Glendon, *Rights Talk,* 40.
15. Ibid., 47
16. Sandel, *Democracy's Discontent,* 12.
17. Ibid., 12.
18. Alan Wolfe, *Moral Freedom: The Search for Virtue in a World of Choice* (New York: Norton, 2001), 195.
19. Sandel, *Democracy's Discontent,* 19.
20. Ibid., 13–14.
21. Ibid., 14.
22. This account follows that of Glendon, *Rights Talk,* 50–61.
23. Ibid., 51.
24. Ibid., 54.
25. Sandel, *Public Philosophy* (Cambridge: Harvard University Press, 2005), 128.
26. Glendon, *Rights Talk,* 56–57.
27. Quoted in Sandel, *Public Philosophy,* 129.
28. Deborah R. McFarlane and Kenneth J. Meier, *The Politics of Fertility Control* (New York: Chatham House, 2001), 34–38.
29. David O'Brien, *Constitutional Law and Politics,* on *Roe v. Wade,* no. 2 (1973): 1237.
30. Glendon, *Rights Talk,* 58–59.
31. Sandel, *Democracy's Discontent,* 21.
32. Michael J. Perry, *We the People: The Fourteenth Amendment and the Supreme Court* (New York: Oxford University Press, 1999), 159.
33. For a more complete discussion of how abortion politics have harmed American democracy, see William E. Hudson, *American Democracy in Peril,* 5th ed. (Washington, D.C.: CQ Press, 2006), 65–142.
34. For a cogent account of abortion politics, see Melody Rose, *Safe, Legal, and Unavailable: Abortion Politics in the United States* (Washington, D.C.: CQ Press, 2007), 67–81.
35. Ibid., 72.
36. Ibid., 102–120.
37. Ibid., 89–102.
38. Rose, *Safe, Legal, and Unavailable.*
39. Ibid., 31.
40. Ibid., 31–32.
41. Ibid., 37.
42. Unless indicated otherwise, public opinion data cited in this paragraph are taken from a variety of polls compiled at publicagenda.org: www.publicagenda.org/issues/frontdoor.cfm?issue_type=abortion.
43. Rose, *Safe, Legal, and Unavailable,* 46–47.

44. For a discussion of the issues involved in intact D&E, see Justice Ginsburg's dissent in *Gonzales v. Carhart,* 550 U.S. Supreme Court (2007).
45. Philip Selznick, "The Jurisprudence of Communitarian Liberalism," in *Communitarianism in Law and Society* ed. Paul van Seters (Lanham, Md.: Rowman and Littlefield, 2006), 28.
46. Mary Ann Glendon, *Abortion and Democracy in Western Law* (Cambridge: Harvard University Press, 1987), 18.
47. Quoted in ibid., 16.
48. Ibid., 16.
49. Melvin Urofsky, *Lethal Judgments: Assisted Suicide and American Law* (Lawrence: University Press of Kansas, 2000), 3.
50. Ibid., 4.
51. Ibid., 11.
52. Ibid., 41.
53. Ibid., 45.
54. Ibid., 77.
55. Ibid., 48.
56. David O'Brien, *Constitutional Law and Politics,* 1288.
57. Urofsky, *Lethal Judgments,* 61.
58. This account follows Elaine Cassel, "The Terri Schiavo Case: Congress Rushes in Where Only Courts Should Tread," FindLaw Legal News and Commentary, writ.news.findlaw.com/cassel/20050324.html.
59. Urofsky, *Lethal Judgments,* 65–85.
60. O'Brien, *Constitutional Law and Politics,* 1296–1297.
61. Ibid., 1299.
62. Ibid., 1298.
63. Ronald Dworkin, et al., "Assisted Suicide: The Philosophers' Brief," *New York Review of Books* 44, no. 5, March 27, 1997, www.nybooks.com/articles/1237.
64. Ibid., 9.
65. Ibid., 10
66. See discussion of this point in J. Bottum, "Debriefing the Philosophers," *First Things* (June/July 1997): 26–30.
67. Stephen L. Carter, "Against Doctor-Assisted Suicide," *New York Times,* July 21, 1996, sec. 6, 28.
68. Dworkin rather unconvincingly addressed this slippery slope argument in the *New York Review* introduction to Dworkin, et al., Philosophers' Brief: "Assisted Suicide."
69. Cass R. Sunstein, "The Right to Die," *The Yale Law Journal* 106, no. 4 (January 1997): 1141–1145.
70. Ibid., 1141.
71. Ibid., 1143.
72. Ibid., 1145–1146.
73. O'Brien, *Constitutional Law and Politics,* 1306.
74. Public Agenda Web Issue Guide: www.publicagenda.org/issues/frontdoor. cfm?issue_type=right2die.
75. Urofsky, *Lethal Judgments,* 102.
76. Pontifical Council for Justice and Peace, Compendium of the Social Doctrine of the Church, Washington, D.C.: USCCB Publishing, 2005, 81–83.

77. Daniel Callahan, *The Troubled Dream of Life: In Search of a Peaceful Death* (Washington D.C.: Georgetown University Press, 2000), 40–56.
78. Ibid., 40.
79. Ibid., 50.
80. Stephen L. Carter, "Against Doctor-Assisted Suicide."
81. Jeffrey Rosen, "The Day after *Roe*," *The Atlantic Monthly,* June 2006.
82. Daniel Callahan, *The Troubled Dream of Life.*
83. Michael Sandel, *The Case against Perfection: Ethics in the Age of Genetic Engineering* (Cambridge: Harvard University Press), 2007.

Chapter 7 Conclusion

We started this book on a wide, lonely sea with an iceberg lurking beneath the water; we will end it in New York City's Central Park on a sunny spring afternoon. On the glorious day that I was there in the spring of 2007 the park was full of people engaged peacefully in a wide variety of personal pursuits. There were the skaters on rollerblades speeding down car-free roads blocked off for the purpose, passing many a dog and his mistress on their daily walk. Open fields were filled with families enjoying picnics on blankets spread on the grass, while nearby nimble youngsters tossed Frisbees or footballs and played catch. On well-kept playing fields evidence of more organized sports was in action, like the bounce of basketballs on the basketball courts, the crack of bats on the baseball diamond, and the flash of tennis balls passing over nets on dozens of tennis courts. Many visitors, like my wife and me, were in the park for less purposeful reasons, simply wandering aimlessly on its many paths or observing the action from the benches. In doing so, we were never too far from a vendor's cart dispensing ice cream, cold sodas, and other goodies, or from friendly park officers coping with emergencies or providing directions. The vibrancy and variety of New York City found its way into the park in the form of agile break-dancers showing their stuff to a hip-hop beat or in a Mozart melody wafting from a string quartet. Central Park provides more than just human-made entertainments, however; its visitors commune with nature in the shade of its trees and the beauty of its well-tended foliage and colorful flowers, sparkling lakes, and vistas across rolling lawns.

Nothing contrasts more with the libertarian view of life than a beautiful public park teeming with urbanites enjoying their leisure. People of all income levels, ages, and ethnicities gather in freedom within a public space designed specifically to bring them together. Nothing bars their entry into the park and no fees are charged to partake of most of its amenities. When Frederick Law Olmstead, the renowned landscape architect, designed Central Park over a century ago, he clearly envisioned the scene I encountered in 2007.[1] Olmstead saw public parks as democratic spaces meant to be accessible to citizens of all classes, especially the poor, who otherwise would not have an opportunity to enjoy nature. The park was built and always has been maintained with public funds, but it also has benefited from private philanthropic contributions. Although Central Park belongs to New York City and its citizens, its day-to-day management is the responsibility of the Central Park Conservancy, a private, nonprofit organization under contract to the City Department of Parks and Recreation. This mixture of public and private responsibility reflects a communitarian ethos that draws on all parts of the community to support this verdant masterpiece in the heart of the city. A visitor to the Big Apple will encounter numerous symbols of individual liberty and enterprise in the city, whether in its majestic skyscrapers, Wall Street exuberance, or artistic achievements on Broadway or at Lincoln Center, but without Olmstead's communitarian monument, Central Park, the city would not be the magnificent wonder it is today.

Americans can be thankful that Olmstead spread his communitarian vision to public parks and other public spaces throughout the country. After completing his work on Central Park, he went on to design other parks in New York City and in many other major American cities such as Boston, Chicago, and Atlanta. In the parks Olmstead designed and in the many others they inspired, Americans can appreciate how common spaces can bring us together for our mutual benefit in ways private pursuits in the marketplace cannot. A libertarian vision of purely private spaces fenced in and accessible through locked gates open only to those with a key could not produce a public park. Unfortunately, the success of libertarian policy ideas over the last three decades has made the United States look increasingly fenced-in in our common spaces and moved us away from the communitarian ethos that animates places like Central Park. It is now time that we reverse this libertarian policy tilt and renew the communitarian vision found in Frederick Law Olmstead's parks.

A renewed communitarian vision will involve balancing the value of individual freedom with the claims of community and the common good. This does not mean discounting the importance of individual freedom, but only acknowledging that freedom can only be realized for the majority of citizens with the support of community institutions. As discussed in chapter 1, what philosopher T. H. Green called *positive* freedom can be realized for most people if the community assists individuals in overcoming obstacles such as poverty, illness, and ignorance that prevent them from flourishing. But a communitarian vision also points to political values besides individual freedom that must be pursued if the common good is to be achieved. Unlike libertarians, who see individual liberty as the sole purpose of government and the goal of community life, communitarians recognize it as one of several values important to the common good. Along with liberty, communitarians believe that public policies must be concerned with solidarity, security, equality, and morality.

A common flaw in most libertarian policy solutions, as revealed throughout this book, is to ignore the mutual dependence that all of us have on one another. Whether in their conception of private retirement accounts, proposals for "consumer-driven" health care, or the right to physician-assisted suicide, libertarians' policies leave individuals to fend for themselves in instances of vulnerability when the help of others is crucial. While personal responsibility for one's fate is a worthy ideal, all of us, no matter how self-sufficient, will encounter times when our survival will depend on those around us and the community institutions that can provide support. Only recognition of our solidarity with others will allow crafting policy solutions that offer these societal supports. Community-rating for health insurance, guaranteed income from Social Security at retirement, public support for prenatal health care for pregnant women, and universal access to utilities are all examples of policies that recognize that the well-being of each of us depends on ensuring the well-being of all. Solidarity with each other and future generations also requires supporting cultural institutions that protect our common heritage and national parks and forests for posterity. Evaluating public policy alternatives according to how they affect social solidarity is as important as considering their impact on individual freedom.

Promoting solidarity, as the previous paragraph suggests, can be one way of promoting the important political value of security. Little of life can be of value, as political philosopher Thomas Hobbes recognized long ago, if we cannot feel secure. While Hobbes was concerned with the physical dangers of life in a state of nature where life is "solitary, poor, nasty, brutish, and short," people in modern societies need protection not only from physical dangers but from economic hazards, threats to their health, and exploitation from giant corporations.[2] Much of the government regulation described in chapter 3 involves providing such security. Admittedly, there is often a trade-off between individual freedom and security. Whether it is submitting to searches at airports or fastening a seat belt in our cars, individual freedom must give way to some degree if we are to be collectively safe. Taxes do deprive individuals of the freedom to spend all the income they earn as they might wish, but unless government collects sufficient revenue it cannot provide security from either foreign enemies or hazardous consumer products. Some insecurity can never be banished from human life, but well-crafted public policy can enhance how secure we can be in the enjoyment of our freedom.

Individuals pursing their self-interest through exchanges in free markets always will benefit unequally. The ability of Adam Smith's "invisible hand" to create rising prosperity for the society as a whole produces winners and losers in a market economy. The incentive to win in competition with one's fellows is the driving force of modern capitalism. Over time, these inequalities can accumulate and divide society sharply between rich and poor. While some inequality ought to be expected and can prove beneficial as an incentive to productive effort, political observers going back to Aristotle have recognized the danger extreme inequality poses to the common good. Communitarians take this danger seriously and see the need for policies that prevent this imbalance. As pointed out in earlier chapters, one of the most serious dangers of the libertarian public policy turn of the last three decades has been how it has increased economic inequality in the United States. A crucial component of a communitarian renewal ought to be public policies that reverse this trend. A return to a more progressive tax policy, programs to provide more educational and other economic opportunities, relief from the growing burden of health insurance premiums and co-pays, and guarantee of a living wage for all workers can all contribute to promoting this political value. The common good does not demand absolute economic equality, but it does require that prosperity be widely shared among all citizens. Reversing the rapidly growing inequality in the United States today has to be a priority for a more communitarian America.

It is tempting to regard public policymaking as a morally neutral endeavor, as simply a matter of finding value-free efficient solutions to policy problems without regard to their moral import. But all public policies require moral choices and trade-offs, whether they concern judgments about the morality of leaving people in poverty or without access to life-preserving health care or how taxation reflects the moral obligations that citizens owe their community. Public policy also has to address what moral standards ought to be promoted in society and how this should be done. Communitarians understand that the moral dimension has to be a part of any public policy debate. The libertarian claim that moral questions can be left to personal, private moral choice ignores (as argued in chapter 6) how that decision inherently endorses the choices individuals might make for themselves. Yet there might be good reasons, in cases like pornography, substance abuse, child care, and perhaps abortion and physician-assisted suicide, for socially acceptable moral standards to be determined through democratic deliberation rather than individual choice. Such deliberation can produce reasonable community standards without imposing draconian limits on individual freedom.

In privileging individual liberty and autonomy over all other political values, libertarians adopt a dogmatic posture that prevents a thorough analysis of how to resolve public policy problems. As one conservative critic of libertarianism has observed, libertarians resemble Marxists in their inability to break free of a rigid dogma. According to Robert Locke, "If Marxism is the delusion that one can run society purely on altruism and collectivism, then libertarianism is the mirror-image delusion that one can run it purely on selfishness and individualism."[3] Only a rigid adherence to dogma can account for libertarian pursuit of the same policy formulas, from tax reduction to deregulation, no matter what the facts and historical circumstances. As we saw in chapter 2, libertarian tax cutters have seen tax cuts as the correct policy solution, whether the budget faced surpluses or deficits. And relying on market forces rather than government regulation is always the answer, even in cases, such as health markets or electricity markets, in which they work neither efficiently nor fairly. Unlike libertarians, communitarians embrace the complexity of the world and the necessity of examining multiple policy options. A communitarian focus is on the best policy outcome for the community, not on a rigid adherence to a particular policy instrument or formula. Sometimes the community is best served through individualist approaches and reliance on market exchanges, but under other conditions, collective needs only can be met through government intervention. Surely, this sort of policy flexibility is what the United States needs in facing the policy challenges of the twenty-first century. Without an ability to consider a broad spectrum of policy means, complex challenges like global warming, oil dependency, economic inequality, international terrorism, and globalization cannot be met. The policy challenges of this century call for policy pragmatism, not ideological rigidity.

Addressing these challenges also will require faith in democracy. Even though libertarianism, with its emphasis on individual liberty, seems democratic, strict adherence to its doctrinal principles ultimately requires limits on democracy, even authoritarian politics. As one libertarian-leaning economist has written, when the public rejects "rational" policy solutions, then the preferences of a democratic majority ought to be ignored.[4] Rational, in this instance, always means the sort of market-oriented policy solutions that libertarians advocate, with no consideration to how they might negatively affect individual lives and, hence, be unpopular. Certainly, popular preference for the economic security that Social Security provides would have to be overcome if the libertarian goal to replace it with private accounts were to be met. Often in the past, the use of rights as "trumps" to overrule popular preferences foiled democracy. As pointed out in the last chapter, the "right of contract" trump that the Supreme Court employed in the early twentieth century prevented either the state or federal governments from enacting child labor laws, limits on hours, minimum wages, and a host of needed labor protections in an industrial society. Libertarians look back fondly on the *Lochner* era of restrictive Court decisions impeding popular social policies as a golden age to which we ought to return. Because so much of the libertarian agenda is unpopular, creating a libertarian world could only come about through limits on the popular will. Those certain of the truth of their ideological dogma may easily succumb to the temptation to contravene democratic politics if necessary to carry out their vision.

The libertarian vision of the United States' future contrasts sharply with that of the open, democratic public park. If libertarians have their way, our country's future will be one of fenced and gated spaces accessible only on an individual basis to those who can afford the price of admission. Only those with adequate returns to their private investment accounts will pass through the entry marked "security in retirement." Access to health care will demand the price of admission to cover high insurance deductibles and sufficient discretionary resources or luck in avoiding illness to accumulate adequate funds in health savings accounts. Increasing inequality will channel citizens into separated existences equivalent to a park that reserves its amenities depending on ability to pay. A deregulated economy will parcel out every aspect of human existence such as access to utilities, consumer product safety, or availability of transportation according to one's ability to negotiate a deal in the market-place. With a price tag on everything, consciousness of a common life and mutual responsibilities among citizens is unlikely to survive. Few Americans will find such a fenced and gated world appealing and, perhaps, this is the best defense against the libertarian illusion. A deeper understanding of public pol-icy alternatives and the limitations of simplistic libertarian solutions are our best hope for defeating this cramped vision and finding policy solutions that serve the common good.

NOTES

1. For insight into Olmstead's vision, see Charles E. Beveridge and David Schuyler, *The Papers of Frederick Law Olmstead: Creating Central Park 1857–1861* (Baltimore: Johns Hopkins University Press), 1983.
2. Thomas Hobbes, *Leviathan,* ed. Herbert W. Schneider (Indianapolis: Bobbs-Merrill, 1958), 107.
3. Robert Locke, "Marxism of the Right," *The American Conservative,* March 14, 2005, www.amconmag.com/2005_03_14/article1.html.
4. Bryan Caplan, *The Myth of the Rational Voter: Why Democracies Choose Bad Policies* (Princeton: Princeton University Press, 2007).

Index